Dave Barrett
&
William Miller

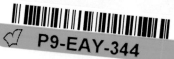

Barrett

A Passionate Political Life

To Bob
Best Wishes
Dave Barrett

Douglas & McIntyre
Vancouver/Toronto

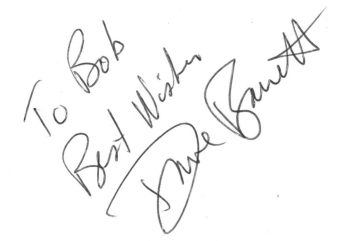

95 96 97 98 99 5 4 3 2 1

Douglas & McIntyre
1615 Venables Street
Vancouver, British Columbia
V5L 2H1

Canadian Cataloguing in Publication Data

Barrett, Dave, 1930-
Barrett

ISBN 1-55054-426-8

1. Barrett, Dave, 1930- 2. Politicians—British Columbia—Biography. 3. British Columbia—Politics and government—1972-1975.* I. Miller, William, 1942- II. Title.
FC3828.1.B37A3 1995 971.1'04 C95-910542-5
F1088.B37A3 1995

Editing by Barbara Pulling
Jacket and book design by George Vaitkunas
Jacket photograph of Dave Barrett by Alex Waterhouse-Hayward
Typeset by George Vaitkunas
Printed and bound in Canada by Imprimerie Gagné Ltée
Printed on acid-free paper

The publisher gratefully acknowledges the assistance of the Canada Council and of the British Columbia Ministry of Tourism, Small Business and Culture.

Barrett

To the thousands of pioneers and activists in the CCF and the NDP, whose sacrifices and efforts have made British Columbia and Canada better places to live

To my parents, Sam and Rose Barrett

To Shirley's parents, Alex and Hilda Hackman

To my teachers, who gave so much of themselves

To our children, Dan and Mary, Joe, and Jane and Wayne, who not only were challenged to live this experience but threw themselves gladly into the maelstrom

To our grandchildren, Hannah and Andrew

And above all to my partner, Shirley, who really made this happen

Contents

Prologue: A Time for Change

I arose early on the morning of August 30, 1972, polling day in British Columbia. After my wife, Shirley, and I had voted, I spent the rest of the day at my campaign headquarters on Austin Avenue in Coquitlam, where an army of NDP volunteers were busy telephoning and arranging transportation for people who needed a ride to the polls. Around 5:00 P.M., I headed home for dinner.

I was keyed up, but optimistic about our chances. I had even told Shirley and our three kids, Dan, Joe and Jane, that I thought our moment had come. I could feel it in my bones. Harvey Beech, my campaign manager, felt the same way. But he and I had agreed not to talk about it. British Columbia had elected the first socialist opposition in the Commonwealth in 1911, but it had never elected a socialist government. The CCF, and later the NDP, had come close, but always our hopes had been dashed.

Both the radio and the TV were tuned to election news when I got home. We would catch a snippet of a radio broadcast in the kitchen, then move into the next room to see what the television was showing. All five of us were in constant motion. I know we must have eaten something, but I don't recall having any dinner that night.

The telephone rang every few minutes. Early results were favourable to the NDP, and I got calls from excited party members and reporters, some of whom wanted directions to our house. About an hour after the polls closed, there was a news flash that Premier W.A.C. Bennett had conceded defeat. The calls came nonstop after that. It was the first time a lot of people in this province had ever voted for a winner.

British Columbia was barely a hundred years old in terms of organized government, and it had been a paradise for buccaneers, high-rollers, land speculators and developers. It was the last frontier, and a long succession of governments had seen it as their primary duty to facilitate the quest for spoils. Social Credit Premier W.A.C. Bennett had ruled the province for the past two decades, a time marked by massive infrastructure development, construction of highways and power megaprojects, and immense resource giveways. Fortunes had been won and lost, with the proceeds going directly into the deep pockets of the corporate elite. Now all that had come to a screeching halt. The Bennett regime had been toppled.

Shirley and the kids and I were happy but still calm as we left the house. A few reporters had gathered outside, and they agreed to follow us to my campaign headquarters. Harvey and Peggy Beech were there, along with a group of volunteers, canvassers and party faithful. We hugged and shook hands all around, then set off together for the Coquitlam recreation centre.

I don't think any of us were prepared for the scene that awaited us there. The place was jammed, and people were spilling out onto the street. They were laughing, crying, dancing, singing. Socialists had been relegated to the political wilderness for so long in British Columbia that many people were in a state of disbelief.

My family and I were surrounded as soon as we stepped out of the car. I had no handlers to disperse the crowd, so we just moved slowly through the friendly, excited throng. People touched us. They wished us well. I recall a few expressions of thanks. Some of the party veterans had tears streaming down their faces. I shook lots of hands. Gradually, people made room for us to ascend the platform.

I have attended dozens of election rallies, but this one was like no other. The room was packed, euphoric. The excitement even affected the reporters, who swarmed us as we climbed onto the stage. The dream that had sustained three generations of ordinary folks in British Columbia had finally come true. People began cheering as I stepped up to the microphone. The next thirty-nine months would never be forgotten.

One

Son of a Jewish Fruit Peddler

I grew up in the East End of Vancouver in the 1930s and 1940s in a house crammed with books and brimming with lively political discussion. Our major entertainment was a radio, and that fuelled the discussion. The East End was strong socialist turf where people voted for CCF members both federally and provincially. The turf battles were between the CCF and the Labour Progressive Party, which was the Communist party. As far as my family was concerned, the only really important people were CCF stalwarts E. E. Winch and Harold Winch, who were both members of the provincial legislature, and later on CCF MLA and MP Grace MacInnis and MP Angus MacInnis.

There was a handful of stately homes in the East End, which extended from Main Street into the bowels of Burnaby, while the rest of the housing was modest, with a sprinkling of apartments. We lived in a working-class neighbourhood with a rich ethnic mix of European and Asian immigrants. High unemployment was chronic during the Depression. I recall people coming to the door asking for food in exchange for work around the house. It was the other side of the tracks.

My father was a very gentle Fabian socialist. Although my mother voted CCF, she was a Communist who thought Joe Stalin was a pretty good guy. The newspapers were extolling his virtues, writing about the heroic Soviet army fighting against the Germans at Stalingrad. I followed the war very closely. My mother was active in antiwar activities such as protesting against the shipment of scrap iron to Japan. She also worked to raise money for Dr. Norman Bethune while he was in Spain and later in China. I recall as a child being in a parade protesting against Fascist intervention in the Spanish Civil War. I sat on a float with a Mercurochrome-stained bandage around my head to make me look like a bombing victim.

My father, Sam Barrett, was born in Winnipeg in 1898 and grew up there. His father had come from Europe in the 1880s and was an interpreter in the Manitoba court system. My father joined the Manitoba 44th in 1915 and saw combat in France with the Canadian Expeditionary Force. He spent ten months in the trenches and was wounded twice. One of his knees was permanently damaged. A gassing had damaged his eyes, and they gave him trouble off and on until 1957, when he lost his sight permanently and received a pension after a long battle with the Veterans' Administration over the original cause of the injuries. After the war, he spent some time in California, where he joined the International Workers of the World, known as the Wobblies, before coming to Vancouver.

My mother, the former Rose Hyatt, was born north of Odessa, in Russia, and she arrived in Canada in the early 1920s. There was a pogrom after the 1917 revolution and my mother's family went as refugees to Bucharest. They were brought out of Rumania by an international Jewish refugee agency and later immigrated to Canada. The train they boarded in Montreal dropped families off all the way across the country. My mother's family was dropped in Vancouver, and my mother and father met there.

It was an arranged marriage, and a failure. My father was nine years older, and they were both very stubborn and very, very bright. Neither would bend. If either one had given just a little bit, it would have been a fabulous marriage, but they were too stubborn and proud. They split up just prior to my twentieth birthday. Their commitment to the kids, however, was total. It was almost like a tacit agreement. There was generosity, affection and genuine love from both parents, but it was separate, not together. Overall, my memories from childhood are very, very good.

Ours was not a religious household, but we were Jewish and we had cultural patterns that we followed and acknowledged with the religious overtones. I recall there was a confusion once about why other kids had a Christmas tree and we didn't.

I was born in Vancouver on October 2, 1930, the youngest of three children. My brother, Isador, is four years older and Pearl, my sister, is two years older. We were poor, but so was everybody else. I sold the *Star*

Weekly for a time, then I began delivering the Vancouver *Sun* and went on to work in the mailing room. When I was in high school, I used to play hooky one day a week and go down and work there. We got five bucks a day. Later on, when I was in conflict with the *Sun*, sometimes humorously and sometimes not so humorously, I once threatened that as a former employee I might go so far as to cancel my subscription.

I also shook hides at Burns' packing house. They would take hides from slaughtered cattle and roll them with salt, all the remaining blood and some of the guts still there. Then they would store these hides in big packs in a warehouse for about six months. A group of us would go in at this point, pull the hides out and, three people to a side, lift them and whack them down on the racks to shake the salt off. All the crap would go flying around and it would stink like hell. So did we. You could shower and scrape and scour yourself but you still stank and no girl would go near you. We got paid very good money though, nearly a buck an hour. We were known at school as the Burns group.

On Saturdays, I worked for my father, selling fruits and vegetables. He was peddling from a truck until the late 1940s, when he opened a retail-wholesale store on Powell Street. He used to park his truck at Pender and Main streets. We would sell off the truck. We sold great numbers of tomatoes, and lots of grapes for home wine-making and to bootleggers. I saw every restaurant in town through its kitchen as we peddled through the downtown alleys.

One day my father and I were parked on Powell Street across from the Marr Hotel, where there was a huge beer parlour. It was a miserable day, very rainy. At that time streetcars ran up the centre of Powell Street. So it was also very noisy. Business was slow as we tried to sell bananas off the truck.

I looked across and saw there was a building for sale halfway down the block at 453 Powell Street. I said, "Pop, why don't you buy that building?" My dad phoned the real estate agent, made a down payment and we were in business. The building cost $3,200, a small fortune. We built some rough shelves to hold the produce and put up a makeshift office, but it was a very rudimentary setup. There was no cash register, just a large bushel basket where my dad threw the money. We sold on volume, the way we had always done off the truck.

My dad had a habit, when somebody came to the truck, of taking a banana and peeling it for them. If we had a big watermelon, he would take a knife, whack the melon and then cut it into wedges for the kids. Whoever came to the truck got something to eat. My dad never paid a nickel for advertising, but his sales techniques made him a fixture in that location. He ran the business the same way after we moved into the store.

On opening day, my dad parked the truck in its usual spot and hung a big sign on it with the store's address and an arrow pointing the way. My father, Izzy and I were gussied up in brand-new white coats. The store was an instant success. We offered red-hot deals and we worked on margin. We bought huge volumes of bananas and tomatoes just on the verge of being ripe, then we had twenty-four hours—forty-eight hours at the most—to get rid of them. Business just took off. Within six months, it wasn't uncommon on Saturdays to see people lined up outside the store waiting to come in.

It wasn't long before my dad had to hire a crew to help out during peak times. These were usually kids from the neighbourhood, or the occasional down-and-outer from Skid Row. Eventually he had to get an accountant to unravel the mysteries of wages and deductions. Customers would pile their bags in one spot and the person serving them would come over and add everything up. Then the customers would pay and take their parcels out the door while the money, hopefully, would go into the bushel basket. There was no way of monitoring anything.

If people didn't have enough money, my dad would give them credit. He didn't even ask their names. Or if they had a $10 bag of fruits and vegetables but only $7 in their pocket, he would say, "Fine, seven bucks." Very quickly he evolved into an owner-greeter. He was a natural character and he had great fun joshing the customers. The Vancouver *Sun* did a write-up on him: Sam the Banana Man. There was a photograph of my dad with his hat tossed back on his head and his white coat on, peeling a banana for a customer.

My father's easygoing approach to business used to bother my brother and me. We couldn't understand how he was making any money. On some Saturday afternoons, to our complete amazement, he would stride into the middle of the store and announce: "Okay, everything's free. We've made enough money today. We'll give the rest away."

We lived on McSpadden Avenue, a one-block street just off Commercial Drive. Our rent was $6 a month. During the Second World War, it rose to $20 a month. The idea of buying a house, as I recall, was never discussed. McSpadden also produced William Esson, who is chief justice of the Supreme Court of B.C., and Frank Iacobucci, now a justice on the Supreme Court of Canada. I was invited to attend Iacobucci's swearing in in Ottawa a few years ago, and of course I saw Bill Esson, who was also there for the ceremony. Kim Campbell, the minister of justice at the time, announced that Esson, Iacobucci and I had all grown up on the same street, and she called for an immediate investigation of the water.

We were products of a school system that was ruthlessly driven by what was called streaming. They gave us IQ tests, and if you were above a certain level you went to one high school, and if you were below that level you went to another high school, which is totally unfair. After Laura Secord Elementary I went off to Britannia High School, where my brother had been before me. I did very well in school until Grade 8, and then my interest in my studies started to slack off dramatically. When I entered Britannia I had to join the army cadets, and that was my first run-in with authority. I was not receptive to the rigidity, discipline and inane delegation of power to peers who were only two or three years older and acted like martinets. I rebelled to the point where I spent most of my time cleaning old Lee-Enfield rifles.

Occasionally the cadets would march up Commercial Drive. One day my best friend, Joe Warnock, and I didn't return from one of the marches, which took us past the Grandview School of Commerce, an all-girls school. Joe and I broke ranks, dallied over lunch and got into a lot of trouble. We wouldn't have made good soldiers.

The expectation at Britannia was that everybody participated in something, and I developed a passion for rugby. I was not very good. I would work my way up to the nineteenth or twentieth position, but there are only fifteen players to a side, so I had to wait until somebody was injured in order to play. But I just hung in and hung in because I wanted to play so desperately. I played hooker, in the middle of the front row of the scrum.

Eventually, Joe Warnock and I got kicked off the senior team for behaviour problems. The coach was a great guy but we rubbed him the wrong way, and we were unceremoniously dismissed. So we went on to play for the intermediate team. One of the teachers, Dave McKenzie, was the coach. McKenzie didn't really know anything about rugby, so Joe essentially took over running the team. But McKenzie spent a lot of time with us. He fashioned a team out of a bunch of rejects, and we became real contenders in the intermediate league. We just missed playing in the championship game.

One September, Joe and I were given detentions right up to the end of the year. When we protested, we were told, well, we'd probably get them anyway, so why not fill them out in advance? We were really angry. After about three days in detention, Miss Clark, the teacher who ran the operetta, came into the detention hall and asked for volunteers. "If you sing in the operetta, you'll get out of detention," she said. Up shot our hands, in we went to the operetta. It took us about six months to figure out it was a setup. But it was a wonderful setup. Suddenly there was a whole new world of exciting people at school, and I would have missed them without those detentions and the operetta. That's how they operated at Britannia. I was still playing rugby, but they obviously felt we should be doing other things too.

I had a social studies teacher named Monty Saunders. He had this big tome by a guy named Shapiro, with everything broken down into dates and times and, although I liked history, I found it a bit boring. Then one day we were sitting in Saunders's class when a bright spring afternoon turned suddenly dark and whappo, a thunderstorm hit. He was reading from Shapiro. Suddenly he slams his book down and turns on a little lamp on his desk and then turns off the main light in the room. And here we were in the midst of this storm that became even more explosive because of this sudden drama. We were puzzled until he reached in his drawer and brought out a book and started reading. It was Edgar Allan Poe's story "The Pit and the Pendulum."

We were about sixteen years old, macho, ready to take on the world. And this guy starts reading "The Pit and the Pendulum." That's the closest I ever came to losing bladder control in a classroom. It was frightening, intriguing, scary and enticing. By the time that class was over, I could hardly wait to get to the library to find out who the hell Edgar Allan Poe was.

Many of the teachers at Britannia were like that. They could seize the moment, leave the curriculum and bang, hit you with an experience that leaves an imprint for life. These were public school teachers. I didn't know until I left there what a gift I had received from that school. When people attack public school education, they make a serious mistake. If they can generalize in their criticism, then I can generalize in my praise. Whoever you were, whatever you were, at Britannia you were somebody. There was room for everybody, and that was because those teachers cared.

There are people I've met through my career who went to Britannia, and the East End is still in their blood. Socred Attorney General Robert Bonner was a Britannia grad. Another was Wesley Black, also a Socred, a bluff, hail-fellow-well-met character and a very decent man. I didn't know Bonner or Black then; they were a generation ahead of me. Bob Williams, who later became a colleague and a minister in our administration, was several years behind me. The school had a seventy-fifth reunion a few years ago. It was jam-packed with people from all over the world.

I grew up in a home where education was highly valued, and my mother and father expected me to go to university as my brother had before me. My brother got his B.A. and his Masters from the University of British Columbia, and he has a doctorate from the University of Washington. He was a fisheries biologist with the U.S. Department of the Interior, and highly regarded in his profession. He was in charge of the La Jolla lab in California. When I was premier, my mother telephoned me in Victoria one day all breathless to say that Izzy, already an internationally recognized researcher in ocean sciences, had just earned a Ph.D. with distinction. There was a pause and she asked if I got the message. I said, "No, Mom, what's the message?" And she replied, "When are you going to return to school and make something of yourself?"

Unfortunately, there wasn't much pressure on my sister, who was very bright and competent. She left school early and went to work and then got married. She is still married to the same fellow, Solly Barrat, who fought and was wounded with the American ski troops in Italy in the Second World War. They have a wonderful family and have lived in Seattle since their marriage.

Despite the pressure and the expectations, I fooled around a great deal and did just enough to get through at school. I was enjoying all the surging emotions of being an adolescent in the East End of Vancouver. By that time, we had seen it all—people using drugs, bootleggers, the seamy side of life. I remember going to Monty's Pool Hall on Commercial Drive when I was sixteen, where I saw a guy holding one of those little Zippo lighters under a spoon. He had a needle and he was taking a fix right in the back of the pool hall. It was fairly normal to see these things in the East End in those days. We all knew it was going on, but we also knew it was something you didn't mess with. You saw it, you shut up about it, but you knew it was there.

This was the social inoculation of living in the real world. It wasn't the antiseptic suburbs. Things weren't really violent, not the way they are today. But there was the same kind of hysteria among the older generation about the adolescents. Young people wore zoot suits in those days, large draped outfits that looked several sizes too large. I was never in the vanguard of fashion, but I wore zoot suit trousers, strides as they were called, made by tailors in Chinatown. The *Sun* and the *Province* would publish stories every so often warning against the dangers of "Zoot suit gangs" and the mythical underworld of "Hoodlums in zoot suits." I was puzzled by the stories. But on reflection, I realize the reporters probably had hangovers and were working to deadline and had to produce a story. I guess it sold newspapers.

After graduating from Britannia, I went to Seattle University in the fall of 1948. It is a Jesuit university. To support myself, I got a job in a clothing outlet, Fleischman's, on Olive Street. I lived with my sister for three months, then moved into one of the dormitories. The following year, I moved into Veterans' Hall, where there were rules about drinking, gambling and fooling around, all of which were ignored. Both the U.S. and Canada were desperate for competent, skilled people after the war. The universities were thrown open to veterans, and I think it changed university education for the better. The idea of a university imposing social rules on people who had acquired life skills during wartime was ridiculous, and I arrived in that atmosphere. Good timing.

There was a lot of gambling in Seattle, pool halls and little tobacco stands. The cities were much more open then; Vancouver was the same way. This guy was running a little bookie joint down where I worked folding trousers. I made a bet on Truman, who was running for president against Dewey in 1948. The odds were 10-to-1 against Truman. But I just knew Truman was going to win. Dewey was an uptight stuffed shirt, while Truman had called a reporter a son of a bitch for criticizing his daughter's musical talents. I didn't care what the pollsters said, I knew a guy like that had to be close to Americans' hearts. I mean, how could a guy who called a reporter a son of a bitch lose an election? That's something I would find out later on wasn't universally true, but anyway, I put a ten-dollar bill on Truman and won a small bundle. I was happier than hell.

I had a wonderful time at university, but I was on academic probation much of the time. I was the only Jewish student in residence, but I didn't feel any sort of racial prejudice or isolation. As for religious pressure, it was nonexistent. I do remember that when Truman fired General Douglas MacArthur there was a tumultuous reaction among the American population. In the midst of this ferment, a plane flew over the university and dropped leaflets. I picked one up and it said, "Stop the Jewish-Catholic conspiracy against America. Vote General Douglas MacArthur for president."

Seattle University was very small, very intimate, so very quickly you knew the teachers. The president of the university was Father Lemieux, a generous, open man. I walked into the reception area outside his office with one of these pamphlets and told his secretary I wanted an appointment. Father Lemieux said, "Oh, Dave, yeah, come on in. What's up?" I laid the pamphlet on his desk. He said, "Don't be upset about that, Dave." "I'm not upset, Father." He said, "You're not upset?" "No," I said, "I just want to know if there is a deal. If there is, I want my piece of the action." He burst out laughing and threw me out of his office. It was that kind of atmosphere.

I was receiving $15 a month from my father to help with my rent and other expenses, and sometimes I gambled it. In the fall of my third year he found out about that, so the money was stopped. I came home and got into a hell of a row with him and he said, "You want to gamble, gamble on your money. You want to go to school, you go to school on my money." I wasn't about to take this, so I quit school. To raise money, I bought a bunch of Christmas trees and set up a stand across the street from my dad's store, where people would know me. I made about $150.

A few days later I was sitting with my brother in a restaurant three doors down from my dad's store. Izzy asked what I planned to do. I told him I would like to go back to school, but I didn't have enough money. I had made only $150, and there was no damned way I was going to ask the old man for a nickel. He could shove his money where the sun doesn't shine. So my brother said, "Well, do you really want to go back?" I said, "Yeah." And he loaned me $300.

I went back to Seattle for the spring term. That summer, I worked for the Jolly Green Giant canneries just outside Walla Walla, in Washington State. I worked with Mexican migrant workers, and we worked thirteen hours a day, seven days a week. We got no overtime until after fifty-six hours a week. I managed to stash about $800 over the summer. Among my experiences there were a lesson on capitalism, a lesson on bigotry and a lesson on plain theft.

The lesson on capitalism came with the requirement that we eat in the company cafeteria, with the cost of our meals deducted from our paycheque. If we went to the local grocery store to buy food to avoid cafeteria bills, whatever price was marked on the item would be doubled at the cash register. It was a two-tiered price system, one for the locals and one for the cannery workers.

The second lesson was the treatment of the Mexicans who worked at the cannery. They were forced to sleep in the fields while the whites slept in barracks. On the last day, when we were about to be paid off, we noticed that the U.S. immigration service had been called in by the company to round up the Mexicans and ship them out as illegal immigrants. I hope they got paid.

Finally, I had deposited all my pay in the branch of the Seattle First National Bank in Dayton, Washington. Unusually for me, I had kept all my deposit slips. When I arrived in Seattle to claim my funds, I discovered only about half of the money had been deposited in my account. After some fuss, I produced my deposit slips and my accounts were made good. Obviously, somebody was stealing at the Dayton end. So much for a small company town.

At the end of summer, I came home and met my brother in the restaurant down the street from my father's store. Izzy was getting ready to go back to university. I peeled off $300 and shoved the money across to him. We were having a meal, and he just looked at the money and kept on eating. I looked at him and said, "What the hell's the matter with you? Take the money." He said, "What the hell is the matter with you?" and shoved the money back. We did this a couple more times, and then he said, "You know, you are even dumber than the old man thinks you are. Where in hell do you think I got $300 from?"

I couldn't say a word. I picked up the money and walked down to my dad's store. I had tears streaming down my face. To discover that my father had financed my return to university by having my brother loan me the $300 was just too much. He knew I would never have accepted it from him, so he cooked up this ruse with Izzy so I could finish my education. I just went over and hugged him. I couldn't say a word.

While I was attending Seattle University, I would come back to

Vancouver at least once a month and stay in the house on McSpadden. Joe Warnock and a bunch of other guys from Britannia were going to U.B.C., and we would hang out together. One night we ran into a group of girls and I met Shirley Hackman. She was from West Vancouver and was working for B.C. Tel. The following night there was a beach party down on Spanish Banks where we built a bonfire and drank beer. It was a wonderful, warm evening in May. Shirley was with a guy named Herbie. I opened a beer for Herbie and proceeded to get him liquored up. Finally Herbie fell asleep and I made my move.

Some of us had gone swimming without bathing suits, and I'm sitting there with my trousers on, drying my underwear on a stick. I got to talking with Shirley. One thing led to another, and pretty soon Shirley and I started going around together. We dated for two years. She went around with other guys and I went around with other girls but it was still pretty steady.

I always had jobs, all kinds of jobs. The summer I met Shirley I was twenty and working on a CNR train between Vancouver and Edmonton. The following year I worked for the City of Vancouver, pouring hot tar on cracks in the road, then shovelling sand on them. Goulashing, it's called. I also cut grass with a scythe that summer. I belonged to the Vancouver Civic Outside Workers Union, which was very militant. Wherever I was, I always joined a union because of my family background.

I was just scraping by in the classroom, so it took me an extra six months to graduate from university. I finished my B.A. in 1953 and returned to Vancouver. One day Shirley announced that it was time for us to set a date to get married. I told her that was not a very romantic way to go about it; wasn't I supposed to get down on my knees and ask for her hand? "I'm not waiting for that," she said. "I'm ready to get married, and if you are not going to marry me then I'll go out with someone else." And she meant it.

I remember sitting down and thinking, I'm only twenty-two. I knew I was going to get married someday, but I really didn't know what love was. I mean, I didn't hear rockets shooting off or see stars or anything, but I really liked this woman. I was very happy with her and I liked to be with her. I finally decided to phone and ask her out. She said, "No, I'm going out with somebody else."

"What?"

"Yes," she said. "I'm going out this Saturday night with someone else."

"Well, are you busy all next week?"

"I don't know yet," she replied.

At that point, I was about to lose it. The next time we went out I said, "Okay, let's get married," and we set the date for October 16. My father was not too happy about it. He thought I was too young to get married. My mother reverted to her traditional role: she went right up the wall. This progressive mother of mine wanted me to marry a Jewish girl, and Shirley was Anglican. My mother called my sister, who rushed up from Seattle. My sister was very supportive during that time.

The fact was, my parents didn't even know Shirley. My dad had met her once or twice. My mother knew I was going around with somebody, but she had been in a state of denial. When confronted with the knowledge that I was really serious about getting married, she went into a deep cultural dive and spent a week in mourning. She was losing a son. There was heavy-duty pressure on me to end this thing.

Shirley's mother and stepfather weren't too pleased, but they weren't really unhappy, either. Shirley had been living on her own as a working girl for a couple of years and was pretty independent. I got along with her mother and stepfather very well, but they were concerned about what she was doing. Besides, they certainly weren't in a position to throw a wedding party for their daughter.

Shirley and I decided to put on our own wedding. We rented a hall, bought the booze, invited all our friends and family, and had one hell of a party. We got married in a civil ceremony that lasted about ten minutes. My mother came with my sister and she was in tears. My dad slipped me fifty bucks, but he didn't attend the ceremony because my mother was there. They were split up by then.

The wedding was in the afternoon and that night we had the party. The whole thing cost $300. Three days later, we were broke. We scrounged up 27 cents, bought a savoy cabbage and cooked it for dinner. For forty-two years now, we have had a savoy cabbage every fall. It's a treasured memory. I remember what Shirley said at the time. "We're broke," she said, "but we're not poor. There's a distinction."

Two

Higher Yearnings

I was a case worker at the Children's Aid Society when Shirley and I were married. I had been working there since shortly after I graduated from Seattle University with a degree in sociology and a minor in philosophy. While I was at university I had become interested in the doctrines of Thomas Aquinas. Aquinas held that legitimate power springs not from the divine right of kings but from the commonwealth of people. To my mind this was a reasonable, orderly approach to life, and it was very useful in helping me sort out the questions we all struggle with. But I was at a loss as to how I would earn a living. With my grades, I felt academia was out of the question. Social work was an application of what I had learned in school, so that's where I focussed my job search. My application to the Children's Aid Society was accepted immediately, partly because there were very few men in the profession.

It was my first real job, and I was required to wear a tie. I borrowed $2 from Shirley to buy one, but I didn't know how to tie it so I had the salesman knot the tie for me. I would slip it over my head in the morning and hang it on the door at night. Ultimately, that tie rotted apart, much as my attitude towards the social work establishment deteriorated once my eyes were opened to how indifferently kids are treated in our society.

I had a caseload of seventy-eight kids, all in foster homes. One seventeen-year-old kid, who is now a very successful businessman, had come from Britain through the Fairbridge Society, which sent disadvantaged youths to homes in Canada. He was really smart, but totally screwed up. I was having a hell of a time with him. I spent a lot of time with him in the office, which is how you did it in those days. That was going nowhere, however, so I tried a different approach.

I was playing with the ex-Britannia rugby team, and one day I decided to take him to practice. We were just a bunch of old boys, and they didn't care who you brought. He got thumped around in the scrum and jostled in the line outs. A little machismo and rough and tumble was sprinkled into the stew. I took this kid a number of times and we began to bond.

One day my supervisor, Jack Saunders, called me in. It was very intense. They were worried about my relationship with this kid. "Yeah, he's a real jerk, but there's a lot in this kid and this is the only way I can get close to some of it," I said. I knew I wasn't being very clinical, but my supervisor was obviously more concerned about something else. So I asked him point blank what it was. He said, "We are concerned about homosexuality."

I got really involved with my kids. What I saw at the Children's Aid Society and later in the prison system crystallized in me this anger, still unresolved, about how kids are screwed by the establishment. But I wasn't aware of this at the time. I was just doing the job I wanted to do. I was twenty-two, living a great life and going with Shirley and my supervisor hits me with homosexuality. I burst out laughing and said, "Hell, Jack, am I missing something?"

He didn't see the humour in that. He was a fine supervisor and we got on very well. But he was reflecting the homophobia of the times. My style was different. I tried different approaches. I complained about the wages. Already, I was swimming upstream. I also found I was ill equipped to deal with some of the problems. In one instance, I was expected to discuss menstruation with the foster parents of two teen-aged girls in my caseload. The only problem was, nobody had ever discussed it with me. I went to the nurse's office and asked for some help. The nurse sat me down, pulled out some charts, and gave me a basic lesson on human development.

Not long after, I left the agency to take a position as program officer in the young offenders unit at Oakalla, an aging, overcrowded provincial prison in Burnaby. I was making $200 a month at the society and at Oakalla I could make $255, so off I went. I soon found myself at odds with the establishment there, too. My immediate boss was Merv Davis, one of the most thoughtful, progressive and inventive social workers I had ever worked with. But the custody side of the prison was very rigid, and my first run-in came when I wanted to take a softball team I was coaching out into the community to play games. It was a knock-down, drag-out fight. I won, but at a cost.

Once I began having these difficulties with the powers that be, I realized that if I was ever going to get anywhere in social work, I needed professional training. I applied to the U.B.C. school of social work and was turned down. So I drove down to Seattle University to speak with Father Harrington, who taught sociology. In the first course I took from him I got a D. He stopped me in the hallway one day and apologized for giving me such a low mark. Imagine. "Why, Father?" I asked. "Well, Dave," he said, "if you had come to class, I'm sure you would have done better." The Jesuits taught humility along with creating guilt.

Father Harrington told me to write to St. Louis University in Missouri. "There's a good school of social work there," he said. "You apply and tell them you went to Seattle University." I got the distinct impression he was going to phone somebody, although he never said that.

When I applied to St. Louis University in the spring of 1954, Shirley was pregnant. People were counting. It was a big thing in those days. Everybody was very relieved when Dan was born on August 9, 1954, ten months after we were married. I was excited as hell about becoming a father. But I was also uncertain about our future. Then one day I received this letter from Father Scheller in St. Louis. It was about three pages long, analysing every reason why I shouldn't become a social worker—my grades, my work habits, you name it. The last paragraph said, "The admissions committee has made an exception in your case and we are accepting you on academic probation." Shirley and I were just jumping with delight. Obviously, Father Harrington had phoned up and asked them to give me a break. And the fix was in. We found out years later Father Scheller was the entire admissions committee.

We rented a place in a fairly new low-rental housing project in St. Louis county. We bought a mattress and slept on it on the floor, and we had a big wicker laundry basket for Dan. We had saved $900, but it didn't last long. Our rent was $83 a month and all we were sure of was $85. That's what my dad was sending us. Since I had been accepted on probation, I had agreed to attend school full time, with no work on the side. But I quickly found that was impossible, so I quietly looked around for a job and found one at the YMHA, the Jewish counterpart to the YMCA. I was a group worker with teen-aged kids. This proved to be a great opportunity to meet young, aggressive social workers from all parts of the U.S., and I really treasured that time with them.

We had arrived in St. Louis towards the end of the McCarthy era, which saw many fine people's lives and careers ruined because they were branded Communists or Communist sympathizers. Neither Shirley nor I were actively engaged in politics, but we were interested in everything going on around us. Once Oregon Senator Wayne Morse came to town and was scheduled to speak at the Jewish Community Center. By that time, he was sitting as an independent, after having been elected as a Republican. He eventually became a Democrat. As a liberal progressive, Morse was a remarkable figure in those days. Shirley and I got a baby-sitter and went to hear him. There must have been five hundred people there, and we noticed there were men in dark suits taking pictures of everybody who was going into the hall. We quickly deduced that this must be the FBI or the CIA, engaged in the silly practice of the United States spying on its own citizens.

There were many exciting things happening in St. Louis in those days, some good and some bad. One of the bad things was the development of the Pruitt-Igoo housing project, named after two war heroes, one black and one white. They developed high-rises and placed people, mainly from the downtown black community, into these giant, monolithic, human filing cabinets. Anybody with brains would have understood those buildings were a disaster waiting to happen. But it was public housing and people thought it was progress. Twenty years later I returned for an honorary doctor of laws degree from St. Louis University and arrived just as they were blowing the project up.

There was an incredible controversy brewing in St. Louis about ending school segregation. It was absolutely strange to Shirley and me. The parochial schools were segregated as well as some public schools. I picked up the newspaper one morning and howled with laughter at a speech made by the newly installed Catholic Archbishop Ritter. He said, "We are now going to deal with segregation in parochial schools. You can either accept integration or be excommunicated." I love that kind of leadership where choices are very clear.

I worked for the YMHA on the q.t., and did my university placement at the St. Louis Family and Children's Service. This was an upper-middle-class agency that dealt with "the poor," and I was beginning to see the same attitudes that I had bristled at as a social worker in B.C. Sometimes economics rather than the welfare of the child was the determining factor in adoption placements. My supervisor was Don Schlegel, who had been a social worker through the Depression and was one of those open-minded, decent, almost selfless people the U.S. is noted for producing. I learned a great deal from him in the field. At first, I was committed to keeping my mouth shut because I had been in trouble in Vancouver for speaking out, but slowly I opened up about what I really felt. He was a very good influence, trying to teach me to exercise control and not to go bursting into things like a bull in a china shop.

At the same time, he had a lovely touch of healthy paranoia about the system. He taught me, for example, to make three carbon copies of everything I did, all the social work reports, all the summaries, all the correspondence. He always carried the third copy in his car. Whenever he was dealing with police or other agencies and they said they had never heard from him or received a letter, he just retrieved the file. This little device helped when I was a young MLA. I always had the file. I called it the CYA experience—cover your ass.

I had a professor at St. Louis University, Dr. Catherine Radke, who had escaped from Germany in 1935 with just a suitcase. She was only about five feet tall. She had a deformed hip and walked with a painful limp. She was brilliant and disciplined but also very Germanic and quite different from the laid-back American Jesuit professors I was used to. By reputation, this woman was frightening, demanding and very tough. I had made up my mind and pledged to Shirley that I was going to shut up and just write what I needed to write and do what I needed to do to get through school. No taking risks or getting into fights. I wrote a paper for Dr. Radke and gave her the rote answers I assumed she wanted. When I got the paper back, there was red pencil all the way through it. The woman who owned this red pencil was obviously angry. At the bottom was an almost indecipherable scrawl saying, "See me about this."

I thought, "My god, what have I done?" I had only been in school two months and already I was in trouble. I made an appointment and she said, "Sit down, Mr. Barrett." She looked at me very crisply. Time was not to be wasted with her. She was really living up to her image and I was scared to death. "Is this what you really think?" she asked, holding up my paper. Before I could even answer she went on a tirade. "Every seven years, on a cycle, we get some students we think are worth teaching. This is the seventh year. You might be one of those, but I don't know."

She told me, "Never write this kind of stuff again. I want to know what is in here." She took her finger and pointed it at her head. "I demand that from you. Now you can leave." I hadn't even said a word. I just crawled out of there.

That was the beginning of the most exciting and stimulating relationship I had with any teacher. Dr. Radke was a German social democrat, a Catholic, who had been head of the Cologne social services department. She was involved in the democratic politics of the left, was an outspoken critic of segregation and exulted in the archbishop saying "integration or excommunication." She became my academic mentor, but only after I graduated did she allow herself to become a personal friend. She really liked Shirley and enjoyed visiting with her on social occasions at school, but she never showed any warmth or undue attention to me as a student. The second year, she made me go through hoops. I thought she didn't like me. But what she was really doing was educating me. Everything I had felt instinctively was reinforced by this woman; all my arguments and emotions were honed into a professional rage. I became a crusader inside the profession, and she played a major part in that.

Money was a chronic problem. At one point I considered transferring to Washington University, another fine school in St. Louis, in a bid to tap into their somewhat broader scholarship program. I went in to see Father Scheller, and before I could even finish what I was saying, he said, "I think you are going to be pleasantly surprised." Within a month, towards the end of my first year, I discovered that I had won a Catholic scholarship worth $2,500. I hadn't even applied for it. It was awarded to me because it was incorporated in a work-study program at the St. Louis County Juvenile Court and I was interested in corrections.

Shortly after it was announced that I had won the scholarship, I got a note in my student's pigeonhole to go and see Father Henle, dean of graduate studies. I thought I had screwed up the scholarship or something. I wasn't exactly Mr. Goody-Two-Shoes as a student. I had a buddy named Joe Boleddo, and occasionally we would go off campus at lunchtime and hit a place called Girardello's, where we'd drink beer and talk about how we were going to change the world. Then we would return to class with beer on our breath.

I had these thoughts on my mind when the secretary took me into Father Henle's office, where he was writing at his desk. I sat down and he kept on writing. I sat there, not saying a word. A minute seems like a long time when there is silence. Probably about thirty seconds went by and I said, "Excuse me, Father, why did you call me here?"

"Oh," he said. "It's quite all right. Congratulations. I just wanted to see the first Jew I know who got money out of Catholics." And then he burst out laughing.

Many years later, in the spring of 1973, as premier I took a delegation to New York to meet the banking and investment community. British Columbia had done business with Salomon Brothers for many years, and we also had extensive discussions with Moody's and Standard and Poor's, the two bond-rating agencies. On the three-man Moody's team was a vice-president named McArthur. He said very little during the two hours we spent there going through the accounts. They were worried about socialists and we had recently brought down our first budget, but we had a solid economy and they were satisfied. It was a good meeting. As we left McArthur's office, he said, "Oh, Mr. Barrett, before you go, I have a message for you."

I was taken aback. "You have a message for me?"

"Yes," he replied. "I am on the board of Catholic University of America in Washington, D.C., and Father Henle is president of the school."

I looked at him. I must have had a very weird look on my face. I had only met Father Henle that one time in his office. "You're kidding," I said.

"I almost wrote the message down because it seemed so strange," McArthur said. "But I remember exactly what Father Henle asked me to say. He said, 'Now that you've made it to the big time, Dave, send the money back.'"

The summer before I began the work-study program at juvenile court, I read a book by John Deutsch about how U.S. training schools messed children up for life. One of the most damning, searing chapters was on the detention centre in Boonville, Missouri. Not long after I finished the book I spent my first day in court. Judge Noah Weinstein, just elected, was taking the bench for the first time. This sixteen-year-old kid was on trial and the prosecution said he should go to Boonville. I gasped and said, "No." I'm a student, sitting in the back, about twelve people in the room, and I've opened my mouth.

The judge looked at me and said, "Who are you and what are you doing here?" I told him I was a student at St. Louis University, and he said, "What do you mean saying no about Boonville? Have you ever been there?" "No," I answered, and he said, "Court's adjourned. This case will be dealt with next week. You, you and you stay here." He pointed at me and another student, who was from the Washington University School of Social Work, and our supervisor.

I thought, It's over. Pack our bags: we're going back to Vancouver. He asked a series of questions and I told him who I was and that I was Canadian. He asked the other student for her name and then said, "Okay, you and you are going to Boonville. I've never been there and you've never been there. Go for a couple of days and write me a report."

We started hemming and hawing and he said, "You don't have any money, do you? You're students." He took out his wallet, peeled off $200 and said, "Take this." We spent a day and a half at Boonville and wrote a scathing report. The prisoners, who were all kids, were crammed together with no privacy and inadequate toilet facilities. There were no services to prepare the kids for the day when they left the institution. The staff seemed to be doing their jobs, but with little sensitivity. It was just a dumping ground. When we presented our report to the judge, the other student said she had spent her $100, but I gave him about $15 change. "Now I know the difference between Americans and Canadians," he said. "You gave me change. With Americans, there is no change." From that day on, he never sent another kid to Boonville.

I discovered later that Noah Weinstein was a real power in both the Democratic Party and the Missouri legal system. During my work-study, he took me under his wing and actually by-passed the supervisory structure by assigning cases directly to me. He treated me like his personal social worker.

One case involved two black kids, one of whom was a chronic bicycle thief. The older one, a fifteen-year-old, had already been to Boonville, and the other was just twelve. The police are in court and Judge Weinstein is ushered in by the clerk. Everyone stands and he sits down. He just sits there. There was a deathly silence and I wondered if the judge was sick. There was only a handful of people, including the two cops, the kids, staff from the attorney general's department and some flunky lawyer for juvenile court. The judge is staring at the cops. This goes on awhile and the cops start fidgeting. One takes his hat off and the other takes his hat off. Still, the judge is staring at them. I knew I was witnessing something, but I didn't know what it was. Then the cops took their guns out of their holsters and walked out of the room and left their guns outside. "Now court will proceed," the judge said.

The older kid received a stern lecture and got placed on probation. Then Judge Weinstein turned to the twelve-year-old and said, "It seems to me we have a serious problem here. To correct the problem, I'm buying you a bike. If you come back in this court again, I'm taking the bike away and you're going to be in big trouble." We never saw the kid again. That was the end of it, and you could have criminologists from here to Timbuktu and hold conferences and never arrive at anything as simple and effective. I'm not saying it would work in every case, but it was a demonstration to me that you can cut through all the bullshit and do something very practical.

At the same time, Shirley and I were having a hell of a lot of fun. We discovered the DeBolivar strip, where they had jazz bands. Occasionally we would get a baby-sitter on a Saturday night, hit the strip and buy a pitcher of beer for fifty cents. Shirley would type my school papers, and one night I refused to finish a paper because I was tired. "You have to finish the paper," Shirley said. "It's due tomorrow." I said I was too goddamned tired and that was it. We were having a discussion. We never had arguments; we had discussions. "Well, I'm not going to bed until you finish the paper," she said. I asked what she meant by that, and she said, "I'm not going to bed with you until you finish this." I asked if she was using sex as a bargaining chip in our relationship and she said yes. Needless to say, I finished the damned paper. And I'm glad to say I was never threatened with that again.

Our second son, Joe, was born in St. Louis on July 6, 1956, a month after I graduated. Our family was well on its way. By this time we had bought an old Studebaker and we spent a great deal of time together at a local park, where there were swings and picnic tables. We also visited with Don Schlegel and his family.

My dad came down for my graduation. The following month, my mother came and stayed a month and helped Shirley with the kids. This visit was the beginning of a strong friendship between my mother and Shirley that lasted right up until my mother died. This woman, who hadn't wanted her Jewish son to marry a gentile girl, did a complete reversal. Now I was a no-good. I didn't deserve this wonderful woman. They had an incredible relationship.

The work-study program that was part of my scholarship required me to work for a year after graduation as a probation officer at the juvenile court in St. Louis county. My salary was $400 a month. Judge Weinstein had gone off the circuit by then, but I was still very busy, working full time at the court. By the end of the year, Shirley and I wanted to come home. Judge Weinstein offered to send me to law school. I was overwhelmed, but I had to say no. I was asked by a social work agency to apply for a job in India, and I had applied for and made the shortlist for a position as probation officer in Eugene, Oregon. But nothing could match the lure of Vancouver.

Then one day I received a telegram from John Braithwaite, with whom I had worked at Oakalla, asking if I would take a job as supervisor of social training at Haney Correctional Institute at $355 a month. I accepted immediately. I liked Braithwaite very much and it was a brand-new job at Haney. We were going home.

Three

Power for a Purpose

Haney Correctional Institute was a new facility, built at a cost of $5 million, which was a lot of money then. I was responsible for the social program, working 3:00 P.M. to 11:00 P.M., and I had some definite ideas about what I wanted to accomplish. I wanted to bring the concept of a community recreation centre to the prison. I had a staff of fourteen program officers, and I supplemented them with an inmates' council and told them to design a program that ran the gamut from basketball to drama. To run the drama group, I hired a guy named Tony Holland, who had been vice-principal of the Old Vic and later enjoyed a fine career in B.C., including responsibility for the drama program at Langara College.

Tony recruited a volunteer named Barbara Walker, who went on to become the wife of Senator Ray Perrault, to help him. It worked like magic. Their first production won in the one-act category of the B.C. drama festival that year.

At first, the social program was panned by the custodial section. "What the hell are you doing? Lock them in the slammer and throw away the key": that was the attitude. But the program was a success. In addition to the drama group, we ran a damn good basketball team and had interest groups.

Haney was supposed to provide occupational training and rehabilitation for the inmates. There were thirteen apprentice shops, twelve of which required three years of apprenticeship. But the maximum stay at Haney was two years less a day. The average stay was nine months. So we didn't even have an inmate long enough to complete his vocational training! Now who the hell had done the planning and not thought about those things? The whole foundation of this "modern prison" was farcical, but nobody wanted to talk about it.

After about a year of working extremely hard on this three-to-eleven shift, I started to get weary. By that time, Shirley and I had bought a little house in Haney, and I wanted to work days. A job came open for the supervisor of casework services, and I applied. I was turned down. Then a guy named Reg Cook was promoted to business manager from personnel and staff training officer, and I put in an application for his old job. It was pretty obvious to me that the institution was happy with the social program, which was winning all kinds of professional and public relations kudos. They tried to dissuade me from applying for this other position, but they couldn't turn me down because I was the most qualified applicant. I got the job. It was a lateral move at the same category, $510 a month. That was big money in those days.

I spent a year as personnel and staff training officer, during which time I started to do some reflecting. I was concerned that we were not turning out men who were equipped to go to work when they got out of prison. Some of the men were ending up back in jail, an indication that the system wasn't working. I began to raise questions within the institution, and it alienated some people.

Then along came Tony Gargrave, a CCF MLA who, with others in the party, had argued for more thoughtful use of prisons. Gargrave came out to look Haney over and I was assigned to show him around. Gargrave was very enthusiastic about the prison. But I explained to him that the project had been launched without the proper critical analysis, and that was undermining its effectiveness. We had a hell of a talk. I confessed I was a CCFer and I really opened up to him about how frustrated I felt at being powerless to reform the system.

We got on so well I invited him to dinner. I phoned Shirley and told her I was bringing an MLA home. "An MLA? Oh my god, Dave, all we have is wieners." We both had the view that an MLA was some kind of big shot. Anyway, we all ate wieners, and after dinner we put the kids to bed and started talking. Gargrave asked if I had ever thought about running for office.

I considered his question. I had come to realize that the only effective way to change the correctional system would be through the political process. I had been instrumental, with Bing Wilkes, in bringing the

British Columbia Government Employees Association to Haney, and that experience had reinforced my view that political power was essential for bringing about meaningful social change. "Well, yeah, I have thought about it. Lots of times," I said. Gargrave encouraged me to explore the idea if I was really interested, and that was the end of our conversation.

About a week later, I asked one of the union guys who the CCF contact was at Haney. "Oh, it's Hank Tyson," he said. "He's a part-time teacher up here. As a matter of fact, there he is down in the parking lot." I was on the second floor. I dashed down the stairs and out into the parking lot and called out to Tyson. He turned around and I blurted out, "Mr. Tyson, my name is David Barrett. I want to join the CCF. I want to be an MLA." He looked at me and said, "That's very interesting. Let's talk about it." I gave him my phone number and he promised to give me a call. I had made my mind up on the spur of the moment, just like that.

Soon Shirley and I were invited to the Tysons' house. There were five people seeking the CCF nomination in the Dewdney riding where Shirley and I lived. The strongest was Stu Leggatt, who had the backing of Erhart Regier, then MP for Burnaby-Coquitlam.

The CCF had never won in Dewdney, a sprawling cross section of burgeoning suburbs to the west and agricultural communities to the east. The seat was held by Socred Labour Minister Lyle Wicks, who had been one of the founders of Social Credit in the early 1950s and had been sitting as the MLA ever since. The closest we had come was in the previous election, when the CCF candidate was Naranjan Singh Grewall, a successful sawmill owner from Mission. Shirley and I later learned that the election race had been racially charged against Grewall, who was Indo-Canadian, and that Grewall had committed suicide soon after. Parts of the riding had the reputation of being very rednecked.

I decided while we were at the Tysons' to seek the nomination. Unbeknownst to me, after we left Hank and Dora Tyson were whooping and hollering, "We've found the candidate." This was 1958. There had been an election in 1956 and another was expected in 1959. As it turned out, it was called in 1960. The Tysons immediately became strong supporters along with Bill Franklin, a former International Woodworkers of America official. It was through Franklin that I first won the support of the IWA. I retained that support over the years through the leadership of Joe Morris, Jack Moore, Jack Munro and Gerry Stoney.

The CCF was very much a family movement in those days. Every Christmas the party held a concert for the kids, and most fund-raising was done at potluck suppers, with lively debates taking place about democratic socialism. It was at one of these get-togethers the Tysons introduced Shirley and me to Grace MacInnis, daughter of CCF founder J. S. Woodsworth and the woman whose name I had heard so frequently as a child on McSpadden Avenue. Grace was known as a peerless fighter for working people and a pioneer of the party. I was awed at meeting a legend, but she quickly put me at ease with her friendly, open, uncomplicated manner.

In 1959, Dr. Guy Richmond, a psychiatrist who had written a book on B.C. prisons, invited me to speak at U.B.C. Richmond worked for the province's corrections branch, and we had met during his frequent visits to Oakalla and Haney. The university was hosting an international congress on corrections, and Richmond wanted me to give a critique of the keynote speaker's presentation. There were a hell of a lot of people throughout the corrections system who should have been given a whack at this, but I got the nod and I was flabbergasted. I couldn't wait to get home and tell Shirley. When I told the Tysons, they said it would be a good opportunity for Grace MacInnis to hear me speak. It was arranged that Shirley would go to the conference with her.

The keynote speaker was an internationally renowned corrections expert from Holland, Dr. Otto Baan, who gave an enlightening explanation as to why prisons are so advanced in that country. During the Second World War, all the Dutch politicians were thrown in jail, and the ones who survived came out saying the system was crazy. They went on to establish a system of diminished responsibility, which says if you are incapable of making rational decisions you may go to jail but you are going to get treatment while you are being held in custody. If you are capable of making rational decisions and you break the law, that's where punishment comes in. Severe punishments would only occur when people were deemed not to have diminished responsibility.

It made sense. It still makes sense. In my critique, I made an impassioned plea about adopting this concept, especially for twelve-year-old kids and young offenders. I was very nervous. I recall that my voice was a bit shrill at times. But I knew what I wanted to say. When I saw Shirley after the meeting I asked her how it had gone. "Oh, it was great, Dave," she said. Then I asked her what Grace MacInnis had thought. "She just leaned over and said, 'He'll do,'" Shirley told me.

After that I threw myself into the nomination fight. The Dewdney constituency had set up panels in the spring of 1959 in Haney, Mission, Agassiz, Coquitlam and Port Moody where candidates would strut their stuff prior to the nominating convention in the fall. I was very critical of the social welfare system. I attacked the way we were spending more money to break families up than to keep them together. I was knocking welfare waste from a different angle, and my speeches were getting covered by the local press.

About halfway through this series of panels, the warden at Haney called me in. I told him that yes, I was seeking the nomination. He wanted to know if I thought this was appropriate behaviour, and I asked if there were any rules against it. "Well, you are a civil servant," he said. "Fine," I said. "What are the rules? I am the personnel officer, and I am not aware of anything in writing preventing me as a civil servant from seeking the nomination." And there wasn't anything.

From that day forward, however, the heat was on. A little later, I was called into a meeting with E.G.B. Stevens and Rocky Smith. Stevens was head of corrections for the province. Smith was assistant director of corrections. They had called me in to Stevens's office to discuss my political activities. I recall they were both very uncomfortable.

The gist of the conversation was that the government didn't want me to continue running. I again asked what rule I was breaking. Stevens suggested my career advancement could be stymied by my political activity. "Mr. Stevens," I said, "you're not suggesting that if I cease and desist I will get a promotion?"

He burst out laughing. "Oh, come on, Dave."

"If you are suggesting that, Mr. Stevens, I would appreciate you putting it in writing so I can consider it."

I got even more uppity. I said I had my rights as a civil servant to do on my own time whatever I wished to do. "But you are criticizing the department," Stevens replied.

"No," I said. "I am not criticizing corrections. I am certainly criticizing social welfare services, but in a generic sense."

"You are splitting hairs," Stevens said.

"Yes, I am."

Smith, who hadn't said much during the meeting, announced that he and Stevens were taking me to lunch. Later, Stevens and I went to the washroom. We were standing side by side, taking a leak. Stevens asked if I was going to continue in my attempt to unseat Lyle Wicks. I said I was.

"Good for you," Stevens said. "Just between us, I hope you get the nomination and beat Wicks."

I returned to the campaign with even greater determination. I was certain I was going to be fired, and that made me even more desperate to win the nomination. Stu Leggatt was very impressive. I kept thinking what a terrific candidate he would make, but I knew I had to beat him.

I was going through this period of angst when along came Bill Cunningham of CBC TV. Cunningham wanted to do a feature story on Haney, with special focus on the drama group and the basketball team. He brought a camera crew, including still photographer Gar Luney, and we spent two or three days doing the story. Shirley and I got to know Bill, and on the last day of shooting we asked him over. It was very relaxing, just drinking beer and having sandwiches. Then I told him I was getting fired, blurted out the whole story. I'll never forget what he said next: "Don't get fired until you talk to me." At that time, I had no idea how the media operated. He explained that he was not interfering with the news, he just wanted to be first to get the story.

About a month later I got a letter from Gilbert Kennedy, who was deputy attorney general. The letter detailed my refusal to cooperate during the interview with Stevens and said I was still "actively engaged in politics." It concluded by saying that this was not acceptable behaviour by a civil servant and that I was fired. I phoned Cunningham as we had agreed and told him what had happened. He told me to demand an appeal. I was really puzzled by this. The queen was in town, Cunningham explained, and the whole media was going to be focussed on her right through the weekend. "Demand an appeal and delay this thing until she leaves town," he said. I phoned Alf Bennett, assistant general secretary for the British Columbia Government Employees Association and a great human being, and an appeal was scheduled for the next day, a Friday, by deputy provincial secretary Lawrie Wallace. I went to Victoria for the hearing, but the decision wasn't to come down until Tuesday.

On Sunday night, Cunningham phoned: "Okay, you're fired." I didn't know what the hell he was talking about. "I've got Bonner in the can telling me you're fired," he said. I was still baffled, so he talked me through the fact that he had a taped interview with Attorney General Robert Bonner saying I was fired as of Monday. The decision wasn't due until Tuesday. "Now there's nothing else on the wire," Cunningham said. "The queen has left, there are no auto accidents, no fires, no other major stories. You're it."

The next day, I burst into public life in British Columbia. The front-page headline in the Vancouver *Sun* said, "Government fires employee seeking CCF bid in Dewdney." They ran my picture with an elaborate story about a young social worker who had lost a $510-a-month job. The story was followed a day later by an interview with Dirk Van der Bent, who had sought the Social Credit nomination in Burnaby when he was a civil servant but hadn't been fired. "It was certainly wrong to fire Barrett," Van der Bent said. "I was never once told there was anything wrong with my seeking the nomination."

I don't really believe Bonner wanted to fire me. What may have happened is that the Socred members in Wicks's constituency became agitated and put on the pressure to get me out. I don't suggest it was Wicks himself. To this day, I don't know what role he played. But within twenty-four hours my name was known across B.C. and I was martyred. I'm on radio, television, and I haven't even been nominated. My stock really shot up among the CCF membership in Dewdney.

Some very touching things happened as well. I don't think they would happen today. Maybe it was a hangover from the Depression. People still had bitter memories of hardships, jobs lost. Farmers started to leave eggs and vegetables on the doorstep of our little house in Haney. People were just incredible.

I finished work at Haney Correctional Institute on July 24, 1959. In August, I got a call from the John Howard Society, which does prisoner rehabilitation work. Their supervisor of counselling services had left. I was invited to apply for the job and was interviewed by the board chairman, J. D. Hobden, an Anglican minister and a great social reformer who had devoted his life to the society. I had figured I would be blacklisted in the profession because I was a hot potato. I later learned that Hobden was a very close friend and long-time associate of E.G.B. Stevens. We had a wonderful little English lunch in West Vancouver. Hobden said he would like me to join the society but needed to get one thing clear.

"We have no opinion about which political party any of our staff belong to," he said in his very proper British manner. "I just want you to tell me that at no time during your staff hours will you be busy on political activities." I gave my word and he said, "Fine, you will hear from us." I was told within a couple of days that I had the job. It turned out to be one of the most rewarding professional experiences of my life. The executive director was Merv Davis, whom I had worked for at Oakalla. Also on staff were Norm Levi, who later became a minister in our government, and Gloria Cranmer-Webster, a talented woman who is now a noted anthropologist and curator.

Meanwhile, the nomination fight continued. I campaigned with a vengeance. All my time off on weekends was spent sewing up that nomination. Then October 16 came. It was not only the day of reckoning for the nomination, it was Shirley's and my wedding anniversary. All the candidates showed up for the nomination meeting except Stu Leggatt. He was in the New Westminster Drama Club and decided to skip the nomination in order to attend a play rehearsal. To this day, I think he simply decided he didn't want the nomination. He was being pushed by Erhart Regier and a woman named Laura Albers. Regier was the MP for the area. Albers was a hard-nosed guru of the CCF in Dewdney and ran a significant part of the party out of her kitchen. A CCF pioneer from the prairies, she was shrewd, tough and in her late sixties when I met her. Leggatt was her political protégé, as Regier had been before him. Stu was eventually elected as MP for New Westminster and then MLA for Coquitlam-Moody and today is a close friend.

There were about 160 people eligible to vote at the nomination, and I got 116 votes. I won on the first ballot. Regier came up to me right away. He had a speech handicap. "G-g-g-good enough to beat my b-b-b-boy," he said, "you're g-g-g-good enough to w-w-w-win the election." He had a problem with alcohol. But to this day, I have never met anyone as politically skilled or astute as Erhart Regier was when he was sober. I mean anywhere—federally or provincially. Not my American political friends or my British political friends. Not anyone I know in Australia or New Zealand. He knew exactly where to expend time and energy for the best results. He organized the constituency on a poll-by-poll basis and kept the party machinery in place between elections, giving us a running start the next time around. Nobody could touch this Mennonite Sunday school teacher with a strong Christian conviction about social justice. "I w-w-w-want you to m-m-m-meet Laura Albers," he said. Leggatt had been their candidate, but neither was fazed by what had happened. The nominating convention was over, and now they were going to work for me.

I began a long political apprenticeship with Regier and Albers. I was immediately suspect to some of the old guard in the party and their ruffled feathers needed smoothing. In their eyes, I was a Johnny-come-lately. I had only joined the party during the year I ran. It wasn't like today, when you can join the party overnight. Another problem was my sense of humour. You couldn't be both humorous and a socialist with some of these people. At the same time, I came into contact with some of my childhood heroes. I met Harold Winch, CCF MP in Vancouver East and former MLA in Burnaby. My god, I was even on a first-name basis with Grace MacInnis!

It was during this time that I began the close personal and political friendships that continue to this day with Dave Stupich, Jimmy Rhodes, Alex Macdonald, Eileen Dailly and others. I also met Harvey and Peggy Beech, strong party supporters from the Coquitlam end of the riding. They, too, had been backing Leggatt. Harvey, a switchman for the CPR in Coquitlam, later went to work for me and continues to be a close confidant today.

The ten months leading into the 1960 election were very busy, very tumultuous. I went to work every day and I kept my pledge, kept the politics separate from what I was doing as a supervisor at the John Howard Society. Then I would rush home at night, have dinner with Shirley and the kids, and be off somewhere. It was quite an adjustment for our family. Shirley was pregnant again, with our daughter, Jane, who was born on June 24, 1960. She was dubbed our election baby.

Shirley wasn't at all sure what I was getting myself into, but she played the role of the demure candidate's wife to perfection. While I was driven by my ambition to become an MLA, Shirley started thinking about the party. She became a true social democrat, so eventually we were both engrossed in something that would become a central part of our lives. Her criticism, positive and negative, was very valuable throughout my years in politics.

The election was called for August 1960. The main issue was public ownership of B.C. Electric, which the Socreds had traditionally opposed and the CCF had favoured. Premier W.A.C. Bennett promised during the campaign not to take over the utility. (He seized it a year after the election and created B.C. Hydro, triggering a court case that cost the province $30 million.) My personal campaign focussed on waste in welfare services. Ironically, in light of what has since happened, most recently in Ontario, I was told by other CCF members that I would never win on that issue.

The east end of the riding, from Mission to Agassiz, was traditionally Socred territory. Albers's strategy was to push me into this area, where we had always done poorly at the polls. Farmers there had to pay a special tax on the dike beside the Fraser River that protected their land from flooding, and I promised to fight against that tax if elected.

The western part of the riding was largely a new population that had poured into the sprawling suburbs of Coquitlam, Port Coquitlam and Maillardville. I was invited to speak in Maillardville by Father Lawrence, who worked at the Haney Correctional Institute. It was a Sunday afternoon in the church hall after services. Father Lawrence introduced me in both French and English, since there were many French speakers in Maillardville, which had always voted Liberal. He told them I had studied with the Jesuits for six years. Then I got up and gave a brief speech. At the end, Father Lawrence thanked me with a grin on his face. "It's all right to vote for Monsieur Barrett," he said. "He is not a Catholic, but at least he is not a Protestant." Everyone burst into laughter and that broke the ice for me. When the votes were counted a month later, I had won every single poll in Maillardville.

We knocked on doors, had little parties for workers and held all-candidates meetings. Wicks did not participate in the all-candidates meetings, and I think that was a severe blow to him. I assume it was a calculated decision by the Socreds to keep him out of the spotlight. I knew nothing of strategy or tactics. I just went to everything and anything I could to make an appearance. I worked very energetically, but at one point Dan and Joe wanted to go fishing so I took a Saturday morning off. The boys and I walked through Haney to the river, our fishing poles over our shoulders. People waved as we went by. The campaign committee was divided about whether I could afford even that little time off. But I insisted. Shirley and I were determined to maintain our family life.

The wind-up rally was scheduled the last week of the campaign at the agricultural hall in Haney, with MP Harold Winch featured as guest speaker. Winch, who had been CCF leader in B.C. from 1938 until 1953, was a major draw with tremendous cross-party appeal, and the place was packed. Bill Franklin was chairing the event, and he had brought in folksinger Jean Mohart, who was known throughout the party for warming up crowds. The place continued to fill, and soon people were literally hanging from the rafters. The fire marshall had to ask them to climb down. The mood was very positive and upbeat.

Laura Albers sent me outside to meet Harold Winch and bring him into the hall. The meeting was to start at 7:30 P.M. The time arrived, but there was no Winch. At 7:50, a green Ford drove into the lot. Someone was slumped over in the passenger seat. I looked closer and realized it was Winch. The driver got out and went around to help Winch out of the car. He was pickled. Everybody knew Winch had problems with alcohol, and my first thought was that the whole rally was down the tube. Winch seemed incoherent, and his suit looked like he had slept in it. I didn't know what to do. Here was one of my heroes, and as far as I was concerned he had just blown the campaign for me.

I introduced myself: "I'm Dave Barrett and I'm the candidate." Winch replied, "Thash nice." As we walked into the hall, music was coming out the door and people were clapping in time with the songs. When they saw Winch, the crowd exploded. And as we walked down the middle aisle towards the stage, I could see Winch growing taller, his slouch disappearing. The baggy suit started to fill out, and the wrinkles vanished. It couldn't have been more than a hundred feet from the door to the platform, but in that distance Winch underwent a complete transformation. He strode right up, shook hands with Bill Franklin and waved to the ecstatic crowd. He was in complete control.

I was still worried. I went over to Franklin and told him Winch was loaded. Franklin asked Jean to play one more song and then went to speak to Winch. I could overhear their conversation.

"How are you doing, Bill?" Winch said to Franklin.

"I'm fine, Harold, how are you?"

"Never felt better. What's the name of our candidate?"

"David Barrett."

"What's that again?"

"David Barrett."

Franklin gave a rousing introduction to Winch, who went to the microphone. "I'm here tonight," Winch said, "because I want to share the platform with an East End boy whom I've known since his childhood, David Barrett."

I have had some electric moments in politics, but nothing quite like that night. It was my first major rally, my first really large crowd. Winch spoke passionately about the needs of people, about decent working conditions and wages. There would be absolute silence until he made a point, and then the audience would explode with enthusiasm. At the end he came over and grabbed me by the arm. We stood side by side, my arm raised with his.

Winch returned to his seat. As Bill Franklin was making the standard appeal for funds, I glanced over at my hero and saw that another transformation was taking place. Winch began to shrink inside his suit and it became baggy again. The wrinkles reappeared. In a matter of seconds, he was totally drained, exhausted and a little bit drunk. The driver and I walked him back to the car amid a standing ovation. The money came in by the bucketsful.

The glow of that meeting lasted for the rest of the campaign. Everything went like clockwork. All our work bore fruit on election night. In the previous election, the Socreds had won with 10,000 votes to the CCF's 7,500. This time around, the Socreds held their 10,000, and we went from 7,500 to 12,500. The votes added were primarily from new voters in the west end of the riding, but we also did very well in more established parts of the riding such as Haney and Mission. The news media dubbed the Dewdney win "the upset of the election." A political neophyte, I had defeated Labour Minister Lyle Wicks. When I entered the House a few months later, I took my seat next to Tony Gargrave.

Four

The Rough and Tumble Road

My first weeks in the House were very disconcerting. I had never seen the legislature before, I had no idea how government worked and I certainly had no experience in debate. This must have been fairly obvious. At that time, people sat behind MLAS on the floor of the House on opening day. During the Throne Speech, a lady asked me to fetch her a drink of water. She apparently thought I was a page. It was a humbling experience.

I will never forget the first time I saw CCF Leader Bob Strachan clash with Socred Highways Minister Phil Gaglardi. Strachan, an ex-carpenter, had been leader of the party since 1954. I don't recall the issue, but it was a wild, violent, crazy exchange. Gaglardi was an evangelical minister as well as a politician, and he was then at the height of his form. He was yelling, and I was cowering behind Strachan. Then, to my horror, Strachan turned and motioned to me to come closer. In the midst of Gaglardi's tirade, Strachan said quietly to me, "Dave, do you know that the Jews are a lost tribe of Scotland?" He then went on to explain that when Jews dispersed after the Babylonian captivity, significant numbers had wandered into what is now Scotland and had settled there. It was all so bizarre, I just burst into laughter. After that, I was able to relax a bit.

Later that same week, I had to stand up and comment on the Throne Speech. There was a strict House rule in those days that you could not read your speech. On the desk in front of me was a glass of water. Partway into my speech, I reached for the glass and my hands were shaking so much I spilled water all over my hand, soaking the blotter on the desk. I just managed to put the glass down without tipping it. To this day, I find it impossible to take a drink in the middle of a speech, no matter how thirsty I am.

At first I was very serious, judgemental and rigid in my speeches. Over time I became more humorous, less dogmatic, and I recognized points made by others, even though I disagreed with them. I also learned never to make a mistake in a speech. I got up one day during mining estimates, saying we should be processing all our resources in British Columbia. I said we were importing bauxite. The Socreds jumped on me, saying the reason we imported bauxite was that there wasn't any in British Columbia. I was really burned about that, and embarrassed. Luckily, I was able to turn things around somewhat by going into the legislative library and digging up an old study that had found traceable amounts of bauxite in, of all places, Victoria. I went back into the House with that information, and we all had a good laugh on the Socreds.

I met some very impressive people in the CCF caucus, among them John Squire, Arthur Turner, Ran Harding and Lois Haggen. I learned a lot from these people during my early years as an MLA about how to survive in the bear pit of B.C. politics. In the Liberal caucus, I particularly remember Gordon Gibson Sr., Allan MacFarlane and Harry McKay.

MLAS were paid $5,000 a year when I was first elected, so I continued to work at the John Howard Society. Sessions lasted a couple of months, and the pay covered all expenses. By 1965, I decided it wasn't fair to the society that I could only work there eight months of the year, so I signed on as a supervisor with the Jewish Family Service Agency on a contractual basis. In 1968, I was hired as a personnel officer at Belkin Paper Box Company in Vancouver. The job was flexible enough to allow me to be active in politics and earn a living at the same time. During the session, I would go home to Haney on Fridays, spend the weekend with Shirley and the kids, and return to Victoria Monday morning.

In the legislature, I started as agriculture critic and then went on to social welfare, parks and recreation, and industrial development. It was relatively rare for MLAS to speak outside their own constituencies, but I eventually started receiving invitations to speak at clubs and constituencies around the Lower Mainland. I gradually became one of the party's fund-raisers, and because of that was sometimes invited to speak in other provinces.

It was on a trip to Saskatchewan that I first encountered T. C. Douglas. The first time I heard him speak at a fund-raising rally, I was struck by how entertaining he was. His speeches were actually political sermons but, my god, was he funny! He used self-deprecating humour and put people totally at ease. He was no evangelist, but the messages he gave were far more powerful than anything I had heard before. I wanted to have some fun in politics, and Tommy Douglas became a role model.

By the time of the 1963 election, I had served three years. I knew where the washroom was and I had survived the Socred onslaught. The CCF had become the NDP in 1961, changing its name to reflect the broader base that resulted from the party's adopting close ties with labour that year. Lyle Wicks had left politics, and I was running against Socred Dick Lester. Lester was a very good candidate. Hints were dropped that he would become a cabinet minister if he was elected. It quickly became obvious that it was not going to be an easy win for me.

I did not know it at the time, but the hardest election for an incumbent is the second. If you win that one, your future chances are much better because you have built a rapport with your constituency. NDPers survive by serving their constituents. If you do your job properly, you begin to attract a grudging respect and sometimes even win support from people of other political persuasions. Constituency work came naturally to me because of my background as a social worker.

The last all-candidates meeting of the 1963 campaign was in Mission. Lester had done very well until then. There were a Liberal and a Tory in the race, but neither was a contender. Mission was always a dicey area, right in the middle of farm country. The key issue was the milk quota. I didn't understand it then and I don't understand it now. All I knew was that no matter what decision was made on the milk quota, the farmers didn't like it. The candidates drew straws, and we were limited to six minutes each. Lester got up, and halfway through his presentation he started talking about the milk quota. He promised to straighten it out if elected. The people in the audience who were happy with the milk quota didn't want it straightened out, and those who were unhappy didn't know how he was going to change it. I sensed he was losing the crowd. The chairman tapped his gavel to remind Lester his time was up, but Lester refused to stop and went on for another two minutes. Finally the chairman banged the gavel down. By this time the crowd was really uneasy.

I had gained considerable experience as a speaker during my three years in the legislature. I stood and gave my standard spiel. Then, about a minute before my time was up, I told the audience I was going to talk about the milk quota. "First of all," I said, "I know just enough about the milk quota to keep my mouth shut." The crowd burst out laughing. "Secondly, if my opponent thinks he's going to tell W.A.C. Bennett how to fix the milk quota he's in for a big surprise. Bennett will tell him in no uncertain terms just who is running the show." I got tremendous applause, and I walked out knowing I had scored more than a draw.

I was right. I was reelected in 1963, but with a smaller majority. The NDP took 14 seats overall, compared with 16 for the CCF in 1960. The Socreds won 36 seats, the Liberals 5. After the election, the government moved to undertake a long-overdue redistribution of seats in the Lower Mainland. Suburbs there had been growing like crazy, leaving a disproportionate number of voters in some ridings. The western part of my riding was sliced off to create the new constituency of Coquitlam. Shirley and the kids and I were living in Port Coquitlam by that time. I won that seat in the 1966 election, this time with an increased majority, while Socred George Mussallem took the remaining portion of Dewdney.

The 1966 election marked the beginning of change. That was the year strong newcomers such as Bob Williams of Vancouver East and Eileen Dailly of Burnaby North took their seats in the House. The new group also included Tom Berger and Dr. Ray Parkinson, both from the two-seat riding of Vancouver Burrard. They, along with Williams, were appalled at the working conditions we tolerated. The NDP was confined to one room in the legislative building in those days. Only Strachan had his own office and staff. There were fifteen of us in one big room with four tables spread around in a square. We each had a couple of feet at a table that acted as our desk. We kept most of our files there too. We had a four- or five-woman secretarial pool.

Some of us, myself included, had railed against this situation. We felt we should stage a protest, but we were in the minority. Then one day I went in to work and there was Williams, sitting at his desk right in the middle of the hallway with a secretary taking dictation. The press reported the incident, and by the next year the NDP MLAS had individual offices. Williams's action taught me an important lesson about using demonstrative behaviour in a responsible way to achieve an objective.

In those days, W.A.C. Bennett was absolutely ruthless in the House.

He refused to put time limits on legislative hours. We had what came to be known as "legislation by exhaustion." Sometimes the House would sit all night, through the next day and all night again. The little dining room we had would be open upstairs, and people could drag themselves there or into the press gallery for a cup of coffee or something stronger, depending on who was around or what was happening. There was always a beer or a bottle in the press gallery, and the minions of the fourth estate would be twirling away all through the hours. A lot of them were drinking as heavily as some of the politicians, so the reporting at times became as slurred as the speeches. While all this was going on, Bennett would slip away to his room to rest.

There was no Hansard at the time, no official record of parliamentary debate. There were only press reports. Television interviews took place occasionally, but a large segment of the province wasn't even aware the legislature was sitting. You just had to grind through the three-month-plus session and hope for the best.

Bennett and the Socreds had been in power since the collapse of the Liberal-Conservative Coalition in 1952. Bennett had been a sitting member of that coalition until he crossed the floor to join the Social Credit party and lead them on to twenty years at the helm. Those decades were marked by massive infrastructure development, by construction of highways and power megaprojects. The one-time Kelowna hardware merchant undoubtedly propelled British Columbia along the road to economic expansion, but he also presided over the immense resource giveaways of this province. Wealth was pissed away, through Crown grants, timber licences, whatever. Just squandered. And the Bennett government had offered very little in the way of social policy.

Bennett couldn't put ten words together that made any sense in an impromptu speech. But he knew what buttons to push. He would throw bait to the Opposition and then play us like a virtuoso. We had in our group people who were extremely serious about their politics and their view that society needed dramatic change. Remember, we were still debating such things as socialized medicine then. I'm talking here about Strachan and MLAs like Arthur Turner, Rae Eddie, Leo Nimsick and John Squire. The very fibre of their life was democratic socialism. But there was little humour. When Bennett baited people by calling them Marxists, they would respond in anger to what they considered primitive political insults with no intellectual merit. Then, when he really had them going, Bennett would swing around and throw a wink to the press gallery. The press was always seduced by this.

I learned to banter in response to Bennett's political hand grenades. Later on, when he called me a Marxist, I would say, "Which one, Groucho, Harpo or Chico?" When he called me a Waffle, an acronym for a group in the party some viewed as left-wingers, I called him a pancake. Once I said that if he went too far, knowing how he felt about Quebec, I would call him a crêpe suzette. It was absurd, but it deflected the kind of exchange that ended all debate.

In 1967, the Socreds moved the opening of the legislature to Queen's Park Arena in New Westminster as part of B.C.'s centennial celebrations. There were more than four thousand people in the arena, but television cameras and live radio coverage probably expanded the audience to six figures. It was great show biz, with much pomp and ceremony.

Victoria had always been a protective cocoon for the Social Credit government, away from the prying eyes of an informed public. I don't recall who initiated the discussion, but it was decided in caucus that we would do something dramatic in New Westminster to bring the Hansard issue into the public eye. The ploy came as an amendment to a routine opening-day motion introduced by Strachan and Rae Eddie. It was supported by the six-man Liberal caucus and even by maverick Socred backbencher Ernie Lecours of Richmond. Bennett sat in stony silence. We had mouse-trapped him. The government majority easily defeated the motion, but in so doing they had officially gone on record in front of thousands of people as refusing to provide a Hansard so that B.C. citizens could have a word-for-word account of their MLAS' speeches in the House.

For us it was a magnificent success. Editorials supported our move and criticized Bennett's intransigence. All of a sudden, we had become challengers. We had decided we weren't taking any more crap. A line had been drawn, and I saw it could be exploited.

This was all part of my apprenticeship. I was learning the craft of politics, and eventually I began to do things instinctively as any journeyman does, whether a plumber or a carpenter or a printer. As parks critic in the mid-1960s, I became involved with Cypress Bowl, a mountainous Crown land area in West Vancouver. I was disturbed that land originally intended for use as a park had been leased to friends of the government for development as a commercial skiing operation. I started hammering away at this, often to the dismay of my own caucus. After a time, I began receiving anonymous telephone tips at home. One call advised me that ultimately the area was earmarked for subdivision.

I began raising this issue in the legislature with Resources Minister Ray Williston, who vehemently denied it. I kept pushing, but the harder I pushed the more apparent it became that I was losing the battle. I had no proof. Even my side would yawn whenever I mentioned Cypress Bowl. Then one day I received a letter I will never forget. It was from a women who lived in downtown Vancouver. She was in her eighties and had never voted NDP, but she had been following my struggle to save Cypress Bowl. She said she knew she would never visit Cypress Bowl, but she supported what I was doing because it was such a comfort to her just to know that it was there. A whole new dimension dawned on me about how we, as human beings, are attached to the land, the wilderness. I'm convinced the letter from that woman synthesized in my mind an attitude that ultimately led to my full support of saving farmland through the Agricultural Land Reserve.

One day I received a tip that someone had filed a subdivision application, and that was the break I needed. I did some research in the lands department and found not only an application for subdivision but also an application for B.C. Hydro to bring in power lines and other supportive documents. I made copies of everything and stashed them. I got up in the House the next session and asked if there was a subdivision application. "No." I asked if there was a plan to bring in electricity. "No." Then I rose on a point of privilege, said the minister had misled the House and, before the Speaker could rule against me, tabled the evidence. Well, the shit hit the fan.

I wasn't finished yet. My research had uncovered the fact that one of the companies involved in the Cypress Bowl development was associated with Meyer Lansky, the New York mobster who had fled to Miami and later the Bahamas. The company's main interest was gambling casinos, but for some reason it had purchased a stake in the bowl. I got Joyce Thomas, who started working for me in 1963, to track down somebody in Lansky's organization. (Joyce is a super sleuth. One time I asked her to get me U.S. economist John Kenneth Galbraith on the phone, and twenty minutes later she had tracked him to India!) In no time we had this guy in the Bahamas, and I introduced myself and said I was interested in his development proposal.

I told him exactly who I was, assuming correctly that he would interpret my interest as favourable because of the growth his project would generate. I asked if it was true that his company was going to be spending a lot of money in British Columbia. "Oh, yes, we certainly are," he said. I had a tape recorder going. "Thank you for answering my questions," I said. "May I use this information?" "Absolutely," he replied.

Back in the House, I accused the government of being associated with mob interests. I baited them awhile, then called a press conference. When everyone was in the room, I played the tape. Bang. Headlines. "Crooks involved in Cypress Bowl." After more than three years of fighting this thing, the scandal was out in the open. Today, Cypress Bowl is a provincial park, and the current NDP administration is developing a master plan to preserve it.

In 1968, Bob Strachan announced he was stepping down as NDP party leader. He had managed to stave off a challenge by the forces of lawyer Tom Berger the year before, but it left him mortally wounded. Ray Parkinson was the spear carrier. He and Berger had only been in the House a year when they began the assault, saying that Strachan was old-fashioned, out of touch, and that it was time for new blood. Some of the criticism was quite barbed. The challenge to Strachan had bitterly divided the party for the first time in my experience, and I resented it deeply. Now, with Strachan stepping down, the Berger forces were making their second run, and after some consideration I decided to step into the leadership fight. I had supported Strachan in 1967. In 1968, he had asked me to consider running and indicated I would have his support.

The convention was held in the spring of 1969. The evening before it was scheduled to begin, Harvey Beech and I were sitting in my hotel room discussing my chances. The leading contenders were myself, Berger and Bob Williams. There had been speculation throughout the campaign that Strachan was supporting me, but he had never said anything publicly, and I expected to receive his formal endorsement at the convention. I also counted on support as a result of my organizational efforts within the party. Then in walked Peggy Beech. "Strachan has just announced he is supporting Williams," she said, somewhat out of breath. "The press is on the way up now."

I was still in shock when there was a knock at the door. The media came bursting into the room in pursuit of a hot news item. They wanted my reaction, and fully expected fireworks. Instead, I was lounging on the couch with my shoes off. "That's wonderful," I said. "This is all part of the democratic process." I was churning inside, but I managed to bore the press into leaving. It was an incredible test, because I was really fuming. Strachan had misled me. He didn't even have the courtesy to phone and say that he had changed his mind. That angered me more than what he actually did. I should have been the first to know.

Berger and I were neck and neck on the first ballot. Williams was third. He was too far back to overtake but was very much involved in the drama and wanted to remain on the second ballot. The convention was deeply divided between Berger's backers and my supporters. A series of floor manoeuvres took place and Grace MacInnis, a powerful political influence for both me and Williams, walked over to Williams and told him to withdraw. Berger won on the second ballot by thirty-six votes.

I never did find out why Strachan switched. We never discussed it. I later made him minister of highways with responsibility for implementing the automobile insurance program. I didn't carry grudges, but I remembered. I had been an MLA for nine years, and up until now everything had been fairly simple and straightforward, with clear goals and time to sort things through. But now things had changed. I was entering into a tumultuous time in my political life.

After Berger became leader, I was very much out of the loop. I had made up my mind that I would run in one more provincial election just to show my loyalty. But I needed a change. I formulated a plan to get my doctorate in sociology at Simon Fraser University, then leave politics. That summer, Shirley and I took the kids on a trip to Mexico. We were gone about six weeks. On the way home, we stopped for a few days in Portland, Oregon. Shirley was off with Jane, our youngest, and the boys and I were walking by a newsstand when one of the kids said, "Hey Dad, look at this. The election is on." We went back to the hotel, packed and rushed home.

W.A.C. Bennett had established a tradition of going to the polls every three years, and he had announced an election for August 31. Berger's campaign slogan was "Ready to govern." There was a picture of Berger all decked out in a suit with his tie a little off to one side. The strategy was all wrong, as far as I was concerned. Everyone everywhere had always said the NDP was a good opposition party. They didn't want us to govern. We were still seen as crazy socialists by the majority.

On election night, there was both joy and consternation. The NDP dropped from 16 seats to 12. Berger lost his seat and so did his running mate, Ray Parkinson. The Socreds were returned with 38 seats. I had won in my own riding with the largest majority yet, and the people who had supported my leadership bid were absolutely ecstatic. Peggy Beech was smiling from car to ear because she knew what it all meant. Berger was through and this was my chance. I had mixed feelings. Berger has a great mind and a hell of a talent. I have always had profound respect for him, though not for some of the people around him. His people were simply too slick.

Berger resigned as leader. The party was seriously divided. At the first caucus meeting, held less than a month after the election, I was elected interim house leader, and that meant I was now in a strong position to contest the party leadership.

I abandoned any thoughts about quitting politics. Now I was determined to become premier. But the powerful labour forces that had surrounded Berger still had considerable enmity for me. They were set to thwart me however they could. People like Ray Haynes, George Johnston and Len Guy did not want me crowned leader at the party convention in Chilliwack the following year. They were all heavy hitters within both the B.C. Federation of Labour and the NDP executive.

To this day, I'm not altogether sure why they held such animosity for me. In 1963, I had gotten into a heated exchange at the national convention with Ontario New Democrat David Lewis, who later became national leader. The issue on the floor was whether people could belong to the NDP through their union affiliation and appoint delegates without actually joining the party. I was opposed. For one thing, it would allow people to be members of other parties and still hold power within the NDP. I believed people should at least join the party to have that privilege. More than that, my position has always been that the NDP represents all the people. I wanted the NDP to have labour support, but not to be a labour party. Anyway, my clash with Lewis could have been what branded me.

For many years, the executive of the B.C. Federation of Labour rented space in a party-owned building at 517 East Broadway in Vancouver. This had always been an amicable relationship. But as soon as I became house leader, the Fed executive kicked the party out of its own building. This was accomplished through a small-print clause in the rental agreement that said if the Fed needed more space, more would be made available. Their action was, in effect, a declaration of war.

I quickly called a meeting with some of my close supporters in the caucus: Bob Williams, Eileen Dailly, Jim Lorimer and Alex Macdonald. Bob Williams was a town planner by trade, and I asked him to find us a new home. In a very short time, he had located a building owned by the Finnish church at Victoria Drive and Hastings Street. The price was $45,000. When Williams asked how we would pay for it, I said to Lorimer, "You're a lawyer. Draw up debentures and we'll sell them to members of the party." We offered $1,000 debentures at 6 per cent interest. I bought the first debenture and, within a week, had personally sold twenty-one to other party members. The building was ours. More members bought debentures and very quickly the new building became de-facto party headquarters. When the first executive meeting was called, it was held there. I had won Round One.

I had many loyal supporters on the party executive as well as detractors. The executive was split. One of my supporters, Dave Stupich, was president of the party. But there were plenty of opponents as well, and they were more determined than ever to bring me to heel. If I was going to become provincial leader at the spring 1970 convention, I knew I needed to get out to the grassroots and build support. I now had five months to lock up the convention, but I had no idea what my opponents had in mind to block me.

I needed somebody to protect my back while I was out in the rural areas, and the person I found was Hartley Dent, an Anglican minister from 100 Mile House who had lost his seat in the last election. He had lost his pulpit, too, because he was from Cariboo country, where they weren't going to tolerate an Anglican minister running for the NDP. Hartley was now party provincial secretary, and we had a talk. I told him to think of himself as a machine gunner in a pillbox, with enough food and ammunition to last about six months. I also told him I was determined to forge a more broadly based working people's party and to take it in the direction of far greater political success than it had ever achieved. Hartley was a very charming, uncomplicated, lovely human being. "Okay, Dave," he said.

I bought a second-hand green Volvo and took off. I knew I had a lot of work to do to heal the party wounds inflicted in the previous leadership fight and the subsequent election loss. The first trip was with Professor Martin Robin of Simon Fraser University. We did Prince George, Smithers, Vanderhoof, all the way across to Prince Rupert. Frank Howard of the NDP was MP for the region, but it was mainly Socred territory provincially. There were about eight people at the first meeting. We took up a collection to cover gas and other expenses and went on. Next meeting, there were fourteen people. Same thing. We worked our way right across the north. Then I had to hurry back down to my first meeting of the NDP provincial council.

A member of the party executive was scheduled to present a paper to council called "Towards Democracy." I had been tipped that this paper was an indirect attack on me. It accused the caucus, of which I was leader, of being undemocratic by arbitrarily assigning critics' roles in the legislature when that should have been done by council. This issue had never been raised before, and it was the opening shot in what my opponents hoped would be a long-running battle.

I was ready for them. After they presented their document, I stood up and said that, before naming people as critics, I had referred back to the process of how this should be done. "Look what I discovered," I said, holding aloft an onionskin copy of a 1933 letter to the council from CCF founder E. E. Winch. The letter stated very clearly that the leader was responsible for naming the critics. "Whoever wrote 'Towards Democracy' was well motivated," I said, "but they haven't done their research, because I did it the way E. E. Winch said it should be done. I wouldn't deviate from that." That cut the ground right out from under them. I had won Round Two.

After that, I didn't show up at many more council meetings. All my energy was on the road. I met people. I sent them little thank-you notes. The crowds grew bigger, up to fifty or sixty people on occasion. I came to realize that in the cities and the suburbs, you are nobody. But in rural areas you are somebody, because sitting MLAs don't often visit. This was especially true on Social Credit turf.

I went to the convention at Chilliwack unchallenged as party leader. We held it in the agricultural hall, a large cow barn. The big fight was over election of the party executive, and that was to be the last gasp of the opposing forces. Our slate had Stupich, Lorimer and other faithfuls. The opposing slate was 100 per cent against me. We decimated them in the morning and there was a hell of a lot of scrambling at lunchtime. At one point Norm Levi motioned to me from the floor. "We've just wiped them out," Levi said. "I think it is important that we compromise and bring some of their people in." Someone had approached Levi and he was willing to bend. I didn't say anything, but Lorimer was right beside me. "Screw them," Lorimer said. I listened to Levi, I listened to Lorimer. "Jim is right," I said. "I want the whole executive. I've had enough." An election was only two years away and I wanted to win. I would brook no distractions. End of Round Three.

I now had a firm grip on the party's reins, and the caucus was united. I sensed that the forthcoming election fight would herald the day the CCF and the NDP had been waiting for. But I still had to bolster my public image and strengthen my footing in the House. There was work to be done, and I couldn't wait to get at it.

Four

The Hordes Are at the Gates

When I returned to the House as leader of the party, I immediately resumed work on one of my pet projects, a guaranteed annual income for seniors in B.C. I had tried to make a proposal for a $200 monthly pension many times, but it was always ruled out of order on some technicality. One day I decided to ask the Clerk of the House for help in wording an amendment to the Throne Speech that pertained to my income proposal. They wrote the motion for me, and the next day I submitted it for the Order Paper. That put the machinery in process, and suddenly the clerks realized they were in the embarrassing position of having helped the Opposition. I figured I'd better get the hell out, fast.

I bolted to the office and told Joyce Thomas I was leaving. There was a men's washroom just across the hallway and I could see the door opening. The clerks' door was about seventy feet down the hallway and I could see it opening at the same time. I ducked into the men's room and locked myself into one of the cubicles. I made the right decision. The clerks went looking for me in the office. They came into the washroom, but I was standing on a toilet seat, crouched over so they couldn't see me. One of the clerks, whose name I won't mention, called, "Dave, are you in there?" Dead silence. "I guess he's not here." Joyce, who was totally unaware of what I was up to, told them, "He's probably in the parking lot already."

The next day the motion was on the Order Paper and, of course, it was in order and, of course, it had to be called to a vote and, of course, the government voted against the $200 guarantee for seniors, and that was the headline. A good headline is very important in politics. I carried the newspaper all around the province telling people, "Your MLA voted against this."

One day we received a tip that Socred Highways Minister Phil Gaglardi had been using the government airplane for personal trips. Gaglardi probably spent as much time fending off allegations of wrongdoing as he did performing his duties in W.A.C. Bennett's government. I would watch in fascination every time he got up. He gave a real Jimmy Swaggart performance, British Columbia's Elmer Gantry having a go. One night he was on his feet and all of a sudden we heard this click, click, click. Everybody turned, and on Liberal MLA Harry McKay's desk was a set of those wind-up false teeth. McKay had released the spring on them just as Gaglardi paused. The whole House burst out laughing.

I was on the public accounts committee, but I was unable to get Gaglardi's flight records. So I went to his expense sheet. I wrote down every weekend he had gone to Kamloops, where he lived. I figured he had used the plane ten times to go home during a two-month period. I was really just guessing. I could not prove it without the logs. I wanted to legitimize my assumptions by filing with the committee. But every time I tried, George Mussallem, Socred committee chairman, would slap the gavel down and adjourn.

One day when I walked in with my sheet, Liberal Leader Ray Perrault, who was also on the committee, stood up and said, "How dare you make these unfounded accusations against a minister of the Crown? Mr. Chairman, I demand this member file that information to stop these scurrilous attacks on the minister of highways." Mussallem was taken aback. Before he got the gavel down, I said, "All right, I'll file them." Now I could distribute the information with immunity because it had been filed with the committee. Later, Perrault and I had a good laugh over how we had conspired to get that information on the record. That incident contributed to Gaglardi's becoming known as "Flying Phil."

There's a story I like to tell from this time about W.A.C. Bennett and my father. During the late 1930s, my father used to take frozen fish from the Coast to the Okanagan, sell the fish and then buy fruits and vegetables for sale back in Vancouver. After I got elected to the legislature, my dad would come to Victoria once a session and stay a few days. Whether he had actually met Bennett on one of his trips to Kelowna or not I don't know, but one day in the early sixties I was walking along with my father, who by that time was all but totally blind and used a white cane. Bennett was coming down the steps in front of the legislative buildings. He could be a very gracious, charming guy. When he saw my father he called out, "Hello, Sam Barrett." My dad said, "Who is this?" "It's Cec Bennett." "Oh, yes, Mr. Premier," says my dad, and they start yakking away. Bennett is really schmoozing him, referring to us merchants, us pioneering merchants in British Columbia. At one point, Bennett says, "Well, Sam, what do you think of your son? Do you think he is good enough to be premier?" My dad says, "No, no, no, he's a long way from that."

I give Bennett his due. After we met on the street, he went to the Speaker and requested that a chair be put on the floor of the House for my dad. So the many times my father came over he sat right behind me on the Opposition side. He would sit and just listen for hours. I never saw that happen for anybody else unless they were a visiting dignitary or a politician. For whatever reason Bennett did this, it was a very warm, generous gesture.

Not long after I became NDP leader, my dad was in Victoria again. We bumped into Bennett. "Hello, Sam, how are you?" Here goes the old shit again. Old times in Kelowna. Then "Well, good-bye, Sam." "Good-bye, Cec. Oh, wait a minute," my dad says. I thought, what's coming down? My dad was a very unpredictable guy. "Cec, remember when you asked me years ago whether you thought my boy would ever be premier?" Bennett said, "Yes." "Remember I told you he wasn't ready? Well, he is ready now, Cec." That's the first half of the story.

About a year later, Bill Hartley, NDP member for Yale-Lillooet and insurance critic, stood up in the House and read a letter from a young woman whose husband had been severely injured in a car accident. She was pregnant at the time of the accident, and her husband had later died. Her insurance policy said that no payment would be made if the patient died more than 180 days after the accident, even if, as in this case, there was no doubt death was caused by injuries sustained in the accident. In this instance, the young man had the temerity to die ten months after the accident and she got nothing. Now she had a newborn child to look after.

The attorney general was Les Peterson, whom I liked very much. My father had been Peterson's first client in Vancouver, and Peterson had always been highly regarded in our family. But he was a political opponent, and when he tried to dismiss Hartley and the issue in typical lawyer fashion, I began to get interested. If only the government had said it would consider changing the law or acting on the widow's behalf in some way, we would have been satisfied. But Peterson wouldn't budge other than to say the 180-day limit was "under study." Hartley persisted, and the Speaker complained that he was breaking the rule against "tedious repetition." Leo Nimsick of Kootenay and Gordon Dowding, MLA for Burnaby-Edmonds, also dealt with the issue, and then I waded in.

Peterson was reading a book by now, and I put the question to him: "Will the minister promise this House that he will approach the insurance company and ask for a review and some leniency and show some awareness of the hardship this rigid rule is placing on this widow?" He said no. I repeated the question. And again. I launched into a constant repetition. Sometimes I stood for periods of up to two minutes before repeating the question. But Peterson and Bennett sat silent.

I asked the question sixty-seven times. The Speaker had left the chair, and the deputy speaker was banging the gavel and calling me to order, but I ignored him. I knew this widow with a baby was going to have public sympathy, so I was determined to carry on regardless of the consequences. I had had no time to consult with my colleagues, some of whom by now were whispering for me to sit down. But I was not about to quit. Out of the corner of my eye I saw Bennett pull Peterson over. Then Peterson stood up and filed a motion expelling me from the house for five days.

Outside the House, the hallway was jammed with reporters. The story had all the ingredients. It was a statement of something I believed in and a political opportunity all rolled into one. At a press conference in my office, I said, "This government is so big it is without heart, it is without compassion and it has forgotten the little people out there it is supposed to represent." It gave me a chance to show just who the hell I was. Funny little guy, great sense of humour, but don't mess with me. The young buck had challenged the old man.

There was a hell of a set-to in caucus. Dowding, a great supporter of mine, was practically in tears over my behaviour. Nimsick exploded in fury, saying that I would smear the party name. Others, like Bob Williams and Jim Lorimer, were in approval. Lorimer just chewed on his pipe and laughed.

So I took a week off and the story raged on. Eileen Dailly was interim leader while I was away. Phones were jammed and letters of support came flooding in. Even the obsequious Vancouver *Sun* berated the government over this issue. It also changed the caucus, just wiped away the last vestige of the old style. After Williams's hallway incident, New Westminster, Cypress Bowl and now this, we were galvanized into an in-your-face political force.

It just so happened that when I came back on the Monday after getting ejected, it was the same week my dad was coming over for his annual visit. We rode over on the ferry together with Gordon Dowding. It was planned that I would enter the House just after prayers, and when I came in the caucus would applaud me for having fought for this widow. My dad was already sitting in the House, and just as I made my entrance, Bennett jumped up and said, "Mr. Speaker, we are honoured today in the House to have a special guest, the father of the leader of the Opposition." They all applauded and my grand entrance was down the tube. I had been creamed, totally skinned by that old bugger. And there was my father, beaming away.

Three years had elapsed since the Socreds had last gone to the polls, and in July 1972 Bennett called an election. Polling day was set for August 30. The NDP campaign in 1969 had tried to convey the impression we were all set to take the reins, and that had been perceived as threatening. This time around, all we were saying was that we needed to strengthen the Opposition. That was the strategy I had asked the party and the caucus to adopt.

Before the writ was dropped, Bennett had gone on a tour of the province to test the waters. There was considerable unrest. Bennett and the Socreds were depleting the province's rich storehouse of natural resources at a great rate to feed the profits of major corporations. British Columbians were suffering from inadequate hospital facilities, mental health care services and care for the elderly. In addition, the Socreds had created a climate of confrontation on the labour front with the first compulsory arbitration law and the contentious B.C. Mediation Commission, which had the power to impose binding settlements on labour disputes.

During a stop in New Westminster, Bennett was greeted by a labour demonstration. There was some jostling and shoving, and a picketer hit Agriculture Minister Cyril Shelford on the head with a sign. It was an unfortunate, ugly incident. Bennett's response was also unfortunate. He told the press the incident was the responsibility of "the labour movement and Dave Barrett."

I met with Alex Macdonald and New Westminster MLA Dennis Cocke in Vancouver and told them I wanted to sue Bennett. I was fed up with the way the old man had been trying to smear me during his provincial tour. Alex agreed to draw up the papers, and we left on the next ferry for Victoria. We also notified the press, whom I knew would ask why I was taking this action. Alex told me to say, "I refuse to have my name dragged through the mud by anybody."

I rehearsed that line, over and over, during the ferry ride. When we arrived at the courthouse, it was a mob scene. We had to elbow our way through the reporters and past the cameras to get inside. I slapped down my $20 and filed the suit. Outside, several reporters stuck microphones under my nose, and eventually someone asked the inevitable question: "Why are you suing the premier?"

I gave the answer I had been rehearsing. Just as I finished saying that I refused to have my name dragged through the mud by anybody, I heard a very audible whisper coming from over my shoulder. It was Macdonald. "That's right," Alex said. "Barrett prefers to do that himself." Fortunately, none of the press heard his remark. I dropped the suit after the election.

By the time we hit the campaign trail, the tension in the province was palpable. The landscape of awareness and expectation among voters had been changing dramatically while the Bennett government was aging, and we were in a good position to benefit from that. The T.C. Douglas government in Saskatchewan, after dragging Canada kicking and screaming into a socialized medicare plan, had successfully implemented car insurance in the province, and there was a growing perception in British Columbia that maybe we should be moving in the same direction. People were also beginning to realize that Socred policies were throwing away control of our land, our minerals and our forests. They were receptive to the common sense of the NDP's proposal to charge royalties on all minerals leaving the province.

By 1972, television had emerged as a major player in the media, and this new device was something Bennett didn't understand and could not handle. He was inarticulate. He fumbled and grew steadily more incoherent, and when he got angry the words became jumbled. On a

CBC television show with Jack Wasserman, where he was fielding questions from a group of students, Bennett launched into a tirade about the evils of smoking. This was after Haight-Ashbury, after the whole flowering explosion of youth discovering the world. The lingering aura of the sixties was still very much alive. All that was beyond Bennett, and it showed.

Even the media took notice on occasion. I recall an editorial in the *Province* during the campaign that said trying to talk to the premier was "like having a discussion with the Point Atkinson foghorn. No matter what you say, it blasts back with the same comment every 15 seconds."

This isn't to suggest my own relationship with the fourth estate was some kind of honeymoon. The Vancouver *Sun* made reference to my "eyebrow raising candor" in one edition, then went on to criticize me for wanting to impose heavy tax increases on basic industries like mining and forestry in order to recoup some of the losses from the giveaway years. They called the NDP's economic platform "theatre of the absurd." This was typical. But the usual sycophantic fawning over Bennett's every move was not so evident during this campaign.

During July and August, Bennett crisscrossed the province in the back of a government-owned black Cadillac limousine. His itineraries were secret. This was a new tactic. Even his confidants were at a loss at times as to where he was. Often the only clue to his whereabouts was the local radio station, because he would deluge it with ads a week before hitting town. I recall that only forty people turned out to greet him at a hotel in Kimberley after a week-long media blitz. On one occasion, he used the limousine as a decoy at a hostile rally in Point Grey while he slipped out the back door into an unmarked car with two plainclothes policemen. Another time, he was heckled and booed by a crowd of a thousand people at a gathering in the Vancouver Technical School auditorium. Such public reaction was unheard of in previous elections.

There was even growing dissatisfaction with Bennett among the establishment of British Columbia, with the Howe Street gang and in the corporate boardrooms. Many of them began to look towards Progressive Conservative Leader Derril Warren of Penticton as their fallback. Warren had never held public office and had been a Tory member for only four months when he was elected party leader in 1971. He was tall, thirty-three, good-looking, and had an "aw shucks" way about him on the hustings. He was the young replacement for Bennett. If the old man faltered, so the thinking went, Warren would bail them out.

Then dissent surfaced within the Socred Party itself. During a *Toronto Star* interview, Rehabilitation Minister Phil Gaglardi criticized Bennett and the rest of the cabinet as square pegs in round holes and said the old man would retire shortly after the election. The story went on to say Gaglardi considered himself the only real choice as Bennett's successor.

It was a bombshell, probably the single most influential event of the campaign. It directed the spotlight not only on a pending leadership struggle within party ranks but also on the Socred politician most often tainted with scandal. Gaglardi had been attacked for years for the way his ministry handed out building contracts to party supporters. He had been convicted of speeding and reckless driving so many times his licence was suspended. He responded with capricious misuse of the government Lear jet to shuttle himself between Victoria and his home in Kamloops. The jet was grounded and Gaglardi dumped from his former post as highways minister when it was discovered he had used it to fly his daughter-in-law to Texas. Now he was touting himself as the next premier.

Bennett flew into a rage, and Gaglardi started backpedalling as soon as the story broke. He denied everything, saying the reporter had made the story up. But the damage was done.

From the time the writ was dropped, I was dodging, ducking, bobbing and weaving in the boonies. I was not spending any time campaigning in the metropolitan areas because they were controlled by the establishment, which essentially had the media in its hip pocket. The less attention they paid to me, the happier I was. I didn't even go near the cities until the last week of the campaign. By then, when Bennett said, "The NDP and the Communists are in bed together" and "Dave Barrett is the most dangerous leader the socialists have ever had in B.C.," people just laughed. Nobody saw me as a threat. I was just a social worker, a little overweight, maybe, but quite jolly. A funny little guy.

Our campaign was strictly a shoestring affair. I travelled with Doug Beech from my constituency. On a couple of occasions we chartered a little push-pull Cessna. It was loaded with the two of us, our luggage and the pilot. I remember when we were in Revelstoke, the pilot had to circle around to get up over the mountains. Then we flew to Houston and landed on a grass field and went to the meeting there. The rest of the time I travelled by car. Who was going to believe we could ever win? We didn't even have a campaign bus.

A week before polling day, Bennett tipped his hand that he was worried. The revelation came as he launched a week-long swing through the Lower Mainland by telling a jammed Centennial Theatre in North Vancouver that "the socialist hordes are at the gates in British Columbia."

He had never talked like that before, although he had always made a habit of attacking the CCF and then the NDP as wild socialists. Cedric Cox, an NDP MLA from Burnaby, had visited Cuba in the sixties, and of course we were branded immediately as Communist supporters of Fidel Castro. Bennett was continually baiting us in the House, but he had always been smug and supremely confident during an election. This time it was different. To my mind, his statement disclosed the message from his pollster that he was in trouble.

Bennett's remark was supported by the hamburger poll at the Pacific National Exhibition in Vancouver. The hamburger vendors were peddling Bennett and Barrett burgers, keeping score. Barrett burgers were outselling Bennett burgers two to one. The Socreds sent someone down to give out free Bennett burgers to people passing by, but it wasn't enough to turn the tide around.

Our motto in 1972 was "Enough is enough," and the voters agreed with a vengeance. We won 38 seats; the Socreds got only 10. Bennett was reelected in South Okanagan, but eleven members of his cabinet were thrown out. Phil Gaglardi was defeated, as were Resources Minister Ray Williston, Attorney General Les Peterson, Provincial Secretary Wes Black and Grace McCarthy, minister without portfolio.

The Liberals captured 5 seats, the Conservatives 2. Derril Warren lost, but Liberal Leader David Anderson squeaked home in Victoria. Anderson had left federal politics to run provincially. When I first met Prime Minister Pierre Trudeau, his statement to me was, "Well, Premier Barrett, we both won." I got the distinct impression he wasn't going to miss Anderson in Ottawa.

Our win was considered a phenomenon; it drew journalists to B.C. from all over the country. Around 10:00 P.M. on election night, I appeared with Shirley and our three kids in an auditorium packed with three thousand people in Coquitlam.

The first thing I did was thank Bennett for the service he had given to the people of British Columbia. There were a few boos, and I said, "Just a minute, we live in a democracy. W.A.C. Bennett led the government of this province for twenty years, and anybody who gives that much time to public life deserves credit. I honour him and congratulate him tonight." I said our victory was a vote for change.

Then I told the audience this was Upton Sinclair's victory forty years late. The media never understood that. They never asked what I meant, and I don't believe the comment was even reported. Upton Sinclair was an American novelist, an ardent socialist and a muckraker of great zeal. In 1934, he ran for governor of California on an environmentally sensitive platform that displayed an understanding of the state's natural heritage, the threat posed by rapid population growth and the need to preserve something instead of rapaciously ripping out trees and minerals.

Sinclair was defeated, but the issues he campaigned on were those now facing British Columbia. I knew the direction we had to go in with the forests, with agricultural land, with minerals. The cornucopia would not last forever; it was time we began to husband the province's riches and utilize them for the benefit of all the people.

Early the next morning, I had a call from Gar Luney, who wanted to take my picture. I didn't know anything then about competition among journalists to get the first picture. I said, "Hell, Gar, it's seven o'clock in the morning." I had a hangover; the kids were still asleep. "Please, Dave, I have to have that picture," he said. I relented. I showered and shaved, promising myself I would go back to bed as soon as he left.

When Gar came in, I was still in my underwear, and he said I needed a shirt and tie. So I got on a shirt and a tie and a sports jacket. I sat on the ledge of our raised fireplace in my underwear, no pants or shoes or socks, and he took the picture. The backdrop was one of Shirley's paintings. That was the photograph they hung in the rotunda at the legislature.

Nine or ten days after the election I got a call from Lawrie Wallace, one of B.C.'s top civil servants. I was to come to Government House and be sworn in. Bennett had said on election night that he would hand over the government very quickly, and now he was stepping down. I didn't know that I could have orchestrated the swearing in and asked for something different, with all the cabinet there. I did know that we only had a couple of hours to get to the ferry with the kids. We didn't have the money to fly over from the mainland.

I phoned Government House as soon as we arrived in Victoria to get instructions. As we went up the driveway, my eldest son, Dan, said that the place would make a good nursing home. My long-time secretary, Joyce Thomas, was on hand, as was executive assistant John Wood, who had worked for many years for Bob Strachan. Bennett wasn't there for the swearing in. I never met with him. We never had a conversation, not even pleasantries. He just walked away.

An early photo of the Barrett family, taken around 1940.
Left to right: brother Izzy, father Sam, mother Rose and sister Pearl, with me in the foreground.

Foncie's Fotos

Sauntering along Granville Street in Vancouver in the early 1950s with chum Bill Esson, now chief justice on the Supreme Court of B.C.

Shirley and I on our wedding day, October 16, 1953.

We had a growing family by 1960.
This picture, taken at our home in Haney, shows our sons Joe, *left*, and Dan, with our daughter, Jane, sitting in Shirley's lap.

With Erhart Regier, *middle*, and Tommy Douglas in the early 1960s. Regier had just stepped down in Coquitlam to provide a seat for Douglas, who had become federal NDP leader.

Ken Oakes / Vancouver *Sun*

Being interviewed by Jack Webster on election night, 1972. Shirley is just to the right of Webster, with my mother, Rose, looking over our shoulders. Our daughter, Jane, is front left.

Vancouver Sun

The new NDP cabinet takes the reins after its swearing in in September 1972. Pictured in the House, *left to right*, are Dave Stupich, Norm Levi, Jim Lorimer, Bill King, Dennis Cocke, me, Lt. Gov. John Robert Nicholson, Bob Strachan, Eileen Dailly, Bill Hartley, Alex Macdonald, Ernie Hall, Frank Calder, Bob Williams and Leo Nimsick.

Harvey Beech, my long-time supporter
and confidant, pictured here
shortly after the 1972 election victory.

Steve Bosch / Vancouver *Sun*

Sharing a joke with federal NDP Leader David Lewis
at a 1972 NDP gathering in Vancouver.

Roy Peterson / Vancouver *Sun*

My visit with Quebec separatist leader René Lévesque in 1973 in Montreal created quite a stir.

An official escorts me
during my 1974 visit to China.

Dan Scott / Vancouver *Sun*

As Ebb Tide fullback I put my boot to the leather
in a 1974 match in Victoria.

Deni Eagland / Vancouver *Sun*

Sharing a joke with my predecessor, W.A.C. Bennett, *right*, shortly before Bennett resigned his seat in South Okanagan. With us is Ray Perrault, now a senator.

Six

The Queen Gave Us the Whole Bag

The swearing in for cabinet was held a week after I was sworn in as premier. There was a very simple, quick ceremony at Government House. Right after the swearing in, I turned to the press and said, "The queen gave us the whole bag." The remark was taken as a joke, but this is how the British parliamentary system works. During an election, the people are responsible for determining who is going to captain the ship. Once power has been bestowed, however, it is the government's prerogative to use it. I was quite serious about doing that.

Everybody who had been in caucus before the election was named to cabinet; that was a priority. I designated Gordon Dowding as Speaker of the House, and Hartley Dent became deputy speaker. I raised two issues during our first cabinet meeting that set the course for our time in government. The first came as a question: Were we there for a good time, or a long time? Under that umbrella, we discussed whether we were really going to make fundamental changes in British Columbia, or whether we would try to hang on for another term, rationalizing that we'd get the job done next time around. We agreed unanimously to strike while the iron was hot. Our government represented the first real break from the traditional power base in the province. We were free and unfettered to roam in new directions. We were impatient to do something decent and honest and human. It was going to be a good time for the ordinary people of British Columbia.

My other point concerned the relationship between cabinet and the bureaucracy. I insisted on a hands-on cabinet. There would be no delegating of political decisions to the bureaucracy. The bureaucracy was there to serve the political masters, not the other way around.

We immediately struck a committee to examine how to bring the British Columbia legislature up to the level of services and access of other legislatures in Canada. Very quickly, we instituted a Hansard, a written record of everything that was said in the House. The next thing we brought in was a set question period. The right of the Opposition to stand in the House and ask questions of the government had been entrenched long ago in the British House of Commons and in our own federal Parliament. But it had never been the case in British Columbia.

When we took the reins, Bennett had been running the province for twenty years out of his hip pocket. He had few of the modern bureaucratic tools. He had treated the civil service like second-class citizens. They had no bargaining rights, and they were held in very tight control. A civil servant couldn't make a phone call on behalf of the province of British Columbia without permission from a deputy minister. Nobody could travel out of province. Bennett himself even refused to attend federal-provincial conferences.

As a result of Bennett's noncommunication with Ottawa, transfer payments at that time would be made by mailing a cheque. The finance department wasn't even allowed to establish an account for automatic bank deposits, which would have allowed federal transfers to be made within a matter of hours. This was costing B.C. taxpayers millions of dollars a year in lost interest. I changed this immediately. As premier, I retained the portfolio of minister of finance as W.A.C. Bennett had done. I was ridiculed for this, but I realized Bennett had found an effective tool for monitoring and controlling government.

There were open and frank exchanges that led to sharp disagreements in cabinet, and that was important, but I deliberately kept a tight rein on meetings. We kept with one simple agenda model all the way through government. I refused to have any report given to me that was over one page long, and I refused to have any memos discussing political matters even written. We did not permit bureaucrats at cabinet meetings. Occasionally a deputy minister would be invited to give a rundown on technical problems or some other aspect of what we were discussing, and then asked politely to leave. Joyce Thomas was the only non-cabinet person to appear regularly at cabinet meetings.

Many of the ministers' tasks were derived from pent-up party policies that had been debated at conventions for forty years. Almost every cabinet minister had a single focus: Norm Levi on welfare reform and Mincome, a plan to give everyone over sixty a minimum income of $200 a month; Bill King on devising what was to become the Labour Code; Jim Lorimer on municipal amalgamation and public transit; Dennis Cocke on health care and the ambulance service; Bob Strachan on auto insurance; Bob Williams on a review of forest policy and the tenure of tree farm licences; Dave Stupich on ways to save agricultural land from development; Eileen Dailly on the province's school system; Ernie Hall on modernizing relationships between the government and civil servants, including establishing bargaining rights for the B.C. Government Employees Union; Leo Nimsick on reviewing the whole area of mining taxation; Alf Nunweiler on bringing the voice of the North into the decision-making process; and Alex Macdonald on a review of family law and police training. Frank Calder, who had first been elected to the provincial legislature in 1949, represented the northern riding of Atlin, and I asked him to be minister without portfolio to begin the first serious negotiations at the provincial level aimed at bringing native people and the federal government to the table over land claims.

Minister of Public Works Bill Hartley and his very able deputy, George Giles, embarked almost immediately on a project to spruce up the Parliament Buildings. During my years in Opposition, I had been struck by how badly the buildings had been neglected. In some places plastic sheets had been fitted on two-by-four frames beneath roof leaks to funnel the water into buckets. This was one way Bennett and the Socreds had saved money. We spent $3 million repairing and restoring the buildings, which were built in 1897 for $925,000.

Partway through the first year, I named Lorne Nicolson as minister of housing. His assignment was to establish co-op housing for the first time in British Columbia, together with incentives and mortgage assistance for people to buy a home. Gary Lauk was brought into cabinet as minister of economic development, and Jack Radford as head of recreation and conservation. The highways portion of Bob Strachan's portfolio was turned into a separate ministry with Graham Lea at the helm, and Phyllis Young was named minister of consumer services.

Shirley and I bought a home in Esquimalt, one of the four core municipalities in Greater Victoria, in the fall of 1972 and moved in the following spring. We had been very happy living in Port Coquitlam. We had many regrets about leaving, but once we were in government I could no longer commute. To keep the family together, we decided to move to Vancouver Island.

Esquimalt has a social and psychological makeup similar to that of the East End of Vancouver, although it is situated on the west rather than the east side of the city. It comprises primarily working-class people, down-to-earth folks with few pretensions. There is also a large military establishment, and a growing retirement community. It is a very friendly area, and we quickly felt at home there.

Our government was elected at the end of August, and we had our first session in October. The session only lasted a few days, but it was productive. We brought in Mincome and raised the minimum wage from $2.00 an hour to $2.50. We struck down the Mediation Commission, which was decidedly anti-labour. We also repealed a ban on the advertising of liquor and tobacco and lifted a 6.5 per cent ceiling on teachers' salaries. Alex Macdonald initiated moves during the mini-session to establish a long-overdue provincial police academy, and also set up a sheriffs' department.

From the beginning, we flouted the conventional wisdom that the best strategy for a government was to do all the bad things in the first two years, be benign in the third year and hand out goodies in the fourth year. My attitude was that we weren't there to play politics. We had a job to do, and we were going to do it as quickly and thoroughly and efficiently as possible, and let history be the judge of the consequences. Our agenda was packed from day one right up to the end.

The battle lines were drawn very quickly as the corporate elite realized they were no longer calling the shots. For the first time, power in the boardroom no longer meant cabinet power as well. The tone from the editorial pages, which mirrored the position of the corporate sector, was entirely negative. The corporate sector believes that the God-given resources everyone talks about on Sunday really belong to them. Their view of private property has nothing to do with how the property came to be on earth in the first place, or how they came to own it. We believed in a more open, egalitarian society, with fair access to resources through competitive bids. Clearly, we were out to knock them off the hill.

The first rallying cry for our opponents, both inside and outside the legislature, was sounded after Agriculture Minister Dave Stupich brought in an Order in Council on December 21 freezing all agricultural land in British Columbia from being sold for non-farming purposes. Prime Fraser Valley and Okanagan areas were under seige from urban speculators, and there was no question we needed to assess what really was farmland and what wasn't before the developers got to it. I assumed every rational person in British Columbia would understand the logic of that. We also announced that there would be legislation coming in the spring session that laid down the conditions and structure of an Agricultural Land Reserve (ALR).

The reaction was shrill, hysterical and immediate. We had handed our political opponents a club, and they proceeded to beat us with it. Now the socialists were taking away property rights. Everybody in the opposition jumped on the bandwagon, including the media. W.A.C. Bennett was on a world cruise when he learned of the farmland freeze. He disembarked at Buenos Aires, Argentina, and fired a ballistic missile in the form of a statement that our actions were "worse than anything in South America." His attack just happened to coincide with a Socred motion of non-confidence over the land freeze.

Dave Stupich introduced Bill 42, the Land Commission Act, on February 24, shortly after the start of the spring session. The bill called for the establishment of a provincial land commission with wide-ranging powers to zone, buy, sell and hold land anywhere in British Columbia. We indicated that up to $60 million would be made available for acquisitions. We weren't talking about expropriation, although the Crown has the right to expropriate property for the common good. What we were doing was protecting farmland, which was only 4 per cent of all the land in British Columbia, from getting buried beneath strip malls and subdivisions. But again there was hysteria.

Bennett travelled from hamlet to hamlet preaching against the land bill and urging farmers not to sign anything with our government. His campaign sparked a series of so-called unity rallies, rabble-rousing protests packed with rent-a-crowd mobs bought by corporations. Protesters would have all expenses paid to come to Victoria and demonstrate against our legislation. As for the newspapers, editorial commentary was no longer confined to the editorial pages. There was a headline about our "Taking the land to Moscow." (To that, I retorted, "Are you talking about Moscow, Idaho, or what?") Some radio talk-show hosts took the platform at unity rallies, demanding that Liberals and Tories cross the floor and join Social Credit to stop the socialists. So much for journalistic detachment. The developers went absolutely bananas.

To fully appreciate the atmosphere surrounding this debate, it is important to remember there was no environmental movement per se in those days in British Columbia. The urban areas were confused, and there was virtually no understanding of the importance of projecting the future needs of the population. British Columbia was the boom province, the last frontier. Why would any government suggest we had to protect land in this great, rich wilderness?

Much of the organized opposition to Bill 42 came from real estate and development companies, but farmers began to see the advantages of the ALR, and by the end of the debate the leadership of the farming community was solidly in support of the government. In response to criticism, we amended the bill to include an appeal process for anyone who wanted their property kept out of the reserve. My one regret is that we did not institute an absolute ban against politicians getting involved in the appeal process, because as soon as we were defeated, the Socreds began making decisions from within cabinet.

It was our intention for the ALR to be stage one. Had we been reelected, we planned to introduce major steps in reforestation and the protection of forest land. We could have been twenty years ahead in restoring sustainability to our forest industry. But that had to wait for the Harcourt government to bring in CORE. Frankly, CORE may be too late. People in rural communities who are demanding more and more access to cut more and more trees don't understand that they may soon be out of work anyway. That's what the pillage of previous administrations has brought in this province, instead of a sustainable forest industry such as that of New Zealand or Sweden.

We were too busy working on our legislative agenda to do any image-building as a government. As a result, everything we did was attacked. We were labelled in the media as wild, out of control. To counteract this, I embarked on a series of excursions throughout the province. We had nearly a thousand people turn out for a town hall meeting in Kamloops. There were six hundred in Prince George. Some came in protest, some in support and some just wanting information.

The meeting in Kamloops was raucous. This was still essentially Social Credit territory, the kingdom of Phil Gaglardi, although Gerry Anderson of the NDP had toppled Gaglardi in 1972. I gave my pitch about why we were saving agricultural land, how we planned to protect farmers, and at the same time dealt with a range of other issues, because there was a lot more on the agenda than just the Land Bill. Transportation Minister Bob Strachan had started to work on a government automobile insurance program. Insurance companies had colluded in fixing prices and sharing the market for years. Now, faced with competition in the form of what later became the Insurance Corporation of British Columbia (ICBC), they just walked away without providing bridge coverage, hoping like hell there would be chaos.

This was all simmering as I took my place at the podium. During questions after my speech, a fellow got up and said, "I'm a lawyer here in Kamloops. I am not a socialist, I do not vote NDP, but I am confused. I support the Agricultural Land Reserve but I do not support the NDP. I support the automobile insurance plan, but I don't like socialism." He went through a whole list of things we had done that he approved of, and I said, "Wait a minute." I went back through everything he had said. "But you say you don't like socialism?" I said. "Well, we haven't got enough time to get into a philosophical debate about labels. I want you to feel better before you leave this meeting. From now on, don't call it socialism any more, call it porridge."

The next day, I was walking down the main drag of Kamloops with Harvey Beech and Gerry Anderson when we ran into this lawyer. "I have to tell you something," he said. "Last night, I decided to join the porridge party."

While I was on the road, hecklers began to appear at meetings. A paid goon squad, if I may use the expression. I'm not altogether sure who financed this endeavour. I do know it had full support of the business community and their Socred pals. The hecklers would yell and stamp their feet to interrupt the meetings. Had they been trade union people, the newspapers would have attacked them as mindless thugs. Anyway, I got to know some of these hecklers. I would wave to them. At a particularly tense meeting in Golden, I stood up and said, "I would like to introduce our trip companions in the back row. They are here to assist local initiatives in protest, and should they wish to introduce themselves, I would like to invite them to the podium to do it." They shuffled their feet and their faces went red. I played this game everywhere we went. After a while, they would laugh about it.

Once during this time I was visited at my office in Victoria by an R.C.M.P. official. Apparently there had been threats on my life, and the police wanted to assign someone to follow me on my travels. "It is not in the Canadian nature for politicians to get shot," I told him. "The only politician in Canadian history who was assassinated was D'Arcy McGee, and he was murdered by a cuckolded husband. I am not involved in any such life-threatening activities." I told the official to do his job by all means, but not to follow me.

At the same time the Land Bill controversy was raging, Education Minister Eileen Dailly brought down another momentous change. Eileen was a former teacher. She walked into my office one day and said she wanted to end the strap in classrooms. I said, fine. Eileen asked if I was sure. I replied that I was. She asked a third time, and again I gave her the go-ahead.

Up until that time I had considered myself to be a pretty perceptive politician. I had completed my twelve years' apprenticeship in Opposition and the party had toppled the Bennett administration under my leadership. But in no way did I understand the political significance of this seemingly trivial exchange with Eileen. What she had proposed did not require new legislation, just a policy change. But from the reaction you would have thought that not only had we stolen all the land and shipped it to Russia, we had also unleashed a new generation of hooligans by removing all discipline from the classroom.

Many school boards, teachers and parents were outraged. Mindless editorial writers were outraged. Talk-show hosts launched into an absolutely maniacal attack. Suddenly, there were descriptions of a whole new world of classroom activities that I had neither witnessed as a student nor read about in the newspaper. It seemed that once loving, adoring children left the bosoms of their parents and entered the classroom, they immediately became wild animals who needed the strap to keep them in line.

The issue exploded while I was in Williams Lake on one of my speaking tours. A woman stood up and started berating me. Another woman, a teacher, shouted that the strap was an essential part of classroom discipline.

I told the crowd that we were getting philosophy confused with taxpayers' responsibilities. "Why the hell should we use taxpayers' money to beat your child?" I said. "If you want your child beaten, do it on your time and at your expense. We will not be like free-enterprise governments. We will not usurp parents' responsibilities. As socialists, we don't believe the state has that right. But watch out. If you do beat your kid, you could get charged with abuse."

Our first year in government was really rough around these two issues. We discovered very quickly there was not going to be any honeymoon. Frankly, that made me all the more determined to get as much done as we could.

I had lunch in early April of our first year in office with Alex Macdonald and Jimmy Rhodes, who had compiled a report on liquor distribution in the province. Rhodes had been elected in 1960 in Delta. He was defeated three years later and went on to become a successful small businessman in the printing industry in Cloverdale. He was known as the business-oriented ex-MLA with contacts in the NDP. When we became government, Jimmy was an important link with the business community. They trusted him and we certainly trusted him. The first thing he did was sell off all his business interests and holdings, so there would be no charges of conflict of interest.

Rhodes told Macdonald and me that two cents on every case of beer delivered to the government liquor store had historically gone to the governing party. There was now confusion in the industry as to who should receive the two cents. I told Jimmy without hesitation that they could take their two cents and give it back to the beer drinker; there would be no more kickbacks to the government party. Rhodes's report launched a series of long-overdue changes to the liquor laws, which eventually led to establishment of the first neighbourhood pubs in British Columbia and the lowering of the drinking age to nineteen.

During the time we were modernizing liquor laws, Alex Macdonald called a press conference to announce that he was returning something he had been sent by Ben Ginter. Ginter was a long-time cohort of the Socreds in general and of Phil Gaglardi in particular. He had large holdings in the liquor business. Alex displayed a case of apples, with one apple missing, and a case of whiskey. He announced that he was sending both boxes back to Ginter with regrets that one of the apples had been eaten by his daughter. "But this is not the first time a woman has been tempted by an apple," Alex quipped. He then delivered a stern admonition: "If this is a gift, it is unwanted. If it is a bribe, it is not enough."

In the spring of 1973, I decided to make a trip to New York. The financial mavens who set B.C.'s bond ratings wanted to meet with us and discuss our economic program. Shirley went with me, along with Deputy Finance Minister Gerry Bryson, my press secretary, John Twigg, Harvey Beech, Joyce Thomas and a few others. During our time in New York, we met John Wylie of Salomon Brothers and our underwriters at First Boston. We met with the bond-rating agencies, Moody's Investor Service and Standard and Poor's. I assured everybody we had no intention of changing British Columbia's traditional pattern of doing business. I found there was far more understanding in some corners of New York about who we were and what we were doing than there was in Canada. Bryson, of course, knew everybody from his years under W.A.C. Bennett, and his presence made things go much more smoothly. I'm sure it didn't hurt, either, that we had just retired $30 million of our $250 million in outstanding parity bonds. The total debt we inherited from the Socreds, incidentally, was $3 billion, mainly due to dam construction on the Columbia River by B.C. Hydro. We left New York after three days with our top credit rating intact.

Next we flew to London, where I met with a number of government representatives, including John Nott, minister of state for the treasury, Anthony Kershaw, undersecretary at the foreign and commonwealth office, and Lord Limerick, undersecretary for trade. We also began discussions during our visit with Mark Litman, deputy chairman of the government-owned British Steel Corporation, about construction of a small mill in British Columbia. I was quite disappointed nothing ever came of that. Before leaving London, Shirley and I had a fifteen-minute audience with Queen Elizabeth.

Then off we went to France. Our swing through the continent was aimed at promoting expanded trade links. Britain's recent debate about entry into the Common Market, in my view, had heightened the importance of increased marketing efforts in Western Europe. Our host in France was Amedi DePompignan of A. E. Ames Ltd., one of the lead underwriters in the vast consortium that handled British Columbia issues on the Eurobond market. As in New York, our policy was to maintain the business contacts the previous administration had established.

After a festive lunch with DePompignan and some other financiers, we decided to do some sightseeing. Shirley, Joyce Thomas, John Twigg, Gerry Bryson, Harvey Beech and I were in a large taxi, and someone mentioned that I was Jewish. On hearing this, the driver said, "Oh, Monsieur, we must show you the memorial to Parisian Jews." We were very relaxed and light-hearted as we drove to a dead-end street in what was to us a remote and totally unfamiliar section of Paris. Standing on a small hill was a concrete dome with a circular skylight. It was very unpretentious on the outside, nothing you would remember in detail. As we entered, we didn't see anything until we started descending the stairs that ran down the side of the dome.

A shaft of light extended down from the skylight to a column of marble two feet across. At the centre of the column was a bronze pair of baby shoes. As we descended further we could see that the inside wall of the memorial was a brass plaque, or wall, of names: every Parisian Jew who had been picked up by the Nazis and taken to the camps. After a very convivial lunch and a few glasses of the finest French wine, we were suddenly confronted with this stark, dramatic scene that recalled so much horror. The contrast was too much. I started to cry. I wasn't sobbing, just crying quietly. I wanted out of there. Shirley saw what was happening and gently steered me back up the stairs. I made a pretence of glancing at the names as we went. Once we were outside, I stood off to the side of the building to collect myself. I had never lost control like that before.

Prior to leaving Victoria, I had been visited by the R.C.M.P., who were concerned for my safety in Europe. The Black September group of Palestinians who had broken into the Israeli compound at the Olympic Games in Munich the year before were still active, and there was concern in Europe about any visiting Jews. The R.C.M.P. advised me that they had been in contact with Interpol, and security measures would be taken. There was nothing noticeable in Britain, but when we arrived in Paris, there were armed policemen at the airport and a police escort on motorcycles accompanied us to our hotel. I found this very unnerving. It was the antithesis of my experience as a Canadian politician, and it came as a shock. In particular, I did not like it that someone else was defining what kind of politician I was, not on the basis of my philosophy but on the basis of my religion.

We took the train from Paris to Vienna, where we were met by heavy police protection. We registered at the Imperial Hotel, where I as usual was dressed casually. Gerry Bryson had on a suit. An obsequious little manager immediately rushed up to Bryson and said, "Your Excellency, how glad we are to see you here." I was standing to the side, watching this, and Bryson shook his head and pointed to me. It only took a millisecond for the guy to bound over and begin laying the same thing on me. To impress on me how lucky we were to be at this hotel, he said, "Even Herr Hitler has stayed here." I replied, "Yes, he did, thirty years ago when they would have been chasing my ass down the street to throw me in a boxcar."

In Vienna, we met with one of the deputies to the prime minister of Austria, as well as the usual coterie of bond underwriters and investment analysts. From there we went to Munich, Frankfurt, Dusseldorf and Bonn, where I had a meeting scheduled with West German Chancellor Willy Brandt. One focus of our trip was to examine the European experience with "worker democracy" and the role of union participation in company planning. We were hoping to avoid in B.C. the high rates of alcoholism, sabotage and absenteeism suffered in some U.S. industries. Union activism was very high in West Germany. Brandt was a social democrat, and much of our discussion was taken up with the Socialist International, which is the umbrella for all the democratic socialist movements in the world.

I was really awed by my meeting with Brandt, one of the few German statesmen who had an impeccable record against the Nazis. As we chatted away I mentioned that Harvey Beech, whom I described as an old social democrat, would love to meet him. "Well, where is he?" Brandt asked. "Just outside," I said. "He didn't think it would be appropriate for him to come in."

So Brandt said, "Let's go." He took me by the arm, walked down the long corridor of the building, down the front stairs, right out to the car. "Mr. Beech," he said. "I am very honoured to meet you. Nothing is too good for the old comrades." Harvey just about fainted on the spot. It was a lovely touch, and something I will remember for the rest of my life.

The first major event on my plate after I returned to British Columbia was the Western Economic Opportunities Conference in Calgary. This took place during the last week of July in 1973, and was initiated by Prime Minister Trudeau in an effort to appear more interested in the West. Trudeau had a minority government at the time, and he was in power due only to the good graces and cooperation of federal NDP Leader David Lewis. To say his government was detested in the West would be no overstatement. Of the four western provinces, Manitoba, Saskatchewan and British Columbia were all held by the NDP, while Alberta was held by the Tories.

The agenda was essentially driven by prairie concerns, but we had a number of issues we wanted to raise. One was the old complaint of W.A.C. Bennett's that there was no subsidy for the B.C. Ferry Corporation. Along with that was our special interest in opening the Bank Act to allow provincial governments to expand their share of bank ownership, even to the point of setting up their own bank to compete with the private sector.

With that in mind, about two weeks before the conference I called Gerry Bryson into my office. I instructed him to go to Ottawa and start the rumour that I was planning to buy an American bank and move the head office to Washington State if we couldn't get the Bank Act changed. Within a week, I was confronted in the corridor by a reporter. "Is it true you are planning to buy a U.S. bank and set up its office in Blaine or Bellingham?" he asked. I gave the answer that is best for any politician under the circumstances: "No comment."

Guess what hit the fan. Mandarins across the country were buzzing about it and federal politicians all knew I was out to embarrass them by buying a bank. I couldn't stop chuckling about the naiveté of the press gallery, and others, who had swallowed this without checking.

As it turned out, the conference was pure bunkum and show biz for Trudeau. What he didn't know was that Manitoba Premier Ed Schreyer, Saskatchewan Premier Allan Blakeney, Alberta Premier Peter Lougheed and I had held two excellent meetings to prepare an agenda. We were a great quartet. I especially liked Lougheed. We were all in our forties, a zestful time of life, and there was much banter to season the seriousness of our discussions. I don't know how we would have done as singers, but we did fine as politicians. I succeeded in winning a federal promise to change the Bank Act. Trudeau got so mauled by the four of us that he banged the gavel down at the end of the session saying, "Thus ends the first and last Western Economic Opportunities Conference."

There was an amusing aside to the three-day conference. Among those attending was Jack Davis, who was environment minister in the Trudeau government and later held a cabinet post with the Socreds in British Columbia. For some reason, Davis was always very uneasy with me and, because of that, I found it difficult to communicate with him. I thought of him as a very sincere, bright guy. I was walking down the hallway to the hotel lobby with Harvey Beech when we saw Davis walk into the men's washroom. Harvey urged me to follow Davis in. "Stand beside him, man to man, and just have a little chat," Harvey said. So I walked into the washroom and stood at the urinal right next to Davis, who took one look at me, lost control and proceeded to piss down his leg and splatter his shoes. That was the last time I ever took Harvey's advice on a social matter.

When I returned to Victoria, I called Gerry Bryson in again and told him I was still intrigued by the idea of purchasing an American bank. Three months later, he came back with a report outlining the availability of a bank in California for $35 million Canadian. I still have the report. It was an exciting concept. I never followed through on it, but to this day I wonder what would have happened if we had bought the bank and moved its headquarters to Washington, particularly in view of the value of the U.S. dollar today.

Shortly after the conference, I was confronted with a serious problem of individual behaviour in cabinet. John Twigg came into my office to tell me that Frank Calder had been arrested in an automobile parked in the middle of an intersection. Calder had been drinking heavily at the time of his arrest, I was told, and was in the car with a woman who also had been drinking. The woman had been charged and subsequently paid a fine. Calder had been held overnight in the police station and released the next morning without being charged. Twigg told me this had happened three weeks earlier.

I called Alex Macdonald in and asked Joyce Thomas to get Calder on the phone. Calder was up north. When Joyce tracked him down, I came straight to the point: "Frank, were you arrested in a car with a woman in the middle of an intersection, and were both of you inebriated?" All his answer had to be was yes or no. Nobody in the room with him would have known what the question was. I say this because one of Calder's arguments against me later was that he couldn't discuss the matter since there were other people in the room. He said, "No, that did not happen."

Alex suggested I take the word of a minister, but I decided to pursue it further. I phoned the chief of police in Victoria and put the question to him. His answer was a reluctant yes. I recall my words to him very clearly: "Chief, I want to thank you for answering these very difficult questions, but I want to say something else. I do not want cabinet ministers, prominent citizens or anyone else of status to be above the treatment given other citizens. If I ever hear of you or any other police officer giving special treatment to a cabinet minister or anyone else in a high station, I will have your job. Do you understand me?" He answered, "Yes."

I called Calder into my office as soon as he came back and told him I wanted his resignation. He was thunderstruck. I said, "I want you to hear something very clearly, Frank. I am not firing you because of the incident. It was foolish, but I can deal with that. The reason I am asking for your resignation is that you lied to me. I cannot have any confidence in a cabinet minister who does not give me a truthful answer."

I wish there had been a way around it, but there wasn't. Calder went on television and accused me of being racist. When the press came to me, I said anyone who knew me would not accept Calder's accusation. I refused to discuss the issue, but said if Calder wanted to discuss it publicly I would respond to his comments and that was the end of it.

Frank decided to leave the NDP caucus and he later became a Socred. In the late 1970s, he stood up in the House and made a very touching statement. He was a Socred MLA by then. He was married and had a child. He got up in a very quiet manner and said, "I wish to apologize to the former premier of this province for my actions." Frank is a spectacular leader for the aboriginal people of this province. Our reconciliation meant a lot to me.

From the time we took power, the management of the province's resources was central to our agenda. In early spring of 1973, Resources Minister Bob Williams had come to me with a report about the B.C. operations of the U.S.-owned forest giant, Columbia Cellulose. Colcel was a subsidiary of Celanese Corporation of New York, and it was in the glue to the tune of $70 million, despite sales of $34 million during the final quarter of 1972. Williams's report attributed Colcel's troubles to the fact it was controlled by an absentee landlord. I called in Dave Stupich and Alex Macdonald and the four of us discussed Williams's recommendation that we acquire a major stake in Colcel in the name of the people of British Columbia. After some deliberation, I called in Gerry Bryson and asked him about the possible impact on our bond ratings in New York. Within twenty-four hours he came back saying he saw no impact whatsoever. After some further deliberation, we negotiated an agreement with Celanese to acquire 79 per cent of Colcel stock. The remaining 21 per cent of the shares were publicly traded. We made a down payment and absorbed a $60-million mortgage at 6 per cent to complete the purchase, thus acquiring $250 million worth of assets. We renamed it B.C. Cellulose.

It was a major coup. Even W.A.C. Bennett understood what we had done. We were attacked, of course. Not on the numbers, but on the philosophy behind the deal. We weren't nationalizing anything, as we were accused of doing, but instead taking an active role in the most critical resource industry in British Columbia. This was the first in a series of acquisitions on behalf of the people of this province that ultimately were pissed away by the Bill Bennett government as BCRIC, the British Columbia Resources Investment Corporation.

Our next acquisition was Plateau Mills of Vanderhoof. This was a small logging and sawmill operation owned by the Mennonite community. They wanted to sell, and Bob Williams suggested we make the purchase. Williams had opened an office in Terrace by then, and he was spending weeks at a time in the interior. We completed the deal for $7.4 million, and the announcement was greeted with a banner front-page headline in the Vancouver *Sun* that said, "Terror tactics used in purchase of Plateau Mills."

Without defining what the terror tactics were, the story implied that we had intimidated Plateau Mills president William Martens to force the sale to government instead of an American buyer. The American buyer apparently had told the newspaper that government muscle was used to clinch the deal. This was an absolute lie, and I was furious. I called Martens and asked him whether I or any minister had used terror tactics in the purchase of his sawmill. "None whatsoever," he said. "It has been an amiable discussion. Your offer was the best, and we took it." I asked if a reporter from the *Sun* had ever contacted him and he replied, "Absolutely not."

I then contacted Vancouver *Sun* publisher Stu Keate. Keate put me on hold while he checked into the situation. He came back on and confirmed that nobody had called Martens. "Yet you ran the story," I said. "The story is a lie. You manufactured the story to suit the lie, and I demand an apology." It was a heated exchange. I was very angry. The *Sun* later ran a story with the headline, "Terror tactics in Plateau deal denied." I never received an apology.

In the fall of 1973 an event took place that would have long-reaching ramifications for British Columbia. W.A.C. Bennett had announced at the end of the spring session that he was stepping down in the riding of South Okanagan. The heir-apparent in the minds of many people was Les Peterson, who had lost his seat the previous year after a long period of yeoman service. Peterson had been minister of education. He had been attorney general. He had been a loyal supporter of Bennett and he fully expected to be the Socred candidate in the forthcoming by-election and then go on to become party leader. He flew to the nominating convention only to discover there was strong pressure for W.A.C.'s son, Bill Bennett, to get the nod. Rather than be hammered by the Bennetts, Peterson withdrew.

Bill Bennett of course won the by-election to replace his father. After the votes were counted, W.A.C. Bennett said the result meant "the end of the NDP government." My only comment was that the result was "predictable."

As 1973 drew to a close, our administration had passed ninety-six laws, gone into both partnership and competition with private enterprise, taken steps to save farmland and opened government to new breadths and depths of public access. Government employees had been given bargaining rights, and we had brought in bold new legislation guaranteeing human rights in British Columbia. We had also passed legislation ensuring that 1 per cent of capital expenditures would be used to purchase work by B.C. artists, creating an art bank. Even Prime Minister Trudeau admitted in a newspaper interview that he was "green with envy" over our legislative record. But there was still much work to be done.

Seven

Oil, Politics and Mud

Throughout 1973, we had been wrestling as a government with very serious problems surrounding the sale of natural gas through Westcoast Transmission Corporation of Vancouver to the United States. The international oil crisis had erupted with the Arab embargo and the emergence of OPEC, the cartel of oil-exporting countries in the Middle East. The six largest oil-producing countries on the Persian Gulf had arbitrarily boosted prices by 17 per cent and were threatening belligerently to push them even higher. But in this scenario of surging energy prices, Westcoast was bound by the National Energy Board (NEB) to guarantee both price and supply to the U.S. Pacific Northwest.

Westcoast was the province's principal carrier of natural gas. The company owned the pipeline that sent British Columbia gas into the U.S. and obtained that gas under contracts with the province's producers. Westcoast received an average of 31 cents per thousand cubic feet. On receipt of this gas from British Columbia, however, the U.S. distributor turned around and sold it into the American market at 64 cents, thus pocketing multimillion-dollar profits. The producers in northern British Columbia received only 9 cents per thousand cubic feet. It was in this atmosphere that our government decided to go into the energy business.

Jimmy Rhodes and Vancouver lawyer Martin Taylor were commissioned to do a quick study of energy issues, talking to government and oil company executives from Ottawa, Alberta, Saskatchewan, England and Norway. Then we set up the B.C. Energy Commission in May of 1973 with Rhodes as chairman and Taylor as chief counsel. The hearings that followed found, among other things, that natural gas was sold in both British Columbia and the U.S. at 40 to 50 per cent less than the price of alternative energy. So the province was losing $100 million a year.

Rhodes and Taylor learned in dialogue with Westcoast president Ed Phillips that the company wanted to escape the squeeze between buying and selling. If someone else would acquire the gas, Phillips said, Westcoast would send it through their pipeline under contract arrangements that provided a reasonable return on its investment. From there, it was only a short step to the creation of a new Crown agency to produce, process and market natural gas. B.C. Petroleum Corporation was established in November of 1973 with Jim Rhodes as its chairman. Its first order of business was to acquire Westcoast's 120 contracts with eighty producers.

A couple of weeks later, the deal was struck. B.C. Petroleum would buy gas from producers, then Westcoast would gather it from B.C. Petroleum, process it and distribute it to the utilities and the U.S. buyer on a cost-for-service basis. Prices were set for Westcoast to earn, initially, 9.5 per cent on its investment. Not only did this assure the company of greater profits than it had ever made in the past, it also averted a looming financial crisis due to the recent loss of nearly 20 per cent of its gas supplies to technical problems in the North, where wells had become saturated with water because the gas had been extracted too rapidly.

Our next job was to bring the price of natural gas up to the level of other fuels. The quickest way was to double the price to B.C. Hydro, which accounted for 75 per cent of the market in British Columbia. Under NEB regulations, the U.S. price for British Columbia gas was set at 105 per cent of what provincial consumers were paying. The price at the border would therefore increase automatically to 5 per cent more than what B.C. Hydro paid. A little arm-twisting by Jimmy Rhodes was all it took. After some deliberation, newly appointed B.C. Hydro chairman David Cass-Beggs agreed to a price of 58 cents per thousand cubic feet.

What this allowed us to do was garner the huge profits that had been going to American producers and put them into the hands of British Columbia taxpayers and producers. Within the first four and a half months of operation, B.C. Petroleum made a profit of $19 million, more than three times as much as the Socreds had earned on natural gas royalties in a year.

At that point a major U.S. firm, El Paso Natural Gas Company of Texas, was ordered by a U.S. federal court to dispose of its holdings in the Pacific Northwest, including its 13.5 per cent stake in Westcoast

Transmission. The shares were to be sold on the open market. I received a call from an aggressive young stockbroker from Toronto named Gary Van Nest, who said he could deliver those shares to the government of British Columbia as a package at $22 a share. After a short meeting with Deputy Finance Minister Gerry Bryson, we decided to use B.C. Petroleum profits to purchase the Westcoast Transmission shares on the Toronto Stock Exchange. The acquisition made us the second-largest shareholder in Westcoast after Phillips Petroleum Corporation of Oklahoma. A day later, the market price was up to $23 a share. By the late 1970s, this investment had made in the neighbourhood of $700 million for the taxpayers of British Columbia.

At the end of January 1974, Prime Minister Trudeau scheduled an emergency energy conference in Ottawa and invited all the provincial premiers. This was at the height of the oil crisis. Prices had been soaring internationally. But they had been frozen in Canada since September 4, and the gap had widened from about 40 cents U.S. a barrel at the time of the freeze to more than $6 U.S. by the time the conference began. Among other tensions, the oil-producing provinces of Alberta and Saskatchewan were pushing to have the freeze lifted while just about everybody else wanted it retained. In my view, federal-provincial conferences were a complete waste of time as decision-making bodies during this period. Apart from a lot of grandstanding, not much happened.

Early in the week-long conference I announced our position. I called upon the federal government to exercise its power under Section 92 of the British North America Act to control oil and gas in this country. I further declared that, as premier of British Columbia, I was prepared to surrender our provincial jurisdiction over these resources if Ottawa established its ownership and/or control for all the people of Canada, coast to coast to coast. The reaction of the media, suffice it to say, was one of shock and horror. My fellow premiers ran for cover. The possibility that Ottawa might assert its declaratory power over oil and gas had long concerned both Alberta and Saskatchewan, who argued that natural resources belonged exclusively to the provinces. To further fuel the flames, I proposed that Alberta and Saskatchewan agree to use oil revenues generated by future price increases abroad to subsidize hard-hit consumers in Eastern Canada.

During a lunch break, I was chatting and having a drink with several other premiers. Trudeau came over to me and said, "You know,

Barrett, you and I are the only socialists in this room. I agree with what you are saying in terms of national control."

I looked at him a moment and then replied, "Don't bullshit me. If you really mean this, go down to that conference and stand up and say that you are prepared to take this initiative on behalf of the people of this country. Otherwise, you are nothing but a teacup socialist." Trudeau laughed and walked away.

Later in the conference, I demanded a national public inquiry into the taxes paid by resource firms. The oil companies had been skinning us, and I cited as an example Standard Oil of B.C., which had paid no income tax for seven years. We had been tipped to this when someone leaked handwritten notes about their revenues and tax write-offs. Standard and other oil firms, meanwhile, were fighting attempts to keep domestic oil prices down. It was, and is, a bloody scandal. Canada had the best politicians money could buy, and the oil companies knew it better than anyone else.

At first, federal Finance Minister John Turner rejected my call for an inquiry. Then public reaction started trickling in, and Turner promised to take the idea to cabinet. Of course, nothing ever came of it. All the conference achieved was agreement from Alberta and Saskatchewan to hold off increasing prices until April 1.

That was the backdrop to my first private meeting with John Turner, who subsequently became a trusted friend. Turner suffered a sincere angst about Canadian nationalism, and he marched very much to his own drummer on this issue. This manifested itself publicly in 1988, when as federal Liberal Leader he had the intestinal fortitude to say that if he were elected prime minister he would cancel the Free Trade Agreement the Mulroney government had just inked with the United States. That was when the elites within the corporate sector and his own party abandoned him.

Turner came to Victoria to discuss our natural gas position. The Liberals were preparing a new budget, and Turner was holding private meetings with each of the ten provincial premiers. Ottawa had proposed taxing provincial resources for the first time ever in its budget the previous May. That budget had been defeated and the government had fallen, but the Liberals had been returned with a majority three months later and now they were having another go. I had the distinct impression Ottawa was concerned that other provinces might get the idea that they, like British Columbia, could also make vast sums by marketing natural gas themselves. Turner and I had a long, thoughtful discussion and I came up with a proposal. "If you leave B.C. Petroleum alone," I said, "we will share one-third of our profits with you. But no fixed tax rate." Prior to this meeting, I had announced publicly that I would be speaking to mayors across the province about sharing natural gas revenues with them. The idea had been well received. I was somewhat shocked to discover that these right-wing mayors, who had always despised the NDP, were now anxious to share this socialist manna, but I didn't say much other than to welcome their support. To Turner, I suggested a formula of one-third to the province of British Columbia, one-third to B.C. municipalities and one-third to the federal government.

Turner was under pressure, no question about it. It was obvious he had been sent to deliver a message, and no other message was to return. He agreed not to press for taxes, but said if we lost money through our venture in B.C. Petroleum, I must be prepared to take the political heat. "I think you are on the right course," Turner said, "but you are on your own." We shook hands on that and he never changed his position.

U.S. consumers, meanwhile, were in a ballistic state over the price of our natural gas. Senator Henry Jackson of Washington State was ranting about this "crazy socialist," and the U.S. House of Representatives was in an absolute snit. In response to the American protest, I went to Seattle and gave a speech to the chamber of commerce. The audience was quite hostile, but I was serenely calm.

I told them plainly that I was about to seek National Energy Board permission to raise our natural gas price at the border to $1.00 per thousand cubic feet. We were getting 64 cents at the time. Since coming down to Seattle, however, I had discovered that Louisiana and Texas were getting $1.25. I told them I wasn't too upset about Louisiana getting that much. It was a small, economically deprived area and needed all the help it could get. But Texas was another matter. "I don't want to remind you Americans, but British Columbia is bigger than Texas," I said. "As far as I'm concerned, what's good enough for Texas is good enough for us."

Energy Minister Donald Macdonald went to Washington, D.C., around this time to make a speech about federal natural gas policy, and in the midst of his speech he attacked our government as "savage." When I heard that, I spoke to Attorney General Alex Macdonald, who was on the B.C. Petroleum board, and had him ask Jimmy Rhodes to file immediately for $1.35. I also called for a full public inquiry by the National Energy Board into pricing on natural gas sales to the U.S. within six weeks. A week before the deadline I had set, I received a telegram saying we could charge 99 cents without any hearing. I sent a return telegram that simply stated: "A penny for your thoughts." I never received an answer.

We had a wild encounter with Donald Macdonald at the airport in Vancouver on his return from an Asian tour. Still thinking Macdonald was a logical man, Alex Macdonald, Bob Williams and I agreed to meet with him to discuss our position. The energy minister was very tired coming off the plane. He began to berate us for being socialists, and I didn't like that. Williams didn't like it either. Donald Macdonald became irate every time one of us expressed the notion that resources are owned by the people, not the oil companies. It was going nowhere, so we broke off discussions. I think that led him to quit politics a few months later. He was so angry at us he went out and showed up on the board of Shell Canada.

There is an interesting footnote to our energy wrangles that involved the natural gas producers in British Columbia. They had been screwed, blued and tattooed in the original deal between W.A.C. Bennett and the NEB. They had signed the contract hoping to make a great deal of money, but the changing marketplace soon dashed their hopes. As soon as we set up B.C. Petroleum, they requested a meeting with me and Jim Rhodes. Alex Macdonald was also there. It was an ironic moment: the very epitome of free enterprisers—the rugged wildcatters—were coming to the socialists for help.

We sat down in a committee room and they presented their case. I don't remember the peoples' names, but they were top brass from the arm of the petroleum association assigned to represent independent producers. "We are going to be fair with you," I said. "You were never allowed to bargain before. You tied yourself into a foolish contract. That's free enterprise and we could hold you to it, but we won't. We propose to increase your share of the gas price, effective immediately."

They just about fell off their chairs. I then hit them with the fact that they could bargain annually with B.C. Petroleum for an increase relative to the world price. They could hardly contain their delight. They thanked me profusely. It was a veritable love-in behind those closed doors. Then out we went. The press rushed up to me, and I said I thought we had reached a deal that pleased everyone and then I walked away, leaving the producers to face the cameras. When I turned on the TV news that night, the same guys who had been practically kissing my backside were now attacking the socialist government for disrupting their industry! There is just no gratitude in this world.

After we took power, the legislature started sitting almost year-round. Our agenda was packed and it required politicians of every stripe to work full time. The pay in those days was $12,500 a session, which normally lasted about three months. Since we kept the House working for two sessions, and longer sessions at that, MLAs started getting paid $25,000 a year. Cabinet ministers went to $48,000 annually and I was paid $52,000 as premier.

Naturally, I was attacked for doubling politicians' pay. No reporter ever explained why the pay hikes came about. That's how drivel becomes legend. And no Opposition member, all of whom were busily attacking us as well, ever sent back a nickel. I'm sure the cheque is in the mail.

During the spring session of 1974, some egg producers came forward with serious complaints about not getting a fair share of quotas with the B.C. Egg Marketing Board. I had observed and commented on egg quotas during my time in Opposition, so in my foolish exuberance I got involved. Rather than delegate this problem to the bureaucracy and call for a report, I invited the disputing parties into my office. We had a hell of a row.

As a consequence, the producers who did not want to give up their share said I had warned them of forthcoming legislation and threatened to kick hell out them if they didn't fall into line. They were certainly entitled to their interpretation. My interpretation was that I did not threaten anybody. I did use heavy persuasion. Then Liberal Leader David Anderson rose in the House one day, waving affidavits from chicken farmers saying I had made threats, and said, "The premier is a liar." Anderson obviously thought he had uncovered the scandal of the century. He got himself kicked out of the House a few times over this, and the chicken and egg war was launched.

I was mighty pissed off. I was not about to reveal everything that had taken place during a private meeting in my office. But I realized how stupid I had been to project myself into the middle of this issue. No good deed goes unpunished. Naturally it became a major news story, and Marjorie Nichols of the Vancouver *Sun* was particularly vicious with it. One day I was coming down the corridor and I saw her talking to Peter McNelly, who had left the Vancouver *Province* and was now working for us. I lost my cool and swore at her. It felt great. I called her a venomous bitch and told her to go fuck herself. It wasn't exactly the kind of language that had ever been used with reporters by W.A.C. Bennett or any predecessor of mine. Marjorie wrote an article about it. Her career was born, and it was revealed to the whole world that I knew how to swear. Incidentally, Marjorie gave as good as she got, but I never made an issue of that.

The Opposition and the press went on a sanctimonious tear. But that was nothing compared with what I got at home that night. Once we moved to Victoria Shirley and I had made a pact that I would always be home for supper, unless I was travelling. It had been a wonderful haven for me and kept me in touch with the family despite a busy schedule. But on the night in question, it was humiliating. Shirley gave me one withering look and I knew without her saying anything what was going through her mind: You asshole!

It took me a hell of a long time to recover from that incident. Years later, I mentioned to Marjorie that I wanted royalties for my role in enhancing her journalism career. We had become friendly by that time.

Transportation Minister Bob Strachan, meanwhile, had been successfully guiding ICBC through some teething problems. Legislation establishing takeover of the province's $135-million car insurance business came into force on March 1, 1974. Strachan had been assisted in getting ICBC up and running by John Mika and Norman Bortnick, whom we had hired from the Saskatchewan Government Insurance corporation to become chairman of our operations in British Columbia. Bortnick later went on to give great public service to the succeeding Social Credit government with Dr. Pat McGeer as his minister. McGeer, initially one of the most savage critics of ICBC, later praised the corporation. There is nothing like a deathbed repentance on the road to political Damascus.

One interesting aspect of ICBC was our experience with agents. Commissions had been fixed at 6.5 per cent for years. All the agents were against socialism and therefore opposed to our insurance proposals. When we brought in ICBC we invited all the agents to do business with us and immediately boosted commissions to 7 per cent. We then went one step further and put a cap on the number of licenced agents in British Columbia, grandfathering everybody who was already operating. When the Socreds took over, they cut back commissions and made licences available to anybody who wanted one and could qualify.

We were moving quickly on other fronts, too. Health Minister Dennis Cocke had established an emergency health services commission that eventually took over operation of all ambulance services in British Columbia. The bill, based on an extremely farsighted report by Dr. Dick Foulkes, also empowered the commission to train emergency medical assistants called paramedics and provide for their licencing.

Human Resources Minister Norm Levi introduced the Community Resources Act, which called for the election of community boards that would have power over all social services in their areas. Board members would decide on local services, handle budgeting, distribute welfare payments and operate day-care centres.

In both Cocke's and Levi's bills, our reasoning was that services could best be provided through community involvement. We had found that it was impossible to make the best use of funding for services when there was a proliferation of private agencies. It was necessary to integrate decision-making with delivery, and you can only do that with community participation. Because the Socreds eventually killed our legislation, the great experiment never really got underway. It still needs to take place in this province.

Partway through the spring session of 1974, I received an invitation to go to Japan, along with Gary Lauk, minister of industrial development. We had been experiencing steel shortages in the ferry-fleet expansion launched in 1973 by Bob Strachan and had given some thought to establishing our own steel mill in British Columbia. Several Japanese financiers expressed interest in financing such an undertaking. We led a seventeen-person delegation on the sixteen-day trip.

There was an international steel shortage at the time. Japan was in the midst of massive infrastructure development and the vast bulk of their production was spoken for. But we succeeded in obtaining guarantees sufficient to complete the contracts we had put out to build two new ferries. Once we succeeded at that, the steel mill idea was relegated to the back burner. To guarantee our supply, the producers had to bump British Columbia ahead of some other favoured customers. I was profusely thanking one of the Japanese business leaders during a private meeting when he said it was done "out of a memory." I was puzzled. "We are aware," he said, "of what your party did to defend the rights of Canadian citizens of Japanese descent during the Second World War." I realized he was talking about Grace MacInnis and Angus MacInnis, and the long battle they and others in the CCF had waged on behalf of Japanese Canadians. I was doubly pleased that it had been a factor in our successful negotiations.

Back in Victoria, I had an amusing exchange in my office with Ian Sinclair, chief executive of Canadian Pacific Limited of Montreal. We were still a new government, and many captains of industry and political chiefs were coming to visit. As a socialist government, we were a curiosity for the eastern establishment. Baron de Rothschild had come. I was interested in banking, but not with de Rothschild. Federal Conservative Leader Robert Stanfield had dropped in as well. I really liked Stanfield, whom I found to be a true gentleman and a man of integrity.

I knew my meeting with Sinclair had the potential for being very tense, so I asked Alex Macdonald to join us. Alex's father had been Liberal attorney general years before in British Columbia, and Alex had long links with the establishment, unlike me. Alex has a mind like a steel trap but he conceals it behind the demeanour of a laid-back country lawyer. He also had the ability to consume cigars without lighting them. He would chew them instead. He came into my office with a cigar half-chewed and dripping saliva.

Sinclair arrived shortly thereafter for our scheduled two-hour meeting. I'm no clothes horse and never have been, but even I was struck by the worn appearance of Sinclair's suit. You could have read the Sunday edition of the *New York Times* through the seat of his pants. He sat down in this semidishevelled state, which matched me completely, and the three of us started talking. Alex was there in case of a flare-up; Sinclair and I both had well-deserved reputations for them. But I wanted this to be a peaceful meeting, and it was—until Sinclair got up to leave.

We had held a broad-ranging discussion, and I asked if there was anything else he wanted to raise. There was. "It's the minimum wage," he said. "If we have to pay the chambermaids at the Empress the new rate, we will be putting that hotel operation into the red."

"I'll tell you what," I replied. "Let's you and I go on television. You tell everyone in British Columbia why you can't pay the $2.50 an hour to chambermaids and I'll tell everybody why we should take back every

Crown grant, every forest licence and every piece of property you've got from the taxpayers of Canada and British Columbia."

It was tense. Alex Macdonald reached up and pulled his cigar out of his mouth and said very calmly, "Mr. Sinclair, what the premier really means here is that there will be no change in the minimum wage." Exit Sinclair.

As education minister, Eileen Dailly had proceeded from abolishing the strap in schools to founding the first community colleges in British Columbia. Under the Universities Act, Eileen had also established a government-appointed universities council to oversee development at the University of British Columbia, Simon Fraser University and the University of Victoria—the three universities in the province.

The legislation also provided more than $4 million in special grant money for innovative programs, with the purse strings controlled by the universities council. That's where the trouble started. University professors raised alarms about threats to academic freedom while administrators berated us for tinkering with the system. In our previous budget, incidentally, we had boosted provincial support for universities by $19 million to $130 million for the year.

During this time I received a call from the U.B.C. alumni association, who wanted me to meet with them over dinner at the Empress Hotel. I agreed, although it meant giving up a night with Shirley and the kids. We chatted during the meal, and I quickly realized that I was viewed as, if not actually anti-intellectual, unsympathetic to their problem. After dinner they showed slides of the U.B.C. campus. When they got to Totem Park, with its lovely display of totem poles, I told them to stop and turn on the lights.

It was time to make a point. I asked how many totem poles they had at U.B.C. I forget what the number was, but I was assured they had the greatest collection in British Columbia. "That's wonderful," I said. "I'm glad you brought this to my attention. Now, I'll tell you where I'm coming from. We'll meet again when you can tell me you have as many native students as you have totem poles." I said good-night and left.

Housing Minister Lorne Nicolson had been working hard to institute steps aimed at making housing more accessible and affordable to the people of British Columbia. His executive assistant was a young man named Andrew Petter, who is now minister of forests in the Harcourt government. One of Nicolson's proposals was to purchase

Dunhill Development Corporation of North Vancouver. After some deliberation, we completed the purchase for $5.8 million and formed a Crown corporation, Woodbridge Development. Under this umbrella, we launched the first co-op housing in British Columbia through the E. E. Winch Society in Vancouver and established a program for accumulating land for municipal development. More than three hundred housing lots were amassed and made available on a sixty-year lease basis in Williams Lake. Similar schemes were targeted for Chetwynd, Squamish, Kamloops and other interior locations.

Not surprisingly, developers didn't like our initiative. Neither did the Socreds, who were comfortably nestled in the developers' bosoms. Some developers said it was okay for us to assemble land, but they didn't want us to build on it because they felt it would be unfair competition. Maybe it was, because Woodbridge profits tripled during the first year after our takeover of Dunhill.

In May of 1974 I received an invitation to visit the People's Republic of China. The invitation was extended by the Chinese ambassador to Canada, Chang Wen-chin, during a visit to British Columbia. Although the trip was billed as a trade mission, External Affairs in Ottawa advised us to approach it essentially as a good-will visit.

A few months later, a member of the Chinese ambassador's staff came to my office to work out the details. I was most effusive in saying how honoured I was by the invitation, and he said, "Oh, it's not because of you, it's because of your mother." The Chinese knew my mother had been active on a committee in Vancouver to raise money for Dr. Norman Bethune's medical practice in China. The invitation was in part a token of their appreciation.

We departed on the two-week trip in mid-November. The NDP contingent consisted of Attorney General Alex Macdonald, Health Minister Dennis Cocke, MLA Emery Barnes and me. The delegation also included Denis Timmis, president and chief executive officer of MacMillan Bloedel, and Jack Munro, western regional president of the International Woodworkers of America. Timmis and Munro were interested in establishing a Chinese market for B.C. lumber products. Shirley came, as did Dorothy Macdonald and Yvonne Cocke. Harvey and Peggy Beech were there as well.

The Chinese were very gracious with their welcome. We were the first non-Chinese delegation allowed to visit their oil fields in

Manchuria. We also visited Harbin, where the Soviet army had taken the surrender of the Japanese army at the end of the Second World War.

It was bitterly cold when we arrived in Harbin. We landed on a grass field with rows and rows of Second World War planes along one side. We were wearing great fur hats and blue woollen coats. As we walked past the airport administration building, I looked back and saw Emery Barnes surrounded by a swarm of children. Emery, who is Speaker of the House in the current NDP administration, is an ex-football player and a veritable giant of a man. He is also black. I don't believe those Chinese kids had ever seen either a black person or anyone as tall as Emery, who is probably closer to seven feet than six feet in height. He attracted crowds everywhere we went. Dorothy Macdonald, who has blonde hair, also drew a lot of attention.

Then we travelled south to visit a communal cotton farm that was home to 7,000 people. We had travelling with us a Chinese interpreter, a diminutive gentleman with a very conservative demeanour who was absolutely masterful in his grasp of English. He also had a great understanding of the nuances of both British and American humour. Macdonald used to begin passages of Chaucer and Shakespeare, and this interpreter would pick them up in midpassage and finish the quote. The man was brilliant.

While we were visiting the cotton farm, Emery suddenly dashed down into the field. Emery was born in Louisiana but raised in Portland, Oregon. Cotton fields were part of his cultural awareness, but he had never worked in one. To this day, no one knows what possessed Emery to run into the field, but he started picking cotton and said in a loud voice, "If my mammy could see me now."

We were all having a good laugh when the Chinese interpreter walked to the edge of the field, without cracking a smile, and began singing "Old man liver." He deliberately said "liver" and that put everybody in convulsions, including Barnes, who collapsed right there picking cotton.

On a more serious note, we met with one of Premier Chou En-lai's key aides and other people in Beijing, and there was a great sense of common human exchange between our delegation and the Chinese. Canada was seen traditionally as a friend, but the Chinese obviously wanted the door opened even wider.

By the spring of 1974, our government was embroiled in controversy over Bill 31, the Mineral Royalties Act, which proposed a 5 per cent annual levy on mineral production in British Columbia. Introduced by Mines Minister Leo Nimsick, the bill also contained an escalation clause allowing cabinet to plug into rising world prices by setting a value based on a five-year average. If prices rose more than 20 per cent above the designated value, the government would take half the increase.

Bill 31 was an abrupt departure from the past, when companies were allowed to mine ores without paying any royalties. In our view, however, the resources of the province were owned by all the people, and we meant to see their interests were taken into account. In an interview with Southam News Services, I told a reporter, "If we cannot get a better return, I'd rather leave the ore in the ground until a generation comes along that has far more sense." I think that was the straw that broke the camel's back. The mining industry became the flagship for all the free-enterprise forces trying to scuttle the NDP government.

A series of demonstrations against Bill 31 were held on the lawn in front of the legislative buildings. Press reports said these demonstrations were financed by the mining industry, which would bus people in from the interior. A "spontaneous" demonstration takes a lot of planning, as the mining industry was well aware. Many of the demonstrators would camp out on the lawn. Some of their parties were quite rowdy. During one demonstration, I was called out to speak. The event was televised and a microphone had been set up. Some people advised me not to go outside, but I have never turned down a crowd in my life, hostile or otherwise.

One of the great things about television is that it is sometimes difficult to tell whether the crowd is irate or pleased. I just walked up to the microphone and waved, a broad smile on my face. I thanked them profusely for coming out to support the mineral bill. They were furious, but the cameras were turning. These Neanderthals simply refused to accept the notion that there was a social and financial responsibility in the development of resources. They wanted the public largesse to continue indefinitely. The same thing is happening today with the Hibernia oil project off the shore of Newfoundland. That project amounts to a $2-billion-plus welfare cheque to the oil companies.

Ironically, although the mining industry was saying that we were undermining investment in the province and using them as a political whipping boy, the reality was that they had begun to cut back on spending even before we were elected. A 1971 study by Price Waterhouse had found that the fifty-six-member Mining Association of B.C.

planned to chop capital expenditures between 1972 and 1976 by 86 per cent from the previous four years. Then, in the midst of the hysteria over our legislation, Mike Ryan, a director of Pemberton Securities and former chairman of the Vancouver Stock Exchange, produced numbers that showed mining stocks on the VSE had consistently outperformed those on the Toronto Stock Exchange since we had been elected. The problem with the mining industry is that they always sent the wrong end of the horse to the trough.

Such was the atmosphere in British Columbia when the minority government of Pierre Elliott Trudeau fell, triggering a general election on July 8. Federal NDP Leader David Lewis had forced the election by refusing to back the Liberals' budget. In the midst of the election campaign, Lewis came to Vancouver and said voters who were unhappy with our government shouldn't let that stop them from supporting federal New Democrats. He was merely encouraging people to separate provincial issues from those he was faced with federally. His remarks were seized upon by the media, however, and this reduced the level of debate considerably. Our federal candidates were repeatedly confronted with the same simplistic question: "Who do you support, Lewis or Barrett?"

The upshot was that the NDP took a tremendous beating. Our standing in the House of Commons dropped from 11 seats in British Columbia to just 2. The only returnees were Stu Leggatt in New Westminster and Tommy Douglas in Nanaimo-Cowichan-The Islands, both with sharply reduced majorities. Douglas had first taken the seat in a by-election in 1969, after Colin Cameron of the NDP had died. The 1974 election was the worst showing for the socialists in British Columbia since 1940, when the CCF returned but one member. Lewis lost his seat in the Toronto riding of York South, paving the way for Ed Broadbent of Oshawa to become national NDP leader a year later. In the wake of our setback, I was more determined than ever to stay the course.

During the summer of 1974, my long-standing dispute with the federal government over the shipping of Alaskan oil in single-hulled tankers along the coast of British Columbia erupted. Reports were circulating that U.S. oil companies were planning a massive expansion of refineries and distribution facilities in the Puget Sound area. Oil tanker traffic through Juan de Fuca Strait was slated to double, and this renewed fears of oil spills devastating the British Columbia coastline.

A year earlier, our government had come up with an alternative proposal to the use of oil pipelines and tanker traffic in moving oil to markets. Our proposal called for construction of an Alaska-Yukon-British Columbia railway system to carry crude oil and liquefied gas from the North Slope to the Lower 48 states. A report we commissioned concluded that a railway line from Prudhoe Bay to Lower Post, B.C., with a connection to the existing Alaska Railway, would cost less to build than a pipeline route, a tanker fleet, or both. It would have created about 2,500 jobs for five years, solved the problem of pipeline construction through permafrost areas, and sharply reduced the danger of spills. I had met with U.S. Secretary of Transportation Brock Adams to discuss our proposal and flogged it in Ottawa as well—to no avail. Now it seemed British Columbia was going to have to suffer the consequences.

I laid the blame squarely in the lap of the Trudeau Liberals. When I had spoken in Washington, D.C., to explain our fears about tanker traffic, I was reminded that I was speaking only for one province, not the Canadian government. In the absence of a firm stand from Ottawa, the Americans saw no reason not to proceed.

Provincial Liberal Leader David Anderson had built a significant part of his political career as a federal MP fighting against the oil tanker route through British Columbia coastal waters. Now, when the issue flared, Anderson was caught between a rock and a hard place. It was his fellow Liberals in Ottawa who had fallen down, but he knew where his bread was buttered and he wasn't about to blame them. He lashed out at me for being a "traitor." He blamed the "dishonest Nixon administration" and criticized oil companies for putting pressure on the U.S. government.

I invited Anderson to support our railway alternative, but he was determined to blame the socialists for the fact the federal government had not brought down regulations. That didn't wash, even with the media. What really puzzles me is that Anderson has now been a federal cabinet minister for two years, and I have yet to see him introduce legislation demanding double-hulled tankers. Somebody, not me, is going to call him a hypocrite. An oil-slick hypocrite.

Grace McCarthy had lost her seat in 1972, and that gave her the freedom to get out into the communities and rebuild the Social Credit Party. She had been touring the province and doing her best to stir up animosity towards our government. McCarthy had backed Bill Bennett's installation first as an MLA and then as Socred leader in the late fall of 1973. Now she was spreading the word that the sheriff program launched by Alex Macdonald was really an armed, secret police force. Her fearmongering was backed by some in the media.

The media crossed the line of objectivity frequently during this time. Alan Black, publisher of the Williams Lake *Tribune*, offered to pay the tab for people to send telegrams criticizing our government. Vancouver *Province* publisher Paddy Sherman took us to task at the twenty-third annual convention of the B.C. Chamber of Commerce. Without putting too fine a point on it, Sherman accused us of "unbelievable weakness, arrogance, ineptitude and sheer political and administrative stupidity."

Within that atmosphere, we concluded our legislative session for the fall of 1974 and took a Christmas break. To say it had been a busy year would be a classic understatement. The session that had opened the previous January 31 had run for a record-setting eighty-nine days, with an unprecedented 106 bills rattling through the House. Our contentious Mineral Royalties Act had passed, along with the Islands Trust Act, which sought to protect the Gulf Islands from being ravaged by developers, and a bill limiting rent hikes to 8 per cent annually.

We had also created the Council of the Family, which provided funding to religious groups who had been agitating about the breakdown of the family in modern society. We asked them to make recommendations about how this could be remedied. Ironically, the program was chopped by Socred Premier Bill Vander Zalm in the 1980s. The resulting protest was so loud, however, that he was forced to reinstate it.

We wanted to improve living standards for all British Columbians, in part by transferring a fair share of the province's bounty into the hands of its citizens. But the blizzard of reforms had stirred the opposition to try and solidify a formal coalition of the right. Newspapers carried advertisements almost daily calling on people to get involved in efforts to get rid of the socialists. Many of these ads were paid for by an organization that called itself the B.C. Disaster Prevention Fund, which claimed to have the support of more than 3,000 British Columbians.

Tory Leader Scott Wallace spoke of a unity party, but his plan was dependant on others, especially Socreds, leaving their party to join a new alliance, and only Liberals Pat McGeer and Allan Williams had shown any support. I dismissed these moves as political opportunism. I said they showed lack of political commitment. I was right on both counts, but what I neglected to say was that they were a harbinger of what was in store for us in 1975.

Eight

Not-So-Strange Bedfellows

The beginning of 1975 found our government embroiled in an escalating dispute with the newly reelected Trudeau government over resource taxation. My exchange a few months earlier with Finance Minister John Turner had failed to produce results, and now Ottawa was threatening arbitrarily to impose a first-ever federal tax on provincial oil and gas revenues. A First Ministers' meeting had been convened hastily in Ottawa in mid-December of 1974. Trudeau had used the occasion to launch attacks on me and on the premiers of Alberta and Saskatchewan for our opposition to the federal plan, which was to scrap deduction of provincial royalty payments in favour of imposing federal taxes on oil and gas companies. We argued that this was an unfair burden on the producers. In British Columbia, B.C. Petroleum was expected to make a profit of $100 million on natural gas sales in the current fiscal year, so Ottawa suggested privately that we could easily absorb the $25 million in increased levies on them. We weren't about to fall into that trap.

I sent a telegram the first week in January to Science Minister and acting prime minister Bud Drury, calling for a top-level meeting. I planned to attend with Alex Macdonald and suggested we meet with Trudeau, Turner and Energy Minister Donald Macdonald. The situation was urgent in British Columbia, where the drilling season runs from January to March. Many exploration companies, including Chevron, Pacific Petroleum and Gulf, already had indicated they would not do any drilling that year. Drury wired back saying the matter would have to await Turner's return to Ottawa two weeks hence; the minister was holidaying in Jamaica and planned to follow up that trip with a week of International Monetary Fund meetings in Washington, D.C. In response to Drury's wire, Alex Macdonald let it be known that he was considering taking the matter to the Supreme Court of Canada for a constitutional ruling.

As is often the case when everyone has their backs to the wall, events began to unfold very quickly. On January 20 we reached agreement with Drury and Donald Macdonald over natural gas taxation. The feds were allowed under the deal to levy tax on gas producers at fair market value. In exchange, they promised not to impose an export tax on natural gas for "the forseeable future." We had demanded this guarantee knowing full well Ottawa could use an export tax to cream off natural gas profits as they had already done with oil exports, where they collected nearly $5 a barrel in export tax and allowed only $6.50 of the $11.40 per barrel export price to return to the producing companies and provinces.

We planned to make up for revenue losses by increased export prices for natural gas. In fact, I had already proposed the export price to the U.S. be increased immediately from 99 cents per thousand cubic feet to $1.35, and to $1.93 by the end of the year. B.C. exported up to 800 million cubic feet of natural gas a day to the U.S. As I had proposed to Turner, profits of $180 million annually would be split three ways among Ottawa, British Columbia and B.C. municipalities. The battle over export prices was to dominate our relations with Ottawa for the next three months.

In the meantime, however, we were caught up in controversy over a routine international borrowing by B.C. Hydro to fund projects on the Peace and Pend d'Oreille rivers. The loan had been completed in two tranches of $100 million each and priced to yield interest of 8.70 and 9.52 per cent. The deal was a particularly good one because it was in Canadian dollars, exempting us from the vagaries of currency fluctuation. The deal was brought to me by Deputy Finance Minister Gerry Bryson and I signed it without a second thought. Then the trouble started.

The lender was Kuwait, which was awash in petro dollars like every other OPEC member. Western nations were lining up to access that money for economic expansion, and Canada was no exception. But I was attacked by Saanich MLA Hugh Curtis for doing business with "the PLO." Curtis had recently quit the Conservatives and joined the Socreds. In the wake of that highly principled step, he questioned me as to the "morality" of borrowing from the Arabs. Then Bill Bennett started screaming that I should have waited for interest rates to come down. I told him if he had the clairvoyance to predict interest rate movements, then he was the most brilliant financier on earth.

There also emerged at this time a concerted effort from all sectors of the business community to try to get rid of us in the next election. A group of businessmen formed the 21 Club to raise money for a revitalized Social Credit party. Conservative Leader Scott Wallace had been dropped like a hot potato, while Liberals Pat McGeer, Allan Williams and Garde Gardom were under increasing pressure to follow Hugh Curtis and cross the floor to join the Socreds.

Attacks on the NDP government from outside Canada were stepped up. U.S. senators Henry Jackson and Warren Magnuson of Washington had sought the intervention of Secretary of State Henry Kissinger in bringing both diplomatic and economic pressure against our proposed hike in the export price of B.C. natural gas. The Seattle *Times* wrote a vicious article attacking British Columbia as a bad neighbour, and the article was reprinted in the Vancouver *Sun*. I made another trip to Seattle during this time. In a speech to the chamber of commerce, I pointed out that Louisiana was now charging $2 per thousand cubic feet, double what we were getting. "Why should British Columbians subsidize you?" I asked. "Why aren't you fighting Louisiana?" Bad neighbour indeed!

My policy from the start had been to delegate power to cabinet ministers. As a result, I was confronted in the House almost daily with issues I knew nothing about. These usually were minor incidents or departmental issues that were of no significance in the grand scheme of things. But everything was fair game to the Opposition. They savaged us from all directions. There was no longer any pretence of rational debate. The cumulative impact of their attacks created the impression of a government out of control. It was obvious we were in for a very rough spring, and that would be the pattern right up to the next election. I had been in politics long enough to know that I had tweaked too many noses, kicked too many butts and challenged too many sacred cows to get off easy. But little did I know at this point how rough it was going to be.

That was the backdrop to my address to the Alberta NDP convention in Calgary at the beginning of February. The convention drew a standing-room-only crowd of more than a thousand people. I launched a stinging attack on multinational oil companies and the federal policy of allowing them to control 90 per cent of Canada's nonrenewable resources. I reiterated my position that I would endorse any federal policy that would put energy resources in the hands of Crown corporations. But in no way would I allow oil companies to dictate policy for British Columbia. "Oil won't rot if it stays in the ground," I said. "If the oil companies pull out, we can do it ourselves and make money the minute we start producing. That oil is like money in the bank."

Ottawa began scrambling to calm the waters. The business community may have been up in arms, but what I was saying had strong populist appeal. My attack on multinational oil companies was coupled with direct criticism of Ottawa's energy policies. I took every opportunity to prod the Trudeau government in the direction of public ownership and control of all natural gas and oil.

It was during this time a brouhaha erupted over a prospectus B.C. Hydro filed with the U.S. Securities and Exchange Commission to support a $150-million borrowing request. The prospectus contained information, supplied by the W.A.C. Bennett government, that showed government-owned B.C. Railway had made profits of $1 million a year between 1969 and 1972. As premier, I was chairman of B.C. Rail. I disclosed in the legislature that the information supplied by B.C. Hydro was incomplete. B.C. Rail actually had a deficit of $98.3 million, and two planned extensions into northwestern British Columbia would cost millions more than estimated. I said the previous Socred administration had disregarded engineering principles and built the railway solely under W.A.C. Bennett's great theme of resource roads to resource riches.

Liberal Leader David Anderson did a thorough raking of Bill Bennett over the Socred blunders. One can only surmise that Anderson realized three of his own members were ready to defect to Social Credit and he desperately needed a hook to pull them back. Bennett's reaction was to stall. These exchanges took place on a Friday. Bennett said he wanted to study my charges and documentation over the weekend before making a statement.

Instead, Bennett phoned Wall Street and pointed out the conflict between the financial statement filed in New York and the documents I had tabled in the House. He accused me of violating Securities and Exchange Commission regulations by filing false information, and he requested that the SEC investigate the matter. Of course, there was nothing to it. We had consulted our lawyers and knew we had broken no rules. The SEC investigation subsequently bore this out. But the effect of Bennett's actions on our government was devastating. No one in the media ever questioned his tactics. I was painted as someone who had tried to foist a hokey prospectus on Wall Street to enhance British Columbia's credit rating. The press did no checking, and Bennett came off looking like a hero. He walked away scot-free from the mess created by the previous Socred administration.

In his role as municipal affairs minister, Jim Lorimer had taken on the problem of urban sprawl and unmanaged growth in urban areas. Problems were particularly acute in Kelowna and Kamloops. Both had experienced explosive growth in their suburbs, which were outside the control of the municipal government. The burgeoning populations were putting pressure on schools, hospitals and other services without paying their share of taxes. Lorimer's solution was to force amalgamation of the two cities with their surrounding areas. This, we hoped, would help introduce some planning into the development process. Needless to say, the local politicians had a fit.

Lorimer took screaming abuse over his legislation, but his usual reaction was simply to doze off. The more shrill the debate, the greater the likelihood that Lorimer would fall asleep. We discovered that he had landed at Normandy four days after D-Day and fought his way through France and Holland. He had been through the worst battles of the campaign and had had a nipple shot away in the process. So nothing ever phased him.

In the midst of the attacks on his amalgamation bill, however, Lorimer decided he'd had enough. Several municipalities had threatened to sue him. He walked into cabinet one day and distributed copies of a bill he intended to introduce that afternoon. It stated simply that he could not be sued for anything he had done in the past or anything he might do in future with regard to amalgamation. We all laughed, saying to Jim that he would never get away with it. At that, he struck the table with his fist and said, "I'm fed up with this." We had never seen Lorimer behave like that. He had always been supremely calm. We decided to just let him deal with it.

When the bill was introduced, the proverbial fan, which was really getting overworked by this time, took another hit, and crap sprayed all over the place. The Opposition launched into its usual rant, calling Lorimer an evil genius. It was great show biz for the Opposition, and the press gallery was packed and obviously enjoying the spectacle. I glanced over at Lorimer and saw that he was dozing, as usual. After about forty minutes, which is a hell of a long time in a debate that you are sustaining only through shrill diatribe, Lorimer suddenly stood up and shouted, "I won't stand for this. I have had enough. I warn you that if you keep this up, I will enter this debate in a way you have never seen before."

Everyone in the House was aghast. Lorimer, who never raised his voice, had delivered a booming threat. After a few moments of silence, the House broke into laughter. Lorimer's intervention had broken the stalemate, and everyone could see the absurdity of the way he was being handled on this bill. Lorimer ended second reading, and when the final reading took place, there was very little dispute and the bill slid through without a hitch. Then he went back to sleep. We all walked around in awe and admiration of Lorimer after that.

Jack Radford, who was minister of recreation and conservation, had been working closely with several other ministers on raising the profile of the tourism industry in British Columbia. One of the moves we had taken in this regard was to resurrect the *Royal Hudson* steam locomotive for a daily run between North Vancouver and Squamish. The Socreds, of course, criticized us over this. After they were elected, however, they tried to take credit for it. Grace McCarthy even made a grand tour with the *Royal Hudson* on a special run to San Francisco!

The Canadian Pacific Railway announced around this time that they were going to close their *Princess Marguerite* ferry run from Victoria to Seattle. This jolted the Victoria business community into a mad rush to abandon their free-enterprise philosophy and demand the socialist government do something. We did, but we held out awhile to make them sweat.

In the process of buying the *Marguerite*, we had said the CPR was going to have to sell all its land in Victoria's inner harbour. The CPR was demanding an exorbitant price. I didn't want to get involved directly, so I sent a message through Jack Radford and Resources Minister Bob Williams that unless the CPR got realistic we would discuss all the lands given to them by the federal government over the years and the windfall profits they had made in disposing of those lands, especially in urban areas.

After that gentle reminder, the deal was quickly consummated. We bought the ship and 8.7 acres of CPR-owned land on Victoria's inner harbour for $2.5 million, and Bob Williams established a Crown corporation to run the ferry. Unfortunately, the *Princess Marguerite* was privatized by the Socreds, then sold, and it ended up as scrap in Hong Kong harbour.

At the start of our term in government, I had appointed Eileen Dailly as deputy premier, and she had acted in that capacity whenever I was out of the province. She had been a tower of strength, and this was never more evident than in 1975, when the opposition parties began drawing together under the aegis of the business community to defeat the socialists. She took on more and more responsibility during that fateful year, as well as bringing about dramatic changes in education. One of her most important initiatives was launching a program for aboriginal people to control their own schooling. In co-operation with Atlin MLA Frank Calder, Eileen established the Nisga'a Tribal Council as the school board in northwestern British Columbia. Those schools are still operating under native administration today.

By July of 1975, all hell was breaking loose on the labour front in British Columbia. During the first year of our administration, Labour Minister Bill King had masterfully guided a new Labour Code to unanimous approval by the House. The 153-section act replaced three existing statutes. It removed authority to grant injunctions from the courts and created a ten-person Labour Relations Board to iron out union-management hassles. The board had sole authority to deal with illegal strikes, lockouts and picketing. King had tailored the new code as a compromise between the former situation, where the courts had punitive and legalistic involvement in labour relations in British Columbia, and previous labour legislation in Britain, where prior to 1972 a collective agreement was not enforceable in law. The new code won endorsement from former Socred Labour Minister Jim Chabot, who said it was a genuine attempt by our government to resolve the industrial relations problems that had plagued the province for decades. Unfortunately, the Socreds gutted the bill in their so-called restraint program in the 1980s.

The leading opponent of the new labour code was Len Guy, president of the 200,000-member B.C. Federation of Labour. On the morning after the 1972 election, I had received a call from Guy saying that he and vice-president George Johnston wanted to discuss the forthcoming labour legislation. The NDP had stated for years that should we be elected, we would rewrite the labour laws. We met in my living room in

Coquitlam, where Guy and Johnston came right to the point. In essence, they wanted to write the legislation and have it imposed arbitrarily by our government. I told them we would be setting up a three-person commission to draft the bill and, ideally, government would name someone to that commission, as would industry and labour. They balked at this, but there was no prolonged objection.

Several days later, I met with Bill King and recounted my meeting with Guy and Johnston. King and I were in complete agreement. Then, on entering the first caucus meeting of our new administration, I was stopped by Joyce Thomas. Len Guy was on the phone. He was very agitated, and he told me he had changed his mind. "Changed your mind about what?" I said. "I didn't think we had made any decisions." Guy told me the Fed would not agree to a three-person commission to rewrite labour legislation unless labour had the right to name all three members. I suggested Guy announce his position to the press and he started swearing at me. The conversation broke down quickly after that.

I had had ongoing battles with some labour leaders since I first ran for NDP leader, and now the stage was set for the animosity to continue. In the summer of 1973 we had been hit with a strike by B.C. Ferry workers at the height of the tourist season. Thousands of tourists were stranded on Vancouver Island for five days as we wrestled with the strikers. A year later firefighters went on strike. In the spring of 1975, the very militant ICBC union called a strike that was widely interpreted as a major challenge to our government. Next the forest industry unions stepped up to the plate. Some 13,000 pulp and paper workers walked off the job on July 16. They had just completed a three-year agreement and wanted a $1.50-an-hour increase in one year. International Woodworkers of America leader Jack Munro wanted to stay at the table, where the IWA were seeking a $1-an-hour hike. But secondary picketing by the two pulp unions soon ended that. About a third of the IWA's 47,000 members were already out of work because of soft markets. The pulp unions threw another 10,000 off the job.

Under King's leadership, a strategy was developed by cabinet to steer clear of the forest dispute. We appointed B.C. Supreme Court Justice Henry Hutcheon as mediator, then backed off and kept our mouths shut while he wrote his report. Hutcheon's recommendation, a $1.55-an-hour increase over two years, was angrily rejected by the two pulp unions, partly due to their hostility towards the IWA. Canadian

Paperworkers Union vice-president Art Gruntman and IWA leader Jack Munro clashed frequently during this time; Munro felt his members were being used as pawns in the paperworkers' bid to get a better deal than the IWA had. Then came a surprise strike by the Teamsters over delivery of propane fuel in the province. They were followed by food industry workers, retail employees and railway workers. By fall, 58,000 people were out. Nearly the entire province was on picket lines.

There was a feeling in cabinet that we should get a grip on the situation, but no one was quite sure what direction to take. I kept my own counsel, except for daily discussions with Bill King and Alex Macdonald. King had an impromptu meeting at the Empress with Len Guy. As King recounted the story to me, Guy had been drinking and was feeling no pain. He was in a petulant, aggressive mood. There was a very sharp exchange, and Guy lost his temper and shouted, "We'll get you commie bastards."

What Guy meant by this, only he knew for sure. But his comment led King to become very concerned about the seething turmoil within the labour movement itself. There were many factions, many rivalries, many separate agendas. King had been trying to weave some kind of compromise that would persuade the unions and management to accept the Hutcheon report and end the paperworkers' strike. He had provided the necessary legislative framework, but British Columbia had no collective memory of sensible dispute resolution on the part of either management or labour. Confrontation was all they knew.

In that atmosphere, King, Macdonald and I met again in my office. After much discussion, I turned to Alex and asked him to draft back-to-work legislation and have it on my desk within twenty-four hours. Labour code legislation allowed us to take that step, but it had to be very tightly controlled. Only Macdonald, King and Marc Eliesen were in the loop. Eliesen had come on board with government sixteen months earlier to establish a cabinet secretariat to speed implementation of legislation through the bureaucracy. I received the bill well within the allotted time. I read it through and discussed its implications with King and Macdonald. I asked a few questions, then decided to proceed.

I had great confidence in King's leadership. I had had a personal experience of it earlier, and I never forgot it. In a dispute involving B.C. Rail employees, I had made a public statement that could be construed as interference in the dispute. King walked into my office, right past

Joyce Thomas, and pointed his finger at me. "If you ever do that again," he said, "you'll have my resignation on your desk." I got the message and I never interfered with King again. With that incident in mind, I said to King that with his approval I wanted to take full responsibility for this decision. I wanted the bill printed overnight. It would be presented to cabinet the next day, which was Sunday, and go to caucus the following day.

I went home for supper and spent time with Shirley and the kids. I was very calm, firm in my determination to take this step with all its attendant risks. In ordering men and women back to work in British Columbia, I would be seen as abandoning the party's long-standing adherence to the principle of free collective bargaining. In the abstract, I would have to agree with that interpretation. In reality, however, the economic warfare waged by the fractious unions was jeopardizing the basic safety, comfort and health of the people of British Columbia. We had done everything we could to help the parties arrive at a voluntary collective agreement. There was just one course of action. The only question was whether the caucus was ready to step up to it.

There followed a series of emergency cabinet and caucus sessions. Alex had copies of the bill and we passed them around. Some people were shocked when they saw what the bill contained. I stood up and thanked everybody for understanding the position we were in. I praised Macdonald's legislative judgement and political sagacity. I also praised King's leadership. The bill I had just presented was a historic step in British Columbia, and I acknowledged that it was a very difficult step for an NDP administration. I told people I wanted the legislation introduced in an emergency sitting of the House on Tuesday, October 7. This unexpected move needed to take everyone completely by surprise. We had to hammer home the point that this government intended to lead decisively. If people didn't like what we were doing, they could deal with that in a subsequent election.

After some questions and discussion, I told caucus: "You must decide. I feel it is very important that we take this step. If you cannot support it, however, it will be necessary for you to find another leader. I will graciously announce that the situation is beyond my desire or ability to control and I have asked the caucus to name a new leader." Naturally, some of the caucus saw this as a threat. It could be interpreted that way. It was clearly a measure of my determination.

My comments were followed by extensive, heated debate. Then we put it to a vote. Three people voted against the bill—Rosemary Brown of Vancouver-Burrard, Colin Gabelmann of North Vancouver-Seymour and Harold Steves of Richmond. They all said they opposed the measure because it interfered with collective bargaining. There are ironies in life that come back to haunt us. In 1993, Colin Gabelmann, as attorney general in the Harcourt government, voted for back-to-work legislation against the teachers. I imagine there had been a great deal of soul-searching in the intervening years.

We had notified MLAS on Sunday of the emergency session. To stifle speculation, we had dropped the hint that the session was being called to discuss the twelve-week-old propane distributors' strike. When I introduced Bill 146, the Collective Bargaining Continuation Act, in the House, the tension was palpable. We had moved to end all major labour disputes in the province with a back-to-work order and a ninety-day cooling-off period. The strikes were to end within forty-eight hours. The Opposition was caught off guard. Seven hours and thirty-five minutes later, the bill passed, with only the three NDP backbenchers voting against it.

The Opposition supported the legislation en masse. Len Guy called Bill 146 a complete betrayal of our party policies and of the working people of British Columbia. He also called on all union members to support candidates in the next election who would oppose strike-breaking legislation. Other labour leaders were less damning. Jack Munro of the IWA expressed regret that the government had been forced to take this action. Teamsters President Ed Lawson said his members would obey the order, and he acknowledged that the government showed "considerable courage" in taking such a "bold step."

Had there been any doubt in my mind that we had done the right thing, it was dispelled quickly by the response of the rank and file workers. These people had almost been forgotten in the confrontation between union and corporate management, and they, along with their families, had undergone severe hardship during the protracted strikes. Phone calls, telegrams and letters began pouring in as people expressed their gratitude to the government for showing leadership and ending the stalemate.

The business community was dumbfounded. Immediately, there was speculation that I was going to use Bill 146 as an election issue. I never had any such intention. I was not beating up on labour, as some critics said, in an attempt to get reelected. Our responsibility was to govern, and that's what we had done. I didn't want to have to order people back to work, but I had no choice. I had the best possible support any leader could have from my cabinet and caucus, and I don't regret the decision in the least.

While our government was engaged in the union-management struggles that led to the back-to-work order, there were some vicious slashing and burning activities taking place among the Liberals. Liberal Leader David Anderson had been under severe attack for months, as the Socreds and their allies in the business community tried to lure his members into their camp. Hugh Curtis had already bolted the Conservatives for the Socreds, and there was rampant speculation as to who among the Liberals would follow. Every day brought a fresh rumour about the offer of cabinet posts. The one heard most often had Pat McGeer in the finance portfolio, Garde Gardom as attorney general, Allan Williams in charge of forestry and resources, and Gordon Gibson as mines minister.

In the end, it was McGeer, Williams and Gardom who made the switch. Gibson remained a Liberal and went on to become provincial leader. I remember the day McGeer, Williams and Gardom crossed the floor. It seemed strange at the time to see them joining a gang they had vilified for so many years. Especially McGeer, who had written a highly critical book about Social Credit. They didn't look out of place for long, though. Alex Macdonald summed it up better than anyone. I remember him saying softly but audibly, "They have changed their principles as they change their coats."

Around this time Edmonton publisher Mel Hurtig arrived in Vancouver claiming he had been tipped that the Central Intelligence Agency had investigated me, Alex Macdonald and Frank Calder at the request of the Socreds. Hurtig further alleged that the CIA had provided the Socreds with secret reports containing things that could be used to discredit us. The request to the CIA, moreover, had been made with the cooperation of an unnamed senior official of the U.S. consulate in Vancouver.

Everybody ran for cover. W.A.C. Bennett, Bill Bennett, Socred party president Grace McCarthy, former Socred Attorney General Robert Bonner and John Stutesman, U.S. consul general in Vancouver, all issued strong denials.

But Hurtig held his ground. He refused to name the source of his information, but he certainly provided enough details to make the story interesting. The reports, he said, were prepared by an intelligence agent who had quit the CIA a year earlier. The agent had recently testified before U.S. Senator Frank Church's select committee investigating the CIA. In a telephone conversation with Hurtig, the agent said a consular official had told him the U.S. was concerned that a socialist government was becoming increasingly popular in western Canada.

To this day, I don't know if Hurtig's story was true. According to Norm Levi, one of the officials at the American consulate in Vancouver was in Philip Agee's book about the CIA. This man had been assigned to British Columbia during our government and had left before the end of our term. And I had reason during the time we were in power to suspect a case of CIA infiltration. B.C. Petroleum chairman Jim Rhodes reported to me that he had an employee the R.C.M.P. felt might be a CIA informant. As the R.C.M.P. explained, we were the only petroleum company in North America about which the CIA couldn't find out everything they wanted to know just by picking up the telephone. The guy in question had impeccable credentials, which we later discovered to be bogus. Sometime after Rhodes fired him, he went to work for ex–Socred Attorney General Les Peterson, who was out of politics by then.

Several years after we left government, I asked Joel Connelly of the Seattle *Post-Intelligencer* to request data under freedom of information guidelines about CIA activity in British Columbia relative to our government. Joel gave me a copy of the material he got back, and all the interesting parts appear to have been blacked out.

During the time Mel Hurtig's revelations were in the spotlight, I learned there had been a new round of anonymous threats on my life. This information had been relayed to Alex Macdonald by the R.C.M.P. It came just as I was about to embark on a month-long tour of the province, and Alex responded with a public statement that security had been beefed up for my trip. Then Bill Bennett made a statement that shocked many people. He said an "atmosphere of confrontation" created by the NDP government might have caused the threats. In other words, I had brought them on myself. I was outraged. Even the press, which had been savaging our government, was knocked off its stride. There was an editorial in the Vancouver *Sun* about "Bill Bennett's cheap shot." The writer said Bennett's comment did a disservice "to all but the nuts." For once, the *Sun* and I saw eye to eye.

In mid-October of 1975, Trudeau called a first ministers' conference in

Ottawa to unveil his anti-inflation battle plan. Soaring inflation had been an ongoing issue throughout the year, and all ten provincial premiers had urged anti-inflation leadership from Ottawa.

For my part, I had been highly critical of the way Ottawa was continually fanning inflation by expanding the money supply, then turning it over to chartered banks so they could maximize their own profits. Our response had been to introduce legislation in May that would enable us to establish our own bank in British Columbia. The bill had passed in June. Trudeau and I had also clashed over Ottawa's action in hiking MPs' salaries by 33 per cent while preaching restraint to the country.

Before leaving for Ottawa, I had announced the first major cabinet shuffle of our administration. Bob Strachan had stepped down as transportation minister to become agent general in London. Carl Liden of Delta took over transportation and communications, while Provincial Secretary Ernie Hall took motor vehicles and ICBC under his wing. Leo Nimsick left mines to take over Hall's travel industry duties, and Dave Stupich took up finance, which I had held since we were elected. In other moves, Jim Rhodes was named chairman of B.C. Hydro, replacing retiring head David Cass-Beggs, and George Lechner took over from Rhodes as head of B.C. Petroleum.

The meeting with Trudeau and the provincial premiers was held over the Thanksgiving weekend. I wasn't terribly apprehensive about attending, because Trudeau had publicly renounced the wage and price control measures I felt were so unfair to ordinary people. Then, without fanfare, he imposed them at the conference. I had never before seen such naked hypocrisy. On the one hand, we were all buying the argument of restraint because there were, and are, serious problems in an unplanned economy. Namely, the rich get richer and the weak get kicked in the teeth. But Trudeau was going hard-nosed on wages and by-your-leave on prices. He had come up with a plan that would result in the weak getting kicked in the teeth twice while the rich escaped again.

When I returned to Victoria, I met with the cabinet ministers and asked them to draw up proposals to implement price freezes in British Columbia that would counter Ottawa's single-minded attack on wages. By Order in Council we froze the prices of food, fuel and essential services. To address the problem of low-income people having to do more than their share in the anti-inflation fight, we boosted the minimum wage from $2.50 an hour to $2.75 and announced plans to raise

Mincome rates on January 1, 1976. The price control program was to be monitored by Consumer Services Minister Phyllis Young.

There was an immediate gasp from the business community. First we had ordered strikers back to work; now we had become the only government in Canada to take action on prices. The other shoe had dropped. Labour went nuts right across the country about the Trudeau government's actions. The Canadian Labour Congress was yelling that no province had taken a stand against Trudeau. Nobody noticed that we had taken action on prices. We were lumped with everybody else.

An ironic twist to this is that the people we had ordered back to work actually received higher wage increases than federal legislation permitted because they were still in negotiation when Trudeau slapped on the controls. By a quirk of timing, they lucked out. But that didn't let us out of the doghouse. Some people in labour were still angry at us, and business was angry at us too.

What few business contacts we had began to shrink in 1975. But there were a small number in the business community who, although they were not NDP supporters and never would be, were willing to listen and have a rational dialogue with us. Among them was Jim Pattison, who was always available on the other end of the phone. Adam Zimmerman of Noranda was another. Westcoast Transmission president Ed Phillips was a straight shooter who, although he joined the 21 Club backing the Socreds, had supported our government in establishing B.C. Petroleum.

I had to make a decision about where we were headed. We had instituted numerous changes, but they were largely misunderstood and therefore perceived as threatening. We had failed to win recognition from labour over the price freeze, and we had further alienated business. The revitalized Social Credit Party could raise all the money it needed, and the Liberal defection had ruled out any possibility of a split vote.

I canvassed the cabinet ministers about their views on the current political situation. Some felt we should not even consider an election yet. Others thought we should go to the polls. We were in for a difficult time no matter what course we took. But the call, ultimately, was mine alone.

If we hung on, there was a strong possibility that the Socreds, with their access to unlimited funds and a supportive media, could build even greater public opposition to our government. Almost every editorial writer or public commentator was a critic. Open-line radio programs, perhaps the most potent of all forms of opinion-making, were a daily conduit for attacks on our government. On top of that, I had no idea what outside influences might be coming into play. Our government had clashed over natural gas pricing with U.S. senators Jackson and Magnuson of Washington. They, in turn, had appealed to U.S. Secretary of State Kissinger. The CIA revelations by Mel Hurtig were still on my mind, as was our experience with the B.C. Petroleum employee. Could some form of U.S. intervention be far off?

I had watched elections in Australia and New Zealand, where mobilization of the right wing had been so effective. I remember sitting alone after supper one night, musing that even if we lost we could probably hang on to a substantial number of seats and a reasonably high percentage of the vote. I knew that sooner or later there would be mindless cutbacks under the Socreds, with their blind loyalty to cowboy capitalism. They would squander the assets we had acquired, and jobs would be lost. They would mount an assault on B.C. Petroleum, which had drawn so much revenue back into British Columbia. As revenue sources dried up, the Socreds would start racking up debts, and the economic fallout would be devastating. Four years hence, people would have a much better understanding, and appreciation, of what we had done in government. If we lost this time around, I hoped we could win then, before too much damage had been done.

We had in place a day-care system financed by government—the first in Canada. I knew it would be one of the first targets of a Socred administration. Other programs were threatened—Mincome, Pharmacare, ICBC. In particular, I was worried about the Land Commission Act. We had one of the most comprehensive farm programs in the nation, including an income assurance plan for farmers. But there was strong pressure from developers and speculators who wanted to see the ALR scrapped.

There was still some anger over the back-to-work legislation. But I anticipated that rank and file members would support us. One exception was mining. The mining companies had taken us on over the Mineral Royalties Act and won the propaganda battle hands down. They had sold the myth of free-enterprise individualism even to the poor miner. Another area of concern was the schools. Eileen Dailly had enabled teachers to catch up on wages and pensions and had reduced student-teacher ratios. But the heated debate around the strap still lingered.

I finally made the decision to go ahead. When I told cabinet, there was reluctance on the part of some members, followed by a fatalistic acceptance. After some discussion, everyone rallied behind the call. Caucus was stunned, but they too rallied, and away we went. The election was called for December 11, and I requested a mandate for my leadership in the national fight against inflation. Trudeau had inadvertently given me a hook when he said that the federal anti-inflation program would continue for at least three years. I promised to extend the provincial price freeze on essential commodities if Ottawa didn't pull up its socks. I said I needed support to make the struggle fair, with equal sacrifices for all and favours to none. I also struck at the theme "Don't let them take it away."

Early in the campaign, BCTV laid plans for a debate among the four party leaders to be televised province-wide. Gordon Gibson and Scott Wallace were quick to agree. I realized it was necessary to clarify the issues and what we had done in government, so I threw my hat into the ring. Bennett initially agreed, then later declined on the advice of his spin doctors. His excuse was that there was no time for the debate in his tight schedule.

I encountered huge, enthusiastic crowds as I stumped the province. But there had been renewed threats on my life, and police protection was increased. As expected, there was a token announcement by a high-profile businessman who threatened to leave British Columbia if the NDP was re-elected. This time around it was Peter Brown, president of Canarim Investment Corporation, who said he would move to Calgary. On the other hand, prominent Socred mayor John Baker of Burns Lake praised me for providing "unbelievable cooperation and help" in sharing gas revenues.

I also encountered my first smear campaigns in 1975. A certain lawyer in Vancouver began peddling a story that I had taken a kickback from Kuwait in negotiating the government loan and used the money to buy property in California. The story was circulated throughout the Lower Mainland, and it related to earlier accusations in the House that we were in league with Arab terrorists. Not long after that, I was confronted by a reporter for the Coquitlam *Herald* who asked me to comment on reports that I owned property next to land bought by the government housing corporation on Burke Mountain. In both cases, it was alleged that I stood to make huge profits. Neither story was true, of course, but one or the other cropped up just about everywhere I went.

One of the issues I hammered away at throughout the campaign was the fate of our acquisitions in the event of a Socred victory. In addition to high-profile B.C. Petroleum, B.C. Cellulose and Plateau Mills, we had initiated smaller takeovers of Panco Poultry, Kootenay Forest Products and Ocean Falls Corporation. The *Princess Marguerite* alone had made $100,000 clear profit in its first year of operation. Time and again I challenged Bill Bennett to state his party's policy on these Crown-owned firms, but he never said a word.

On election night, Shirley and I and the kids awaited the results in a tiny, depressing motel room in Port Coquitlam. We had wound up our campaign there. All the blinds were down, and the R.C.M.P. had taped aluminum foil over the windows as a security measure. There had been another threat on my life that day, and police had staked out the hallway. Vancouver *Sun* columnist Jack Wasserman dropped by. So did NDP campaign strategist Gerry Scott. We all sat on the bed and watched the results on television. The atmosphere was one of deflation.

As soon as the results started coming in, I could see that we had lost. I conceded defeat thirty-five minutes after the polls closed. We had skidded to 18 seats from 38 when the writ was dropped. Yet our popular vote stood at 40 per cent, versus 39 per cent in 1972. Cabinet ministers Ernie Hall, Jim Lorimer and Bill Hartley, among others, all went down to defeat. I lost my seat in Coquitlam by nineteen votes. In my concession speech, I congratulated the Socreds and promised the party faithful the fight would continue.

Although I appeared stoical the night of the election, I was seething inside over what I feared would happen to the assets our government had accumulated. I poured out my feelings a week later, when Dave Stupich and I held a news conference to report on the province's financial picture. We had brought down three surplus budgets, and cash reserves had risen from $98.6 million to $143.7 million. Debt in parity bonds had fallen from $253.5 million to $144.5 million, while assets in Crown corporations had grown from $3.8 billion to $5.7 billion.

As soon as Stupich had finished his comments, I made an emotional appeal to the people of British Columbia to be on guard against fast-talking salesmen who might try to get them to sell off their assets. "Don't listen to anyone who says the people shouldn't own assets because it's socialist," I said. "Don't allow any government, ever, to sell you out." My warning, tragically, went unheeded.

Nine

They Gave Hypocrisy a Bad Name

I didn't realize how utterly exhausted I was until after the 1975 election loss. The caucus had been going full tilt throughout our time in government. We had brought down an astounding amount of legislation and then fought a bitter, heartbreaking campaign. It was a sombre ride back home to Victoria from that motel room for Shirley, myself and the three kids. I remember it as a really hard trip. There was the depressing feeling that it was all over.

It had not been an easy election. Once the deal was struck for the three Liberals and one Tory to cross the floor to join the Socreds, the fix was in. The possibility of a split vote had been eliminated, and everyone had joined hands in a common cause to defeat the NDP.

Our kids didn't say much about how they felt. Shirley told me later they were more concerned about me than themselves. At the time we were defeated, Joe was at the University of Victoria and our eldest son, Dan, had completed a year at Simon Fraser University. Jane was in Grade 10 at Esquimalt High, and she went back to school the next day. She could have stayed home, but she chose to go. Her close friends were generally sympathetic, but all of the kids had taken a fair amount of ribbing as the children of a politician. We had a very tight-knit, private family, though, and this gave our kids the confidence and resilience to cope.

Shirley and I decided to take a holiday. We spent the next two weeks in Manzanillo, away from everything, where I could lick my wounds and ponder my future and the party's. It was rejuvenating, but I still wasn't sure whether I wanted to stay on as leader. A lot depended on the mood of the caucus.

While I was away, the caucus deliberated over what the party should do. A series of very tense meetings followed my arrival back in Victoria. There were twenty or so people attending. The majority wanted me to continue to lead the party. But I had lost my seat, so if I was going to remain as leader, somebody would have to resign.

Almost immediately, Bill King offered his seat. But the caucus refused. He was from the rural interior riding of Revelstoke-Slocan, and I was a city slicker. Another solution would have to be found. After considerable debate in a caucus meeting, Bob Williams offered his seat in Vancouver East.

We had agreed that whoever stepped down would become a research coordinator in the NDP provincial office. We knew we were moving into a tough period where the Socreds were likely to launch an assault on our legislation. We wanted somebody working for the party, outside the legislature, who was tough and bloody-minded. Ideally, that person would also have cabinet experience. Williams fit the bill perfectly. He did a superb job for the party and the caucus during that difficult time.

Bill King was chosen by caucus as interim opposition leader. The Socreds were pitching the propaganda that B.C.'s finances were in a shambles because of the socialists. They projected a budget deficit, then went on a spending spree to make sure it happened. At one point, they announced that ICBC was in serious financial trouble. They borrowed $200 million to prop it up, then quietly put the money back a week later. The press covered this ploy, but nobody really attacked the Socreds for playing politics with the provincial purse. It was a trying time for the NDP caucus, and King did a spectacular job.

Bill was also very gracious to me personally. While he was interim leader, he split the leader of the opposition's allowance fifty-fifty with me, saying he was just holding the position temporarily. My protestations were there, but my gratefulness far exceeded them. Anyway, Bill would brook no argument, and he's bigger than I am.

After several months' delay, Bennett called the by-election for June 3. The return to Vancouver East was a very exciting, nostalgic reaffirmation in my political life. As expected, the Socreds attempted to portray me as a parachute candidate. But I had been born and raised in the East End, so the campaign was really a homecoming for me. Shirley, the kids and I lived in Greater Victoria and made it clear we planned to stay there. We wanted to establish a political base in Vancouver East, however, so we borrowed money on our home and bought a house there. We made it available to my mother, who had long since remarried, and her husband, and this is where we stayed when we were in the constituency. My mother had been a long-time social activist in the East End, and now her old political strings picked up all over again.

Vancouver East had changed very little from when I was growing up there. It was still a working-class area, North American folklore's "wrong side of the tracks." There was a shortage of parks, and the schools were neglected. Britannia High School, one of the oldest secondary schools in Vancouver, had never had a gymnasium or a cafeteria until Bob Williams and Alex Macdonald came along. The East End was forgotten by city hall, and this tended to strengthen the cultural and political identity of the residents. There exists among them to this day a deep sense of loyalty to the East End. Williams is a prime example. He has a fierce, abiding, consuming commitment to the area.

The East End, which included both Vancouver East and Burnaby, had delivered up some of the greats of the socialist movement. It had sent to Ottawa and Victoria people like Arthur Turner, E. E. Winch and Harold Winch, Grace MacInnis and Angus MacInnis, and Paddy Neale, who was an MP and then secretary-treasurer of the Vancouver and District Labour Council. It was an immigrant area, particularly post-Second World War Italian immigrants. But there was also a rich mix of Ukrainians, Chinese, Japanese and Indo-Canadians. Scots were very active politically, first with the CCF and later with the NDP. Native-born Canadians tend to be naive and passive about politics compared with immigrants, who have made a definite choice to come to this country and tend to feel very strongly about government and the political process. The passionate political ferment of the East End was further augmented by the first rush of Americans who came to Canada because of the Vietnam war.

I remember an occasion during the campaign when the Ukrainian community asked me to address a luncheon at the Ukrainian Cultural Centre. They also invited my mother, who spoke a number of languages fluently, one of which was Ukrainian. It was arranged for her to sit next to me at the head table. As it turned out, several of her old friends were there, and it was more like a homecoming for her than a political rally for me. There must have been about two hundred people, a warm, beautiful happening. While I was preparing to give my speech, the person who was chairing the meeting asked my mother to introduce me.

This was the first time I had ever seen this side of my mother. I knew what her politics were, and I knew of her passion for social justice. But I had never seen or heard of her speaking to a group. She stood right up and gave a magnificent speech for about ten minutes. I presume it was magnificent; I didn't understand a word, because she spoke entirely in Ukrainian. Towards the end the crowd burst out laughing and I wondered what the hell she was saying. Then it was my turn. I stood up, thanked my mother, made some standard political comments and then told the audience this was the first time I could remember being upstaged at a political meeting by another speaker. I concluded by saying, "I will defer to whatever my mother has said." At that, they just howled with laughter.

After I sat down, people crowded around, hugging my mother and chatting her up. As we drove away, I asked my mother what she had said. "I just told them how difficult it was to raise you," she replied. "I told them what a terrible student you were, what a layabout, but in spite of all that, you still turned out all right, and that is a tribute to me as a mother." Now I understood why the audience was laughing. The joke was on me.

Many people in the riding also remembered my father. His store on Powell Street, which had closed in 1957, and his methods of doing business had been legendary. My father was also known in other ways. He was incredible in his dealings with people. This was a guy who used to take my brother and me into restaurants and, after having a look at the menu, go into the kitchen and pull out a five-dollar bill and lay it on the cook and tell him what we were ordering. Then we would have these spectacular meals brought to the table.

It used to embarrass us the way he would go into the kitchen, and I recall the time I commented on it. "I raised such stupid sons," he replied. "You call the waiter, tell him what you want and he brings the food and then you give him a tip. What did the waiter do? All he did was bring the food to the table. But you go into the kitchen and give the cook a tip and then you get good food."

On many occasions during the campaign, I would knock on a door to have someone answer, "If you're half as good as your old man, kid, you've got my vote." At another door, someone would say, "Oh yes, I know your mother. She helped raise money for the Spanish Civil War."

My campaign manager was Joe Denofreo, whom I had known for years as a social worker before he went to work for CUPE. We have always been friends, but that didn't prevent him giving me orders. He had me out knocking on doors even before the election was called. As soon as the writ was dropped, the first of a series of polls was published showing that I was going to lose.

I was running against a very fine man from the Socreds named Ralph Long, James Siemens of the Liberals and Lester Lavers of the Tories. There were also three independents in the race, including an anti-abortionist named David Bader. I struck up a friendship with Long, who got a pretty rough ride at some of the all-candidates meetings. A couple of times when he was unfairly attacked, I took the mike to point out that we needed rational debate on issues without screaming accusations.

At one point, CBC arranged a television debate between Siemens, Long and myself. The interviewer opened with a question to me: "What makes you think you have the right to run in Vancouver East after your government's record and your being a parachute candidate?"

After that auspicious opening, I began outlining the issues. About five minutes into the program Bader, who had been left off the panel, burst into the studio demanding to be included. The filming stopped and a great argument ensued between Bader, the producer and the interviewer.

I turned to Long and Siemens and said, "Look, he has a right to be with us." I suggested we take the position that either Bader be included or we walk. They agreed, and we joined the fray with Bader, who by now was quite hysterical with his yelling and screaming. Another ten minutes and we all walked out. The program was never broadcast.

Denofreo, meanwhile, was driving me ruthlessly. He sent me knocking on doors with a young woman who was sixteen years old. I dislike knocking on doors, a hangover from my days selling fruits and vegetables. I had become known in the party for my unwillingness to canvass voters. I would go down a street and hit maybe half a dozen houses and then quit. So Denofreo assigned someone to go with me.

One night I was out with this young woman. After the fifth or sixth house, I said I had to pee. I told her I wanted to return to the committee room. She refused, but I was adamant. Here I was, an adult, ex-premier, telling a sixteen-year-old party-faithful kid that I had to pee.

"If you really have to pee, Mr. Barrett, just knock on the door and ask people if you can use their washroom."

I still thought I could intimidate her. "I don't want to go to the damned door and use somebody's john. I have to pee and I want to go back to the committee room."

"If you won't go to the door, there is a tree," she said. "Stand behind that and nobody will see you. Mr. Denofreo told me you would try this and I was to deal with it. He told me when you did I was to, quote, kick your ass up and down the block."

Denofreo sent me canvassing the Italian community with a fellow named Franco Cuzzetto. Franco was a custodian at the Vancouver School Board and a very active, committed member of the party. We were expected to hit fifty or sixty houses in an evening.

The first place we stopped, we were invited in to taste the wine. Italians are great wine-makers, and proud of it. People all over the East End produced wine in their kitchens and basements. We went in and sat down and, yes, the wine was magnificent. I tried not to take too much. Italians don't spit out wine when they taste it the way the French do. Not in the East End, anyway.

So we would have wine and some cheese with it and I would say how wonderful it was. Half an hour or forty-five minutes later, we would go to the next house. Same thing. I had to be careful in my praise. Everybody knew Franco and I would be getting more wine farther up the road, and for me to make comparisons would lose me votes. We only visited five or six houses on those nights. Then pressure started for us to come in and have a meal. Denofreo finally pulled us out of the Italian neighbourhood, but it was the same with the Chinese and Greek families. I put on a massive amount of weight during the by-election.

Bob Williams and his wife, Leah, worked tirelessly on my campaign. So did Alex and Dorothy Macdonald. Vancouver East voters saw Williams as their boy. Macdonald wasn't an East Ender, but he was their boy too. Alex was lawyer to many of those people, and some of them were never charged legal fees or, if they were, it was a pittance.

Denofreo booked a large building at the PNE for the victory party. He knew from canvassing polls what the results were going to be, but he wouldn't share the information with me. On polling day, June 3, I was pronounced winner with more than 70 per cent of the vote. Long of the Socreds was next with 25 per cent. All the pundits had been saying it was going to be a close, tough election fight for Barrett. So much for their clairvoyance. I did not view this as a great victory for me, but a continuation of the emotional tide of East End voting patterns.

Now came the task of rebuilding. We had a good core of former cabinet ministers left: Eileen Dailly, Dennis Cocke, Bill King and Alex Macdonald were still there, and we had Bob Williams working on the outside. There was a strong nucleus to build upon. The House was sitting when I returned, but the session was short and relatively uneventful.

We had the summer off, and I decided to go into the rural areas as I had done after the 1969 election. This time, however, we were stronger. There were ex-MLAS and former cabinet ministers who wanted to run again. And people had been returning to the party after the short taste they had had of the Socreds.

Len Guy and George Johnston had disappeared from the labour scene. The new secretary-treasurer of the B.C. Fed was Jim Kinnaird, who had been deputy minister under Bill King. I spent some time mending fences there and within the party hierarchy. By the fall of 1976, hostility towards me had diminished dramatically.

I travelled around the province with Harvey Beech. I had bought a 1976 Volvo demonstrator from Don Docksteader, my right-wing car-dealer friend and a great character. He kept saying I was in the wrong party, and I said the best thing about him was that he sold socialist-made cars. On one trip, Harvey, Bob Williams, Emery Barnes and I travelled together. We held regional public meetings during this time, sort of mini-caucus meetings. We would hear briefs during the day and top it off with an NDP banquet and a fund-raiser. We had meetings in Vernon and Revelstoke, then Williams returned to Vancouver and the three of us pressed on to Cranbrook. At the meeting there, Emery gave me a very moving introduction, and after my speech we drove over the pass from Cranbrook to Castlegar.

We arrived in Castlegar around 1:00 A.M., with no hotel reservations. We hit a couple of places, with no luck, then pulled into a large motel, dog tired. The three of us walked into the office and the manager looked up and became quite flustered. "Oh, Mr. Premier, I'm so sorry. I don't have a room." I chuckled. I wasn't premier any more. "If only I had known, Mr. Premier," he went on. "I just feel terrible."

Emery hadn't said a word. Suddenly he pushed past me and Harvey. "I want to ask you a question," he said, towering over the minuscule manager. "You don't have a room for this man?" he said, gesturing towards me. "Tell me, what have you got against Jews?" We all laughed except the hapless manager, who was more flustered and bemused than ever.

The year 1977 marked the beginning of fundamental change to the economy of British Columbia under the new Social Credit administration. Our government had acquired assets worth more than $600 million with an investment of less than $100 million. Now, under Bill Bennett, subtle but definitive shifts were taking place in taxation policies and access to resources that ultimately would deny the people of British Columbia ownership of those riches. It was all going back to the corporations.

One of the first indications of this came from Transport Minister Jack Davis, the defeated federal Liberal cabinet minister who was resurrected as a Socred. Davis concocted a scheme to obtain three new ferries in a complicated lease plan that doubled their cost from $46.5 million to $95 million. Then he boosted ferry fares. The Socreds had been elected on a promise to run a no-debt, pay-as-you-go policy. But under the ferry-lease deal with B.C. Ferries and measures taken later by other Crown corporations, the Socreds instigated a huge borrowing program drawn on the credit of British Columbia. Since the borrowings were completed through Crown firms, they never had to be reported in annual government budgets.

Then Mines Minister Tom Waterland introduced a new mineral bill. I got into a heated debate in the House with Waterland over the bill's failure to instigate a planned increase in coal royalties. When the NDP took power, the royalty amounted to 25 cents a ton. We increased it in stages to $1.50 and had announced a further increase to $2.50 just before we were defeated. After a series of talks with Kaiser Resources President Edgar Kaiser, however, Waterland decided not to proceed with that increase. Kaiser Resources had made a $71-million profit the year before, mainly by exporting coal from southeast British Columbia to Japan. Waterland's move, I figured, deprived the province of an additional $11 million.

An interesting political dimension developed over this issue involving Liberal Leader Gordon Gibson and Tory Leader Scott Wallace, both of whom threw themselves into the debate with a vengeance. I cannot think of two more deeply committed MLAS. They made brilliant, prophetic speeches about where the government was going. Both were self-professed free enterprisers, but neither could stand the stench of what was evolving under the Socreds. I suspect it was an irritant to both the media and the business community to hear Gibson and Wallace blasting the Socreds. But there was no excuse for this $11-million give-away to Kaiser. It wasn't enough money to make or break the government, but it was a signal to the rest of the business community that the Socreds were there to be skinned.

The Social Credit government began to display an overt paranoia about civil servants, which became a hallmark for their time in office. In late 1977, Bill King disclosed details of a Socred investigation into the alleged politicization of the civil service. The investigation had been launched shortly after the Socreds were elected. A civil servant named Klaus Ohlemann had compiled a blacklist of Order in Council appointments while we were in government, identifying these people as NDP supporters. At first the government denied the existence of a blacklist. But King had been fed a copy, written by Ohlemann to Dan Campbell, who had been Socred campaign chairman in 1975 and was an aide to Bill Bennett. Campbell had sent the list to cabinet ministers, outlining the need for reducing "a top-heavy bureaucracy." You should have seen everyone run for cover when King dropped that little nugget! Ohlemann, the designated fall guy in the episode, eventually apologized.

Another Socred ploy was an audit by the Clarkson Gordon accounting firm. The Socreds picked Clarkson Gordon to conduct an independent review of British Columbia's finances, but the firm was not given full access to B.C.'s books. They were only allowed to report on the figures the Socreds gave them. The company chose partner Ian Adam to head the review. Adam, incidentally, happened to be on the executive of the Point Grey Socred constituency. He had also done work for Bill Bennett in his Kelowna business. Adam forecast a $541-million deficit.

But the Socreds were handicapped on two counts. One, there were no facts to support their charges of financial bungling by the NDP administration, and two, even the media wasn't buying it this time. The Socreds had been hiding money in Crown corporations to distort the province's true financial picture. The charade unravelled as Bennett and Adam and Finance Minister Evan Wolfe were all tripping over each other, trying to deal with a situation they had created themselves. At one point, Wolfe even admitted in a newspaper interview that the cash transfers were political decisions, not financial ones.

The legislature was a real bear pit during this time. Even though the NDP didn't have massive numbers in the House, we were able to maintain the tension and keep the government on their toes. The government found that many of the changes we had made were worth maintaining. On one occasion Socred backbencher Ray Loewen actually proposed government action that already had been taken during our administration. Loewen had met with a constituent about to lose his life savings in a business venture that was going into receivership. Loewen wanted government to become an equity partner to bail this business out. I informed him that we had passed the Savings and Trust Corporation of B.C. Act, which allows government to do just that. Loewen tried to respond, but Bill Bennett silenced him. Many of the Socred backbenchers were totally unaware of what we had done. They were just anti-NDP, period. It was embarrassing for Bennett and a great moment for us to rub it in.

The Socreds continued their relentless largesse towards the corporate sector. Remember our struggle with the federal government over natural gas royalties? Well, the Socreds had hardly taken their seats on the government side of the House before they wiped out the results of that struggle with two strokes of red ink. They repealed our tax arrangement with Ottawa in what amounted to a $6-million giveaway to the multinationals.

Shortly after he became premier, Bill Bennett named Judge Lawrence Eckhardt to head a royal commission on electoral reform in British Columbia. Eckhardt, a former Social Credit candidate, presented his report to the legislature in June of 1978. Gerrymandering is a euphemism for what Eckhardt's report did to the political map of this province. It increased the number of seats in the legislature by 2 to 57. It wiped out three NDP-held seats—the two held by Norm Levi and Rosemary Brown in Vancouver-Burrard and Bill King's seat in Revelstoke-Slocan—and added two seats in the Socreds' traditional stronghold in the Fraser Valley.

One of the more bizarre changes took place in the Vancouver-Little Mountain riding held by Socreds Grace McCarthy and Evan Wolfe. The riding had been won by Phyllis Young and Roy Cummings of the NDP in 1972. It was diverse, economically and culturally, with Shaughnessy mansions on one side of the riding and modest homes on the other. Eckhardt added a piece of land on the western boundary from a well-heeled, predominantly pro-Socred neighbourhood, disfiguring the riding into the shape of a clenched fist with one finger standing erect. The finger had a distinct tilt to the right. What had been a swing riding was now safe for the Socreds.

We had only forty-eight hours to debate the bill incorporating Eckhardt's recommendations. It was ipso facto, up your gee-gee done. The legislation was rammed through the House. It wasn't until after the 1979 election that sworn statements from commission workers were found alleging McCarthy had interfered in the work of the Eckhardt Commission to give herself a safe seat. Ombudsman Karl Friedmann tried to investigate the allegation but was blocked by the courts. The "Gracie's finger" affair was on and off the front pages for nine months during 1980, but by that time it didn't matter.

Adoption of the Eckhardt report triggered media speculation that a general election was imminent. The pundits began assessing the possible outcome, and there was a common theme that the pendulum was swinging back in our favour. It was suggested that Bennett would not be able to whip up the same holy war against socialism that he had fought in 1975. There were favourable assessments of former ministers like Bill King and Dennis Cocke, and rumours that New Westminster MP Stu Leggatt was about to abandon the federal scene and become a provincial NDP candidate.

It was nice to get good press, but it was premature. Bill Bennett still had a major card to play before hitting the campaign trail. In late August of 1977, he had introduced legislation to establish B.C. Resources Investment Corporation, the now infamous BCRIC. To get it going, the Socreds shovelled in a rich array of resources acquired by the NDP government. Into the pot went 100 per cent of the government stake in Plateau Mills; 100 per cent of its holdings in Kootenay Forest Products' sawmill and plywood plant in Nelson; 9.8 million government shares in B.C. Cellulose, with sawmills at Castlegar, Terrace and Kitwanga, and pulp mills at Prince Rupert and Castlegar; and the 13-per-cent ownership of Westcoast Transmission. To sweeten the pot, Bennett threw in oil and gas exploration rights on 2.9 million acres north of Dawson Creek. The assets were valued at $151.5 million.

BCRIC turned my worst nightmare into reality. On the eve of the 1979 election, Bennett offered everyone in the province five free shares. Then he allowed everyone to buy 5,000 additional shares, raising $487 million in one of the most successful offerings in Canadian history. Nobody twigged to the fact that BCRIC was a Crown corporation and therefore British Columbians already owned those assets. It was a revisitation of Barnum and Bailey, with a new twist: Barnum, Bailey and Bennett. A lot of people fell for it hook, line and sinker. The media did too.

BCRIC was the mother of all Socred scandals, but we who fought it were just voices in the wilderness. And the sound of our voices was lost in the stampede to buy shares. Some of my colleagues in caucus even bought BCRIC shares. Alex Macdonald, Victoria NDP MLA Charles Barber and I were among the most vociferous critics. Vic Stephens, who replaced Scott Wallace as Tory leader after Wallace resigned his seat in Oak Bay in December of 1977, was also very effective. Macdonald refused to take his five free shares, saying they would only be useful for wallpapering his bathroom; they weren't soft enough for any other purpose!

In the ensuing years BCRIC went on a spending spree, paying a premium of more than 100 per cent over market to acquire Kaiser Resources for $600 million, among other ill-fated deals. Kaiser officials Edgar Kaiser and Jack Poole made personal fortunes on the takeover. In 1987, Vancouver businessman Jimmy Pattison called the Kaiser acquisition "catastrophic" for BCRIC. Today BCRIC is known as Westar Group. At their annual meeting in Vancouver early in 1995, Westar shareholders approved a plan to wipe out those famous five free shares and consolidate them on the basis of 125 BCRIC shares for every Westar share. It was the first successful reverse of the alchemist's dream: the Socreds had taken gold and turned it into lead.

Bolstered by the circus atmosphere surrounding BCRIC and a more favourable electoral map courtesy of the Eckhardt Commission, the Socreds called an election for May 10, 1979. Very early in the campaign I received a surprise endorsement from Ralph Loffmark, health minister under W.A.C. Bennett. Loffmark, defeated in 1972 and now a commerce professor at U.B.C., praised me for promoting a $1-billion railway through British Columbia linking Alaska with the Lower 48 U.S. states. He went on to say I believed in the North as W.A.C. Bennett had, while Bill Bennett lacked his father's vision.

The Socreds were in a temporary state of shock, scrambling in all directions to control the damage. But what Loffmark said was true: I did agree with W.A.C. Bennett's strategy of opening the North through railway extension. A rail link would ensure controlled use of resources and preservation of wilderness areas, rather than the wide-open huck-sterism that tends to follow highway construction. My campaign message was that this election was the last chance for British Columbians to have a say in the control of their natural resources. I wanted people to understand that BCRIC had put our acquisitions on a collision course with disaster.

There were renewed calls for a televised debate between me and Bill Bennett. Because the Tories and the Liberals had been decimated in 1975, the networks wanted this to be a one-on-one contest. The by-now familiar pattern unfolded. I challenged Bennett to meet me face to face and Bennett countered with a challenge of his own. In the end, Bennett shunned the meeting. I thought he had made a fatal mistake in ducking another debate. But he got away with it. Instead of castigating the premier for dodging the people, the media virtually ignored the issue. I guess Bennett's timidity over meeting me in front of the cameras was old news by this time.

The last major rally was in Victoria, where 8,000 people jammed the Memorial Arena. It was the biggest crowd of the campaign. I was introduced by Tommy Douglas, who said the crowd was big enough to "scare Bill Bennett out of the other half of his wits." I had seen Douglas draw huge crowds before. But I had rarely witnessed such joyous bedlam as I encountered in that arena. It carried over at the polls four days later, but it wasn't enough. Our strength in the House increased from 18 seats to 26. The Socreds won 31 seats.

The election held some happy surprises for the NDP. The coattails of Charles Barber helped his running mate, Gordon Hanson, to defeat Socred cabinet minister Sam Bawlf in Victoria. Jim Lorimer toppled Tourism Minister Elwood Veitch in Burnaby-Willingdon, and ex-MP Frank Howard passed Agriculture Minister Cyril Shelford in Skeena. Ernie Hall was returned in Surrey. I won in Vancouver East. I was very happy to see Karen Sanford win again in Comox. Sanford had emerged as one of the stronger people in caucus and had really proved her mettle during debate on the Eckhardt Commission report. Had we formed the government, I feel confident she would have been in cabinet.

As I had forecast in 1975, people returned to us in large numbers after four years of Bill Bennett. They had a clearer vision of our political philosophy and were less vulnerable to Socred fearmongering about the socialist bogeyman. We had won 46 per cent of the popular vote. It was a dramatic comeback, but close only counts in horseshoes. The aura of BCRIC and the effect of Socred gerrymandering were simply too much to overcome. Now, in the wake of our defeat, I had to make a decision about whether to remain in politics. In my own mind, I knew I wanted to leave.

Ken Oakes / Vancouver *Sun*

Left to right: Here I am with Socred Leader Bill Bennett, Liberal Leader Gordon Gibson and Tory Leader Scott Wallace as we present our views to a group of religious leaders at the PNE Forum in Vancouver during the 1975 election campaign.

Randy Thomas / Vancouver *Sun*

The banter belies the tension as Prime Minister Trudeau and I exchange quips in 1976 at the Habitat Conference in Vancouver.

Vancouver *Sun*

Bill King, *left*, and Alex Macdonald escort me into the House following my June 1976 by-election victory in Vancouver East.

Federal NDP Leader Ed Broadbent, *left*, and I ham it up
with West German Chancellor Willy Brandt at the
Socialist International convention in Vancouver in 1978.

Steve Bosch / Vancouver *Sun*

Shirley and I wave to supporters
after the NDP's heartbreaking 1983 election loss.

Ralph Bower / Vancouver *Sun*

The new talk-show host hits the deck running in 1984. Here I am conducting my first-ever interview on CJOR with author/historian Pierre Berton.

Kerry Waghorn

As MP-elect, I had my work cut out for me when I went to Ottawa in 1989.

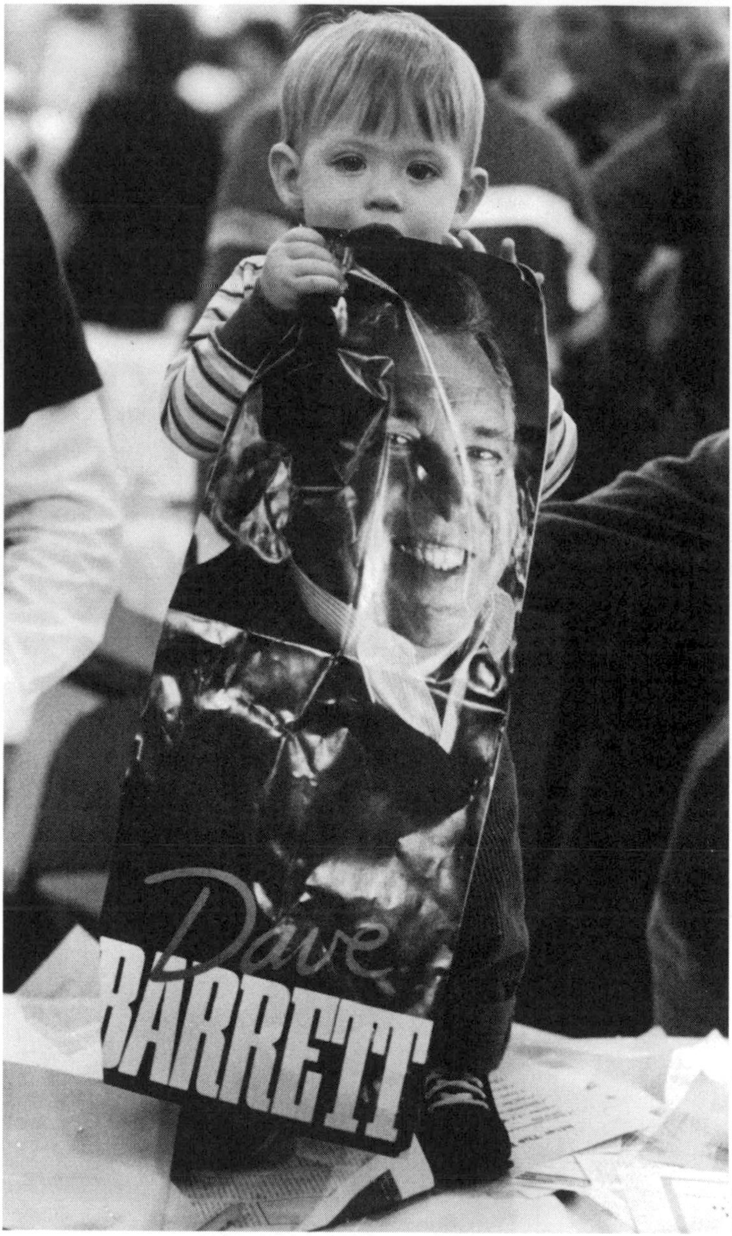

C. McConnell / Toronto *Star*

"What happened, Papa?" Thirteen-month-old Andrew Barrett clutches a campaign poster following his grandfather's failed bid in 1989 to become federal NDP leader.

Gathering of the clan: Past and present B.C. NDP leaders pose at a party fundraiser in 1987 at Union Hall in Victoria. Pictured standing left to right are Tom Berger, Bob Skelly, Mike Harcourt and me, with Harold Winch seated.

The Barrett family in 1992.
Back row: Jane, Shirley, our grandson Andrew, me and Joe.
Seated in front: Jane's husband, Wayne Thompson,
our granddaughter Hannah, Dan and Dan's wife, Mary Heppner.

Ten

Gracie's Finger: Who Really Got It?

Our stunning comeback in the 1979 election was masterminded by Yvonne Cocke, then provincial secretary of the party. Yvonne had used her considerable skills to pull together all the elements within the party and run the best campaign we had ever seen. British Columbia was in the spotlight, and the media took steps to boost their coverage of the highly charged political scene. The Vancouver *Sun* sent columnist Marjorie Nichols back to Victoria after postings in Ottawa and Washington, D.C., while the Vancouver *Province* brought Allen Garr on board to write a regular column. These moves were accompanied by an increase in reporting staff at the *Sun*, the *Province* and the Victoria *Times-Colonist*, as well as more frequent visits by reporters from the *Globe and Mail*, the *Toronto Star*, BCTV and the Seattle *Post-Intelligencer*. There was a sense the New Democrats were on a roll and bound to gain momentum over the next four years. The defeat of Jev Tothill, who had replaced Gordon Gibson as Liberal leader, and Tory Vic Stephens had given British Columbia a genuine two-party system for the first time in many years, so we were expected to be more focussed—and polarized—around issues. Nobody wanted to be left out of the story.

I was pleased and disappointed at the same time. I also felt strongly that it was time for me to go. I had been party leader for the better part of ten years, a long time in the modern political context. Besides, I had suffered two defeats. Many of the caucus members knew I was feeling this way. Some spoke to me about it; others said nothing. Dave Stupich remarked, "Look, we didn't win, but we didn't lose. If there had been a turnaround in just three seats, we would be government by one seat today." From that perspective I owed it to the party to stay for the next election, when the real test would come.

Shirley and I discussed it at some length, and in a very short period of time the issue became a major bone of contention. On one occasion, we got into such a heated discussion in the car that I had to pull over to the curb. Shirley took the position that I could not leave, that the 1979 result was a draw. There is no draw in politics, but she argued that I couldn't walk away from the party at that point. Then we burst out laughing. For the first time ever, we were on opposite sides of this particular issue.

It was during this time that I received an invitation to attend a conference on international terrorism in Jerusalem. Israeli Prime Minister Menachem Begin would be there, along with Labour party leader Shimon Peres. CIA director George Bush, right-wing U.S. Congressman Jack Kemp and my old sparring partner from Washington state, Senator Henry Jackson, were also invited. There were forty-two participants, and I discovered later that only five were from the left. The conference was to take place the first week in July, and I accepted. It would give Shirley and me a chance to get away for a while and reflect on where we were. Before leaving, I met with Hugh Legg, an NDP researcher and a strong critic of unfettered capitalism, to discuss material for my talk.

It was Shirley's and my first trip to Israel. My mother's brother had gone to Palestine when their family left Russia, and I was able to meet him for the first time. His daughters were married and raising families, so I met cousins and second cousins. Two of my second cousins, who were the same age as our children, were officers in the Israeli army. It was my first real experience with the tensions of the Middle East, and it occurred to me for the first time that the same terror existed among Arab families as among Jews. Humans are humans. Terror is terror. I found myself wondering how I would function under that kind of pressure.

The conference was essentially one-sided. Participants were mainly from the U.S., Britain and Israel. The first four days consisted of one jingoistic speech after another before anybody from the left got up to speak. I was particularly impressed with the comments of Frank Cluskey, leader of the Labour Party of Ireland. He gave a brilliant analysis of human behaviour, not on the basis of politics but on the basis of ancient racial tribalism and fundamentalist religion, and it was obvious he was reflecting on the strife in his own beloved Ireland. Merlyn Rees, who had been a cabinet minister in the Labour governments of both James Callaghan and Harold Wilson and was outgoing home secretary, made thoughtful remarks about Ireland from the British perspective.

One of the speakers from Germany was Hans Josef Horchem, an anti-terrorist specialist. He gave an interesting analysis of the Baader-Meinhof gang and the way their actions undermined the authority of the state. But I was troubled by the way he defined attacks on the state as absolutely immoral. In my comments about his presentation I referred to the July 20, 1944, plot against Hitler. Hitler's Germany was immoral, I said, so the only recourse for people of conscience was to take matters into their own hands. I made reference to Thomas Aquinas, who laid out five conditions that provide moral justification for a person to take up arms against the state. I was verbally assaulted later in the elevator by the German delegation, but I stood my ground.

As the only Canadian at the conference, I was expected to comment on the October Crisis of 1970, when British diplomat James Cross and Quebec cabinet minister Pierre Laporte were kidnapped. Terrorists later murdered Laporte, and Prime Minister Trudeau invoked the War Measures Act. Cross was eventually released. My message was very much outside the conference mainstream. Legg had written a thoughtful speech warning governments about overstepping their boundaries in combatting terrorism, thereby posing a threat to their own citizens. Instead of touting Trudeau's actions, the speech criticized what Canada had done, saying police had sufficient powers without the War Measures Act. The media was singled out for sensationalizing events at the expense of factual reporting, thus making news a weapon for exploitation in the arsenal of the terrorist.

The last straw as far as my opponents were concerned came when I drew a connection between terrorist violence and the corporate agenda. "What morality could have motivated an automobile company to proceed with manufacturing a car whose gas tank was proven, prior to production, to blow up on impact? What kind of alienation would have allowed a board of directors to proceed with production of a nuclear reactor when adequate safeguards could not be guaranteed in the plant's construction? The alienation involved in these corporate decisions surely qualifies as a starting point for an enlarged definition of terrorism." It wasn't what they had come to hear. Those of us on the left were totally isolated in the conference from then on.

By the time we arrived back in Victoria, I had resolved to stay on as leader for one more election. Shortly after our return, a major scandal broke involving Social Credit election tactics. It came to light that Socred caucus researchers had advised party members how to play dirty during the last election campaign. Specifically, it was suggested that members write bogus letters to newspapers praising the Socreds and making it appear the letters came from ordinary citizens. There was one letter attacking Norm Levi that had appeared in two newspapers over the signature of prominent NDP supporter Gordon Townsend. The papers apologized after Townsend complained. It came to be known as the "dirty tricks" affair.

As events unravelled, the Townsend forgery was linked directly to Bill Bennett's office. Once Attorney General Garde Gardom ordered a police investigation, the scandal really heated up. The two researchers fingered by government—Jack Kelly and Ellen MacKay—vowed to tell all in the hope of escaping prosecution. Kelly had quit his job after the affair came to light, but MacKay refused to resign or accept a reprimand until the entire four-member research staff was pink-slipped by Socred caucus chairman Jack Kempf. The lawyer representing Kelly and MacKay, Robert Gardner, said the pair would await the outcome of the R.C.M.P. investigation before considering a wrongful dismissal suit against the party.

At the height of the scandal there was a dinner honouring me for my ten years as head of the provincial NDP. I received telegrams poking fun at "dirty tricks" from federal leader Ed Broadbent and Saskatchewan Premier Allan Blakeney. Blakeney sent one telegram, then another to confirm he had written the first. The second was signed with his thumbprint. Broadbent's wire closed with assurances that he had, in fact, written it.

It took the R.C.M.P. three months to complete their "dirty tricks" investigation. By then, Allan Williams had replaced Garde Gardom as attorney general. When Williams received the R.C.M.P. report, he refused to make it public. He said only that there was not enough evidence to lay charges. It was amusing to watch Williams during this cover-up. He had been very sanctimonious about switching to Social Credit after so many years of pummelling them, along with McGeer and Gardom. Now he and his colleagues had jumped into bed with the Socreds and pulled up the blankets. I recall saying at the time, "We don't know who is doing what to whom, but we sure as hell know who is feeling the effects."

Around this time Health Minister Rafe Mair resigned in Kamloops to take up a new career as a radio hotliner. Mair was a very capable minister and frequently gave credit to Dennis Cocke for things Cocke had done while we were in government. It was my opinion that Mair was not at any time in Bill Bennett's good books, and that may have been a factor in his decision to leave. We were favoured to win in the Kamloops by-election set for May 14, 1981; even Bennett was wandering the legislature conceding defeat. One Socred after another marched through Kamloops, promising to build a bridge across one of the many rivers in the riding. I was in Clearwater during the campaign. By then the Socreds had been promising a bridge a day. "I can't top the promises for all those bridges," I said, "but if we're elected, I'll give you a river." It was a promise I didn't have to keep. Socred Claude Richmond pulled it out on polling day with 44 per cent of the vote, compared with 42 per cent for Howard Dack of the NDP.

Because there were only 5 seats separating the Socreds and the NDP in the House, the government really had to keep on its toes. We were looking for a chance to defeat the government on the floor. On one occasion there were four Socreds absent during a debate and we were able to match their strength. We took full advantage. Our researchers had flagged a clause in the provincial Constitution Act that set the maximum number of cabinet ministers at twenty-three. But no more than nineteen, including the premier, could receive the additional $24,000 annually for assuming a portfolio. We zeroed in on Tourism Minister Pat Jordan as the newest cabinet minister. Jordan was shaken by the line of questioning, delivered masterfully by Charles Barber of Victoria. She took the question as notice, indicating she was unable to answer at that time. Barber directed his question to Finance Minister Hugh Curtis, who also took it as notice.

Barber then took a different tack and moved for an emergency debate to discuss this serious constitutional matter. If Jordan had received her extra pay as a minister or any travel expenses, then she was in breach of the Constitution Act. Acting Speaker Walter Davidson said he needed time to make a decision on whether Barber's issue qualified for an emergency debate. I rose and challenged Davidson's ruling, saying he should decide immediately.

By now the Socreds knew all too well what we were up to. They were desperate to avoid the pending vote. Davidson huddled briefly with the Clerk of the House and finally agreed his ruling had been challenged. The stage was set. There would be a vote. Socred whip George Mussallem took a roll-call list and checked which of his members were present. The division bells started to ring, warning all members a vote would be taken in five minutes. All available Socreds showed up, and the vote was a 26-to-26 tie. Davidson was then forced to vote with the Socreds on his own ruling to break the tie. This was only the second time in British Columbia history that the speaker had had to rescue the government by casting a tie-breaking vote. We never got that close again.

The "Gracie's finger" gerrymandering issue resurfaced during this time when two women who had been on the Eckhardt electoral reform commission, Florence Tamoto and Vi Barton, swore affidavits that Grace McCarthy had interfered in the work of the commission. An inquiry by deputy attorney general Dick Vogel dismissed the allegations. The BCRIC issue flared anew as well when share prices started to fall on the stock exchange. The BCRIC fiasco ultimately wiped out the savings of many ordinary British Columbians who had put their homes in hock for as much as $30,000 to buy the maximum number of shares under the government offering. We made hash of the Socreds in the House, but in my own mind I knew the damage visited on the province by these two scandals could not be undone.

I was far more concerned about the fate of B.C. Petroleum. Bill Bennett had said during the 1979 election campaign that he wanted to sell the Crown corporation because, in his view, it would be better off in private hands. B.C. Petroleum had by now chalked up nearly $1 billion in profits for the people of British Columbia. These profits were pouring into general revenues. It was nothing short of miraculous that B.C. Petroleum had escaped getting mired in the cesspool of BCRIC. Now, Bennett renewed talk of selling it off. As it turned out, nothing happened at that time, but it was only a stay of execution: in 1990, at the peak of its insane policy of deregulating energy, Bill Vander Zalm's Socred government, through Energy Minister Jack Davis, handed B.C. Petroleum over to a group of natural gas producers who still operate under the name of CanWest. The group brokers natural gas sales and purchases in Canada and the U.S. and pays royalties to the province. B.C. Petroleum continued to function, administering a few contracts with producers who were not prepared to assign contracts to CanWest. Vander Zalm didn't receive a penny for B.C. Petroleum. And British Columbians to this day have no idea what was given away and how much revenue has been lost.

By February 1982, there was widespread speculation about a fall election. It was then Bob Williams dropped the bombshell announcement that he would challenge Alex Macdonald for the NDP nomination in Vancouver East. I had been picking up rumours, but until Williams announced his intentions I had no firm indication he would actually throw down the gauntlet. Williams's job with the party had ended in the summer of 1979. He had attended the constituency association's annual meeting on January 27 and been elected president by acclamation. But he had said nothing about seeking the nomination. A week later, Alex and I had sent a letter to constituency members thanking them for their support and saying we would both run again. Now Williams's hat was in the ring as well.

My immediate reaction was to schedule a meeting with Williams. Macdonald was in Germany attending a seminar on labour-management relations when Williams's announcement was made. I requested that he return. The nomination meeting was set for March 7, and there was no time to lose. Williams and I met on common ground in the East End and went for a long walk. I asked him not to challenge Alex, but he was adamant. Williams was very protective of his East End turf, and Macdonald was not an East Ender. There was tension between Williams and Macdonald, which is not unusual in two-member ridings.

I told Williams up front that I would not be running again if we lost the next election. Even if we won, I said, I would not serve a full term. After two years, my plan would be to ask the party to call for a leadership convention while I was still head of government. Williams did not believe me.

We parted in disagreement. It was a sad moment for me. Williams and Macdonald were both able, brilliant people who had given a great deal to the party and to the people of British Columbia. Now they were pitted against each other in a struggle that would benefit Social Credit and could hurt our chances in the next election. I had told Williams if he persisted I would intervene publicly and support Macdonald. This was something I had never done before, and I don't think Williams believed I would do it now. But he was wrong. Macdonald and I ran on a slate for the nomination, and we were both successful.

My worries, however, were far from over. I had begun to notice signs of a revolt in caucus against my leadership. Nobody had said anything to me directly, but there was obvious unrest. There was an edge during meetings and around the legislative building different from anything I had ever felt before. This was to be expected after two election losses, and frankly I was surprised it hadn't surfaced earlier. By the summer of 1982 things were getting really hot, so I requested a caucus meeting for late August in Nanaimo. Twenty-three caucus members attended.

I opened the meeting by saying that I knew there were criticisms of my leadership and that I was prepared to listen to them with an open mind. No MLAs had stated publicly that they were opposed to my leadership. But several stood up to criticize me. Some people felt that I had maintained too low a profile and not attacked Socred policies forcefully enough. The biggest gripe was that I had become a one-man show, acting autocratically in defiance of decisions by the party's grassroots and overriding the caucus.

I sat back and watched the proceedings with interest. It was a no-holds-barred meeting. Graham Lea and Charles Barber argued strenuously that my strategy was wrong and I was no longer the right person to lead. They said the party needed new blood, new ideas. They used all the standard, valid arguments that any leader faces over a period of time. At a lull in the discussion, I stood up and said that I was prepared to leave. "But if you are convinced that I should go, I want you to agree right now about who should succeed me, so that we can spare the party the divisiveness of a leadership contest on the eve of an election." I did not want another Berger-Strachan battle. I wanted the caucus to unite and pick a new leader.

Then Emery Barnes took the floor. Emery was normally very quiet during meetings, so his remarks on this rare occasion had quite an impact. He ran through a list of all that I had been criticized for and then said, "Okay, but who have we got to take his place? After listening to what Dave has listened to, I'm surprised he doesn't walk out and tell us all to go to hell. Now it's up to us to put up or shut up." Barnes nipped the leadership revolt in the bud. A straw poll was taken, and only three caucus members voted to turf me. The whole process was very therapeutic, and it united us for the forthcoming campaign.

Early in 1982, Bill Bennett had launched a restraint program that would be the determining issue in the next election. The province was in a steep recession, and Bennett was selling the notion that holding the line on government spending was the best way to dig ourselves out. This was the time of neoconservative U.S. economist Milton Friedman and right-wing political leaders Margaret Thatcher and Ronald Reagan. Bennett tore a page right out of their book. He started by limiting government wage hikes to 12 per cent in the first year and 10 per cent in the second, then reduced the amount by stages to a zero increase. All government contracts were set to expire after the next election.

The restraint program was part of a long-term strategy to get Bill Bennett reelected. After his close call in 1979, Bennett had hired Patrick Kinsella to spruce up his image. Kinsella, who had been part of the Big Blue Machine that got Tory Premier Bill Davis reelected time and again in Ontario, became Bennett's key handler and strategist, and Norman Spector was appointed as Bennett's principal secretary, his right-hand man. British Columbia was into tough times, and Kinsella and Spector presented Bennett as the tough man required to deal with the situation. It was the same strategy Reagan had used in 1980 to defeat Jimmy Carter: a simplistic notion that we have to punish ourselves to save ourselves. Tommy Douglas once described this philosophy as taking money from the rich and votes from the poor with a promise to protect them from each other. But it caught the fancy of an aging population that had lingering memories of the Depression.

While the Socreds were busily preaching restraint from the driver's seat, they were shovelling money off the back of the truck on the $3-billion Northeast Coal development. It was the largest industrial undertaking in British Columbia's history, and the biggest mining development in the history of the country. It was running way over budget, and it was ill conceived from the start. The project involved two open-pit mines in an area roughly a hundred kilometres southeast of Chetwynd and a hundred kilometres southwest of Dawson Creek. It called for a new town at Tumbler Ridge and a new railway line, and it was being undertaken at taxpayers' expense to fulfill economically questionable contracts with ten Japanese steel mills.

The province could easily have met those contracts through increased production from the vast southeastern coal deposits held in BCRIC. But that option was ruled out by Socred Industry Minister Don Phillips, in whose South Peace River riding the Northeast coalfields were situated. "The Japanese wanted Northeast Coal," Phillips said in the House, to the press and to anybody else who would listen. "That's why we are doing it." I could hardly believe my ears. We had used public money through the creation of BCRIC to fund coal development in the southeast. Now we were spending additional billions in the northeast so the Japanese could whipsaw us on price!

NDP industry critic Stu Leggatt led a brilliant fight in the House against the Northeast Coal project. He assembled meticulous research showing that Japan already had contracts in Australia and elsewhere amounting to 80 per cent more than its estimated coal requirements for the next fifteen years. Japan had finished upgrading and expanding its infrastructure in 1978, and therefore would be winding down on coal consumption at a time when British Columbia would be trying desperately to increase shipments. Leggatt forecast that taxes would have to rise in order to pay for the project, saying, "The Japanese get the coal and we get the hole."

The project was a prime example of the short-term economic thinking of the Bill Bennett administration. Had we been reelected as government, we would have amended the Northeast Coal deal to require that at least 30 per cent of the tonnage be carried in Canadian ships built in Canadian yards and manned by Canadian crews. I would also have insisted on the Japanese building a small steel mill and railcar plant in British Columbia as part of the price, since the Socreds had sold off the plant we had built in Squamish.

In 1983, we anticipated going into a spring session, getting a budget structured around the Socred restraint program and then heading into a general election. But instead of recalling the legislature, Bill Bennett embarked on a madcap course of financing day-to-day operations with special warrants approved in cabinet. It was an unprecedented departure from parliamentary tradition, which requires government to convene the House to pass a budget or interim supply legislation. Ten years earlier, when I was premier, Bill Bennett was hollering, "Not a dime without debate" during a campaign to delay our government from passing a spending bill. Now the government under his leadership appeared to be frozen in indecision, afraid to call either an election or a legislative session.

The warrants had to be signed by Lt. Gov. Henry Bell-Irving to take effect. Bell-Irving had announced after being presented with the warrants that he would take time to assess Bennett's request, leading me to hope that he might refuse to sign them. I sent letters to him, Auditor General Irma Morrison and Comptroller General Brian Marson protesting Bennett's breach of custom and the parliamentary process. Although the Financial Administration Act gave the government authority to use special warrants, it made it clear they were to be used only for extraordinary or unforeseen purposes. And routine government expenditures in a new fiscal year were anything but urgent or unforeseen.

In the end, Bell-Irving authorized almost $700 million' worth of special warrants. When I heard that, I knew immediately that he had received a tacit agreement from Bennett either to recall the legislature or to call an election within thirty days. Sure enough, Bennett called an election for May 5.

During the 1983 campaign we found ourselves in a pattern disturbingly similar to that of 1969, with the media constantly portraying us as the likely winner. There was speculation that Socred cabinet ministers Jim Chabot, Hugh Curtis and Jack Heinrich were in trouble. Curtis was challenged by John Mika, who had joined my staff years earlier and by now was a popular alderman in Curtis's riding of Saanich and the Islands. We were depicted as vulnerable in several ridings, but the consensus in the media was that we were likely to come out on top. The Socreds responded with an advertising blitz that was about as subtle as a knee to the groin. One TV commercial carried the message: "The NDP isn't working today, and if it gets elected, you won't be working tomorrow."

Another ad had a headless body dressed in a dark three-piece suit. A voice-over warned people to be wary of the socialists because they were hiding their true colours. Then the jacket came off, followed by the vest and the shirt. When the pants dropped, there was red underwear! It was an effective device. We soon heard that ad had been Grace McCarthy's idea. Two days after it aired, I was scheduled to speak in Port Alberni. I got up in front of a crowd of four or five hundred people and a pair of red shorts came scooting along a wire somebody had strung across the room like a clothesline. "I didn't come here tonight to discuss the colour of my underwear," I said. "I'm going to leave that to your imagination. But I understand Grace McCarthy is behind this idea. I want to assure the people of British Columbia that Grace McCarthy is one woman who will never see the colour of my underwear." I received an unprecedented amount of mail after that, people sending me red boxer shorts, red jockey shorts, red G-strings. I still have them.

Bill Bennett's handlers, meanwhile, played up the underdog image of the Socreds. Patrick Kinsella, the Socred campaign chairman, was frequently overheard remarking to reporters about the difficulties Bennett was having on the campaign trail. "He's got to start looking like the premier," Kinsella remarked to one journalist at the end of the first week on the hustings. I spent that week campaigning in the B.C. interior with Shirley and some party workers. On our return from Powell River, our plane, a chartered DC-3, veered to the right off the runway and onto the grass at Vancouver International Airport. The flight attendant told us to duck down and grab our ankles. The incident lasted about twenty seconds. I congratulated the pilot, Cliff Sandison, on bringing the plane back on course. "It was a little veer to the right that caused all the problems," I said. "As soon as we went left, everything was okay."

By the last week of the campaign, we were still perceived as the front-runners. The Socred restraint program was the primary issue, and I had a sense the message was sinking in about what it would do not only to civil servants but also to small businesses and contractors who relied on government spending. Then, in an interview with BCTV, I said the NDP would probably scrap the restraint program because it was just scare tactics and had no sound economic foundation. The alarm bells sounded. The clip was played and replayed and the election turned around almost overnight. There was still a mood for Reaganomics, and it propelled the Socreds back into power with 35 seats as against 22 for the New Democrats. Our share of the popular vote held almost steady at 45 per cent.

I sincerely wish I had not been so blunt. It would have been far wiser to fudge and just say I would call for a review of the restraint program and then make a decision. I had been walking a tightrope to keep control of the campaign, and suddenly I was the architect of our defeat. I felt terrible. Shirley was with me all through the campaign, and she reminded me gently that I couldn't have done otherwise. I knew she was right. Bennett's wage controls covering 250,000 workers would inflict extreme suffering on individuals and families while letting the rich get away scot-free. There's no way I could have stood for that. But still, it rankles.

Eleven

The Last Hurrah, Maybe

After the May 1983 election, I was determined to do what I had hoped to do after the loss in 1979—reorganize my affairs and step down as party leader. I had a sense of relief that at last I was in a position to move on to other things in my life. Politically, I was burned out. I announced very early on that I would be resigning.

When the session began that summer, the caucus was moving in many different directions. Many people began to treat me with a deference that I had never before been accorded. Some of those who were testing the political winds on behalf of their own leadership bid even began to praise me. There is no greater method of making way for yourself in future than by praising somebody who has just croaked.

Seemingly without conflict, the caucus was nevertheless seething beneath the surface as various individuals were either beating the bushes for potential leadership candidates or viewing themselves in that coveted role. We were also demoralized by the election results. Although we had captured 45 per cent of the popular vote, our strength in the House had declined by 4 seats. The Socreds now held a solid 35-seat majority.

It was in this milieu of post-election self-pity and political infighting that we entered the legislature on budget day, July 7. We were well aware from rumblings we were picking up and references in the Throne Speech that major initiatives were on the way. But few, if any, of us anticipated fully what was in store.

Although Bill Bennett had campaigned on a platform of fiscal restraint, it came as no surprise to us that the $8.4-billion budget was anything but restrained, with a $1.6-billion deficit projection, higher taxes and a 12.5-per-cent hike in spending. The twenty-six bills introduced with the budget, however, were another matter. The Bennett government's legislative program was unprecedented in its attempt to scrap job security in the public service and eliminate social programs. Restraint was one thing, but this was a scorched earth policy. The Rentalsman and the Human Rights Commission were to be eliminated. The province's 200,000 government workers were to be reduced by 25 per cent over the next year. The Socreds also proposed unilateral changes in collective agreements. The just-introduced Bill 2, for example, gutted the government's contract with the British Columbia Government Employees Union, while Bill 3, the so-called Public Sector Restraint Act, allowed employees to be fired without cause after their contracts expired.

A generation had come along that was now participating far more fully in the affairs of state than at any time in the past. Ordinary people had an emerging voice in British Columbia, and they were determined to drag the political process out of the back rooms and into the open for a new kind of democracy. There was a burgeoning environmental movement. There were expanding political power bases around women's issues. Labour was more focussed and the academic community was doing more soul-searching over where it wanted to go and how it wanted to get there. This new awareness had taken root between 1972 and 1975, when people saw they could be empowered. The Socred legislation was a repressive move against that kind of empowerment, a repressive move with a vengeance.

The NDP caucus pulled itself together around the legislation very quickly and started fighting back. We opposed every bill on the legislative order paper. We dragged out debate through adjournment motions and challenges to the Speaker, which also kept the division bells ringing and the Socreds off balance because they never knew when they might be called into the House for a vote. We used every parliamentary device to buy time for people to understand the folly of the Socred agenda.

The NDP council had decided during their first meeting after the election to wait until the following year to select a new leader. I was deeply disappointed. I had hoped the party would move quickly to pick my successor. But I felt morally bound to stay on until a new leader was selected, so I threw myself back into the fray and found my energy returning around the spate of new issues.

I was very, very angry at what was happening to my beloved province. This was my home, and what I saw happening was alien to anything that had ever been experienced in government in British Columbia. The W.A.C. Bennett administration had had the same philosophy as the current Socred government, but they were never out to punish people with such vindictiveness. It was almost as if this government was saying, "Okay, you voted for me. Now you're really going to get it."

We weren't the only ones fighting the Socred legislation. On July 15, Operation Solidarity was formed under the leadership of B.C. Federation of Labour president Art Kube. Soon this expanded to become the Solidarity Coalition, which brought together trade unionists, religious leaders, academics and a broad array of social and community groups. Kube displayed an incredible ability to rally people against what the government was doing, and he called for a general strike that would force the province to its knees unless the Bennett government withdrew its legislation.

The movement gained momentum very quickly. On July 27, more than 20,000 people jammed the lawns of the legislature in a massive protest. We in the NDP had no direct influence over the coalition. I was not in consultation with any of its leaders, although some members of the caucus probably maintained regular contact. We had our hands full in the House. I went out and spoke to the rally at some length, extolling the virtues of the parliamentary system and telling the crowd that what they were doing was not the way to change legislation. Personally, I view demonstrations as a hundred-yard dash. But you don't change the world by hundred-yard dashes in politics. It's the marathons that count. On August 10, 50,000 people marched on Empire Stadium in Vancouver in a similar protest.

By fall, the Socreds were growing very impatient and testy. They had not passed a single bill, and their party convention was scheduled to take place in Vancouver on October 16. They wanted to be able to parade around the convention floor with some key pieces of legislation in their pockets. To accelerate passage, Bennett extended sitting hours in the House in mid-September. By the beginning of October, we were sitting round the clock.

After the House had been sitting all day and all night for a week, we resumed discussing Bill 2 which, like most of the new bills, was still languishing in first reading. It was October 7, and debate had been abnormally good-humoured under the trying circumstances. It was now well past midnight, and we had been debating the bill for thirteen hours. This was one of the most contentious bills on the order paper, because it curtailed the bargaining rights of government employee unions. The Socreds wanted badly to take it to their convention. Since we had given government employees bargaining rights in the first place, we weren't about to lie down and see them taken away.

Sitting in the Speaker's chair was rookie Socred backbencher John Parks, who had narrowly defeated Norm Levi in Maillardville-Coquitlam. (Levi had run there after his former riding of Vancouver-Burrard was wiped out by the Eckhardt Commission.) As an MLA, Parks was quite a heckler, with a tendency to run roughshod over the rules of the House. He was filling in for Speaker Walter Davidson when NDP MLA Chris D'Arcy of Rossland-Trail tried to move adjournment of the House as a ploy to drag out debate. Parks decided to disallow D'Arcy's motion.

I then rose to challenge Parks's decision, and he ruled me out of order. I got my back up at this. It was my right under the parliamentary system to challenge the Speaker, and I was particularly determined to do so in the case of this blatant abuse of power by Parks. It occurred to me that I had come full circle. I had begun as an Opposition backbencher fighting against the things I felt should be changed within the system. Now I was fighting to have recognized the rights granted to me, and to every MLA and MP, by the system. And I was not going to sit down.

Sitting beside me during this exchange was Frank Howard. Frank was one of the toughest and brightest when it came to the rules. He and Arnold Peters had used the rules as MPs to force the Canadian government to change the divorce laws of this country. Frank had returned to provincial politics in 1979, winning a seat in Skeena. He leaned over and said, "You're right. Just don't sit down."

The clerks, meanwhile, were working with Parks. This went on for several minutes. At one point I requested a five-minute recess. I spoke to the clerks and suggested they try to persuade Parks not to return to the chair. I then offered a compromise: if Parks did not return to the chair, I would not return to the House.

The clerks were George MacMinn and Ian Horne. They were not there to get involved in political disputes or grapple with the political ramifications of a ruling. They had merely been trying to help Parks out of this impasse. They gave no indication as to whether they agreed with me, but they did convey my message. The House could move on and it would be a draw. I had sympathy for Parks, and this was a way out for him. I hoped he would understand that he was wrong. But Parks was entrenched, so I had no choice but to press my challenge.

As soon as the House resumed, Parks ordered me to sit down. I refused. I was out of order and I knew it, but I wasn't going to be badgered by him. I was opposing an abuse of power. When you break the rules, it destroys the system, and there was no way I could sit and let that happen. Then Parks ordered me to leave the chamber for the rest of the day. I proposed another recess, but he was adamant.

I sat down and refused to budge. I said to myself, to hell with it. If the Socreds were going to allow this substitute Speaker, who was ignorant of the rules and therefore really not to blame, to steamroll over the House, then so be it. If they wanted to throw me out, they were going to have to do it bodily.

Parks then ordered me ejected. Sergeant-at-arms staff members Dick Nicol, Bill Roach and Jack Dunn waited ten minutes, then converged on me seated in my chair. At first they tried to lift me in the chair, but it tipped over. I fell to the floor, arms crossed. They dragged me through the revolving doors of the legislature and deposited me on the red carpet that runs the length of the Speaker's corridor. I had become the first member in the 112-year history of the B.C. legislature to be physically tossed from the House.

My dispute with Parks lasted fifty-seven minutes, start to finish. Walter Davidson was standing in the corridor during this time, and he could easily have settled the matter. But Davidson had barred news gathering in the corridor on September 27, and he was apparently far more concerned about forcing the media to obey his rules than about upholding the rules of the House. As my struggle with Parks was escalating, Davidson was busy instructing the media not to film or photograph the outcome.

And what did the media do? They were cowed in the face of authority, to their everlasting discredit. It was not a question of supporting or attacking the government, not a question of supporting or attacking me. It was a question of recording an event, and they chickened out en masse. Not one of them had the guts to pick up a camera and photograph me getting thrown out, not one had the guts to take a picture of Davidson yelling at them.

The arrogance of the Socreds around the issue would become even more evident when, nine days later, at their convention in Vancouver, Parks auctioned off the shoe he had worn when he kicked me out of the House for $1,125. Parks's action forced the press to reexamine the events, and as a consequence they began to understand they had failed at a very important moment. This was evident in some editorials of the day. For the moment, though, I was out on my ear. And because I had been physically ejected, I was barred from the House for the remainder of the session.

The Socreds were determined to pass their entire legislative program during the session. Closure had rarely been used in B.C., but now it was employed no fewer than twenty times to cut off debate so the government could make a triumphal march into their convention. Once the Socreds decided to use closure, and there was no public outcry, they seemed unable to stop. It was the end of debate; the government side of the House appeared to be out of control. Boisterous backbenchers would pop up almost at random, as if they had a free hand to invoke closure, and cabinet ministers would pretend they were powerless to do anything but look on.

Bennett adjourned the session at the end of October in an atmosphere of escalating tension. An estimated 100,000 members of the Solidarity Coalition had staged a march around the Socred convention in downtown Vancouver. Then more than 35,000 government workers walked off the job on November 1 after their contract expired, closing liquor stores and offices and bringing highways maintenance to a halt. They were quickly followed by 28,000 teachers and 4,000 employees of provincial Crown corporations. Next on the list were B.C. Ferry workers and municipal workers. Soon more than 200,000 public sector workers were due to be on picket lines in British Columbia. Private sector unions were next in line.

As events catapulted towards a general strike, Bennett knew from the polls that the public was behind him. He had the upper hand. Although it wasn't generally known, the Solidarity movement was showing internal signs of collapse. The BCGEU, which had started the walkouts, was nearing a settlement. Teachers were returning to work, and the ferry workers had served notice they would go out for only four hours. Art Kube had fallen ill, and many on the coalition executive were wanting to settle.

It was in this atmosphere that IWA leader Jack Munro travelled to Kelowna to meet with Bennett in a last-ditch effort to reach a settlement. The meeting took place in Bennett's home. The only three people in the room were Bennett, Deputy Premier Norman Spector and Munro. I received a call from someone who shall remain nameless here, tipping me as to what was happening. The caller said there were points of an agreement, but he was concerned there would be no record. It was to be a verbal agreement and a handshake.

"Look, I'm not party to any of this," I said. "I'm not even aware of what the negotiations are around. But I can tell you this. From my experience, if you want an agreement with Bill Bennett, you'd better get it in writing." That was the only advice I gave.

Tragically and regrettably, the subsequent outcry from labour gave the impression that Munro made a deal without having all the details in writing and was ultimately double-crossed by Bennett. To this day there is undying anger in some segments of the trade union movement over the Kelowna Accord. Some still believe Munro sold out to Bennett. Many community activists still believe they were sold out by labour. I never learned the full details of the agreement, but I'm convinced Munro's only fault was trusting Bill Bennett.

During the time all of this was going on, I was denied entry to the Speaker's corridor, the legislature and the public galleries. I had access to my office and the caucus room, but by now I was truly a lame duck, removed to the back burner of history. Politics is very much the quick and the dead, and I had joined the dead.

I didn't return to the House until near the end of the spring session in May 1984. Bennett managed to keep me out for almost six months by preventing the House from moving to restore me. Even editorial writers said this was going too far. In banishing me, however, Bennett may have got more than he bargained for. Once I was out of the picture, he no longer had a focus of hostility to sustain him. His popularity plummeted between 1984 and 1986. He could not have won another election, and that's what led to the return of Bill Vander Zalm.

I vividly recall one afternoon shortly after I had been ejected from the legislature. The House was sitting when I returned to my office from a caucus meeting and spoke to my staff. They were all there: Joyce

Thomas, Harvey Beech, John Mika, Wayne Harding and Sharon Vance. (Arne VanCampen, another valued staff member, had gone on to a job in the civil service.) It was midafternoon, and I told them I was going home. Never before had I left during the session unless I had a meeting in Vancouver or some other important reason. I had been conditioned from the time I was first elected to spending many long hours in the House. Shirley would come over from Haney with the kids during the session and I would find it very difficult to pull myself away, even for a short time. I remember once telling her I felt like I was in a mental hospital and she was coming to visit me. We both laughed, but that attitude had prevailed until the day I walked in and told my staff I was going home. Everyone was stunned, including me. Joyce asked if I wanted a ride or if I was going to call Shirley. "No," I said. "I'm going to walk."

Our family home is about four miles from the legislative buildings. It was a gorgeous, warm day. As I walked up Government Street, people seemed a little bit taken aback at seeing me. There were some curious looks. Many people said hello. I was wearing a pair of very uncomfortable business shoes, but I was in another head space. My mind was working away a mile a minute as I walked. I was having this incredible conversation with myself. "The House is sitting," I told myself, "and I'm going home. It doesn't matter. It's over. It's over. Now just relax and enjoy the walk."

I recall this conversation with myself very clearly. I had an overwhelming sense of relief that I was returning to private life. All the problems and joys, all the pleasures and pain, all the things I had wanted to do in public life were finished. As I walked I thought how lucky I was. I had a lifetime partner who had been with me through heaven and hell. Shirley had been absolutely selfless in her support, both critical and positive. But I was aware that I had been in politics for the years that are most productive in a person's career, and now I would have to find another source of income.

It is worth remembering that Shirley and I came out of the last of the era of what one might describe as the traditional family. We had already seen in our generation the breakdown of the extended family. But the expectation when we married was that the husband would work and the wife would stay home. I'm not saying that's necessarily the ideal today, but I had given my best years to public service and now I had little to fall back upon. We had debts to pay. I was probably the first non-millionaire to be premier of British Columbia. I realized, too, that as the first social democratic premier, people would not be falling all over themselves to offer me jobs. I would not be sitting as a director in corporate boardrooms. There would be no rewards in recognition of my superior talents at providing the legislation that made sure the rich got richer.

Shirley was there when I got home. She made me a cup of tea and a sandwich, and we just sat and talked. We had sat and talked like this many times in the past, but now there was a whole new dimension to our discussion. Our life had been a roller coaster. Neither of us had been able to predict the course of events. It had been a grand partnership, filled with memorable experiences, good and bad, but now I had to find a new way to make a living. The party had set a date in May for the leadership convention, and it was approaching very quickly. That walk was definitely a psychological turning point for me. My mind was looking in new directions.

Not long after that, Joyce Thomas came rushing into my office and said that someone in Prime Minister Trudeau's office was on the phone. It was Tom Axworthy, brother of Liberal cabinet minister Lloyd Axworthy and one of Trudeau's key aides. I had never met Axworthy and I had no idea what the call was about. We chatted awhile, then Axworthy said, "The prime minister is considering a number of appointments, and I have been asked to call to see whether you would be interested in an appointment to the Labour Relations Board of Canada."

I was startled. Trudeau and I were political opponents. We had had some pretty harsh exchanges in the past. There was no need for him to offer me anything, and I was genuinely touched by this act of generosity. Before really giving it any thought, however, I told Axworthy I wasn't interested. I really should have talked with Shirley before making that decision. The LRB was a ten-year appointment and I had no other prospects. To this day, I don't know why I acted so hastily, but that was the end of the conversation. The door had opened, and the door had closed.

About a month later, I got another call from Axworthy. He asked if I would consider an appointment as ambassador for disarmament. Trudeau was winding down during his last year in office and he was on that great peace-mission kick, which was well received by the public, and to which I believe he was sincerely committed. I told Axworthy I would discuss it with my wife and call him back.

I rang off in a state of excited agitation. I wanted the job. The Cold War was still pretty hot in those days, and I saw the position as a platform for sinking my teeth into an issue that had concerned me for some time—the proliferation of nuclear weapons. Shirley and I had a long talk, during which she asked what the disadvantages were to the job. "We would have to swallow the cruise missile tests," I answered. Canada had recently renewed its agreement with the U.S. allowing cruise missile testing in northern Alberta, despite nationwide protests. The NDP was very much opposed to the testing, and I had spoken out against it frequently. "You wouldn't want to do that, would you?" she said.

Despite Shirley's reservations, I told Axworthy I was interested, and that launched a lengthy series of discussions about how much I was prepared to compromise. The talks were proceeding on a positive track, but tension was building between Shirley and me. Her position was that there was no room for compromise around the cruise missile. Axworthy phoned again, pushing me for a decision. Shit or get off the pot, in other words. I told him that before making a decision I wanted a meeting with Defence Minister Allan MacEachen.

Before leaving for Ottawa, I phoned Remi de Roo, the Roman Catholic bishop of Victoria. Bishop de Roo was known for being outspoken about his progressive views. I told him Shirley and I were having a moral dilemma and invited him to dinner so we could discuss it. "Why are you picking me?" he asked. I answered that all my Jesuit friends were dead. "This is the first time I have ever been asked to substitute for a Jesuit," he said. "I'm not sure if that's a compliment or not, but I would be happy to meet with you."

He came for dinner and we had a long discussion after the meal. Bishop de Roo quickly realized he was dealing with a domestic dispute. He said I had two options. I could shut up about the cruise until I had the job, and then use my position to promote world peace until they caught up with me and fired me for my opinions. Or I could simply turn down the job because of my opposition to cruise missile testing. "You are not lying in either instance," de Roo said. "If there is a clash over the cruise, they will fire you. My own opinion is we have lost the fight on the cruise anyway." He assured us he felt both alternatives were morally acceptable.

This was a very intense time for Shirley and me. Over the years, Shirley had been a strong advocate for peace. She had been active during the Haney days in a group called the Voice of Women, which was opposed to nuclear weapons. After Remi left, Shirley said, "Nothing doing. You've got to state from the start where you stand on the cruise missile." But I still wanted to take the job. To settle the difference, we put it to a vote. The vote was one to one, and I lost.

Nonetheless, I flew to Ottawa in the spring of 1984. I was impeccably dressed for my meeting with MacEachen. I had on a brand-new suit and tie and my shoes were so shiny you could see your reflection in them. I was a walking photo opportunity. I was picked up by car and driven to the appointment at the defence building. Tom Axworthy was with me. The interview began with a long discussion of what the job entailed. I assured the minister of my interest but told him I had a problem. "Well," MacEachen replied, "what kind of wording could we use to get around your opposition to the cruise missile?"

I decided to level with him. I told MacEachen I understood that they wanted me, a prominent NDPer, to lend political credence to their peace program. The Liberals were in trouble politically. The Conservatives, under their newly installed leader Brian Mulroney, were way ahead in the polls. I was prepared to be used for political purposes, but not to endorse cruise missile testing. "Have you spoken against this?" he asked. I assured him that I had, and he said, "Well, how many times?"

The meeting deteriorated from that point. I don't quantify my opposition to an issue on the basis of how many times I have spoken against it, or my support for an issue by the number of times I have spoken for it. "You can have my body," I said, "because I think I can do something with this job that means a great deal to me. But you can't have my soul." MacEachen gave me a look that seemed to suggest he wasn't sure how to take my comment. Axworthy, meanwhile, said nothing.

The meeting came to an amicable end. It was nearly five o'clock, and Axworthy suggested we go for a drink. "I guess I've blown it," I said. "I guess so," Axworthy agreed. "I don't think they are going to carry it any further." I was crestfallen. I had become attached to the image of myself as a roving ambassador and in some small way moving the world towards a semblance of sanity. Now it was over. The job eventually went to Douglas Roche, the former Tory MP from Alberta. I went home on the plane the next morning. Shirley was happy but still a little bit annoyed that I had come so close to accepting the position.

The NDP leadership struggle, meanwhile, was really heating up in

B.C. There was strong caucus support for Bill King. He had all the leadership attributes. Bill has a deep understanding of the human psyche; he is fair-minded, patient and cautious, and he has a passionate commitment to social justice. Everybody who has worked with him has immediately gravitated towards him. But Bill was reluctant to announce. He had lost his seat in Revelstoke-Slocan, and so he was out of the House and out of the action. Other candidates began to come forward. There was Bob Skelly, a brilliant researcher with a thoughtful, academic approach to issues; Graham Lea, who really had nothing beyond a quick wit to propel him to leadership; and Dave Stupich. Dave was a wonderful cabinet minister, but I don't think he would have run if King had declared his candidacy earlier.

Since King was unavailable, a group in caucus decided to pursue David Vickers. Vickers, who had been deputy attorney general when we were in government and now sits as a judge on the B.C. Supreme Court, was bright, quick, thoughtful and sensitive, but he had absolutely no political experience. Dennis Cocke, Colin Gabelmann and Rosemary Brown were Vickers's chief backers.

King finally threw his hat into the ring some six months into the campaign. By then, many people who had been anxious to support him had already made a commitment to Vickers or Skelly.

I did not officially back any of the candidates. I still had scars from my own experience with Bob Strachan, and I had long ago decided I would never intervene as a past leader. I don't think an endorsation from me would have altered the outcome; Strachan's certainly didn't do Bob Williams any good in 1968. It can even be the kiss of death. You have both real and imaginary power in the party as leader. But the minute you step down, you're dead.

During the convention, I deliberately sat in the bleachers with Shirley and Harvey Beech. I was there throughout the process, but it was the first time in twenty-five years I had not taken part down on the floor.

I knew the ultimate choice was going to leave divisions within the party similar to those that followed Tom Berger's victory in 1968. How to heal those wounds would be a question for the new leader to solve. The King and Vickers forces were at each others' throats. There was a feeling of betrayal on both sides. Because of this division, Skelly was able to come up the middle and win the convention, bolstered by the skilled campaign leadership of Gerry Scott. I voted for King, but he had made the same mistake I was to make years later in my bid for the federal NDP leadership: he was too slow in entering the race.

The convention was my last act as leader. Our conventions are mostly business, but Shirley and I were given a wonderful sendoff by the party. It was very touching and emotional. I walked out of the convention hall after it was over with a strong sense of anticipation. A new life, and some exciting new opportunities, beckoned.

Twelve

Flights of Fancy

Sometime in my final year as NDP leader, I had received a call from Ted Smith, general manager of CKNW Radio in Vancouver. He and I had met in Victoria and held discussions about my taking a position with the network as a talk-show host. After the ambassador for disarmament offer from Trudeau fell through, I got back to Ted and we made arrangements to meet again.

Ted Smith is undoubtedly one of the nicest people I have met in the media. As soon as we sat down in his office to discuss my joining CKNW, he produced a bottle of Bells scotch, put it on the table and asked if I wanted a drink. I was startled.

I'm not a teetotaller. I enjoy a beer or a glass of wine, even the occasional cocktail. But Smith's gesture put me in mind of my early days in the legislature. There was a great deal of drinking. I'm no prude, but I was shocked at what being absent from home and surrounded by booze did to people, both politicians and the press.

All this came back to me when Ted Smith placed that bottle on the table. Was I walking into a situation at CKNW fraught with the same dangers that had unsettled me years before? Were problems there so bad people had to be tested for their booze resistance before they were hired? I felt very, very uncomfortable, despite my genuine liking for Smith.

Around that time, I also talked with Vancouver businessman Jimmy Pattison. I had always found Pattison very above board in his dealings. Whatever he said, he kept his word. There was no offer or promise of a job, but Pattison asked if I was interested in coming to CJOR, the radio station he owned. At the time, they were in negotiations with Rafe Mair, who had been hosting a talk show for them. I was interested, so Pattison suggested I call station manager Harvey Gold. Gold told me they were happy with Mair and planned to continue with him.

About a week later I had an interview with Jack Webster at BCTV. It was a wrap-up interview about my stepping down as NDP leader. Webster was at his affable best; he's probably the most superb television interviewer I've ever encountered. As I was leaving the BCTV studio in Burnaby, I received a phone call from Harvey Gold, saying they had reached a point of breakdown in negotiations with Rafe Mair. I met with Gold and we came to a tentative agreement.

My lawyer, John Laxton, who is now chairman of B.C. Hydro, negotiated my contract, and I signed with CJOR in June of 1984. Then I signed a separate contract to do a weekly television interview for CKVU. I was there for one year, and after that I free-lanced occasionally on CTV. I also did a stint on Peter Gzowski's *Morningside* program after Stephen Lewis was appointed U.N. ambassador. I appeared weekly for about a year on the political panel with Eric Kierans and Dalton Camp.

I set up a company for my media endeavours, Barrett Communications Ltd. During the first year alone, I grossed more than three times what I had made annually as premier. I mention this because during all the years I was a sitting member of the House and then premier, I was often the subject of attacks in the media over how much politicians get paid. The presumption exists that somehow you're going to make a fortune in politics. One of the most dangerous things happening in today's world is the attacking of politicians' pay, perks and pensions. To do their jobs properly, politicians—and judges as well—must protect their families and sustain themselves independently, without kickbacks or payola or the influence that provides them cushy jobs later. Carping about pensions only ensures that you'll get politicians who help the rich get richer.

By the time I signed the contract with CJOR, our kids were all doing their own thing. Jane was studying abroad at the University of Western Australia, Joe was enrolled at the University of Victoria and studying languages in Europe. Dan had walked out of university in frustration and was happily working in a shipyard in Esquimalt.

Shirley and I moved to Vancouver and rented an apartment not far from Stanley Park. One day we were walking along the seawall, and I suddenly realized I was no longer responsible for the party, for the caucus, for all those things I had loved doing. The agreement was over, honourably ended by both parties. And I hadn't really understood until that moment how much tension and pressure it had caused and how restricting it had been. I just burst out spontaneously, "I'm free." Shirley and I had a good laugh about that.

A few weeks later, while we were in San Diego visiting my brother and his wife, Fulvia, and their family, I read in the newspaper that the government of Canada had called an election. I was not scheduled to begin the CJOR program until September, but after talking things over with Shirley, I called Harvey Gold and suggested I start work right away. Gold agreed, and Shirley and I rushed back to Vancouver. My producer was a very bright young woman named Anne Garber.

The first guest I had on my program was Pierre Berton. We did what was essentially a Canadian history wrap leading into the election. I also interviewed John Turner, who had succeeded Trudeau as prime minister and was fighting his first election as Liberal leader. Patronage was the major issue, and Turner and Brian Mulroney had had a sharp exchange on television where Mulroney had attacked Turner for endorsing a huge list of patronage appointments left by Trudeau. Lord only knows the extent of the hypocrisy of Mulroney speaking out against patronage, but he put Turner on the defensive for the rest of the campaign.

Covering that election smoothed my transition from politician to talk-show host. I did an open-air commentary on election night. As a talk-show host, I wanted to inform and to entertain. I made it very clear that I was biased, but so is everyone else who sits in front of a microphone. I wanted people to understand there was more to life than right-wing rhetoric or the establishment point of view. Jimmy Pattison and I get along very well, but it should come as no surprise that we have different political points of view. Yet I was never interfered with at CJOR. I picked the guests I wanted. We did the standard book reviews and, on occasion, the nonsense fillers that seem to entice listeners, such as interviewing astrologers or futurists.

On some issues there was no possibility of rational debate. On the question of abortion, for example, which came up frequently, my bias was such that I just couldn't abide the violent rhetoric of some of the antichoice people. I believe a woman has the right to make decisions about her own body. At CKVU I did a show on the Holocaust featuring a group of survivors. I didn't have a denier because I don't think I could have handled that, somebody denying the Holocaust.

I had an extremely interesting exchange with James Irwin, the American astronaut. Irwin was a traditional military man, patriotic and totally committed to the United States. When I asked his thoughts on nuclear weapons, however, I was thunderstruck by his reply. In fact, I frequently replayed it on the air. He described to me in poetic language how he had looked back on Earth from space and realized that this planet was unique in the universe, and the political boundaries humans had imposed on it were petty and insignificant. He waxed philosophically about the global village of Marshall McLuhan. He then said he had come to realize there should be no further testing or construction of nuclear weapons. I asked if he would speak to President Reagan about this. He said he had already done so, without success, but would pursue it again. That interview was a good lesson for me. I had judged Irwin as just another jingoistic U.S. military leader. Instead, he was a man of tremendous insight and sensitivity.

I had a good friend from the NDP named Paul Murphy, an irrepressible Irishman and quite a character. One day I was having coffee with Murphy and we cooked up a scheme to have him come on my show. He would pose as a noted UFO authority named Dr. Ersatz. The day of the show I began by giving him a great buildup. Before I could finish, Murphy broke in with a fake Viennese accent and launched into a four-minute monologue about his scientific experiences and his knowledge of UFOs, and how he had seen them coming down from the sky. I nearly wet my pants. I thought it couldn't possibly go anywhere, that the whole thing was so phony people would just turn off their radios. Then, lo and behold, the board lit up. We were flooded with calls.

The next two hours convinced me that P. T. Barnum was absolutely right about a sucker being born every minute. Murphy fielded calls from people who said they had actually been on UFOs. One caller claimed to have been captured by aliens and taken aboard a spacecraft. A number of people believed strongly that there was an international conspiracy by governments to keep this kind of information from the public. All of which Murphy agreed to.

Finally we got a call from a woman who said, in an earnest voice, "Dave, Dave, this guy is conning you. Ersatz means artificial and phony. He's a phony, Dave." Then she hung up. "What do you say about that, Doctor?" I asked. "Vell," Murphy replied, "she may be right."

We took a commercial break at that point, but when we came back on the air, the calls were coming in from people who insisted that Dr. Ersatz was real. The program didn't exactly rank with Orson Welles's *The War of the Worlds*, but it revealed to me that there are a lot of gullible people out there.

In 1986 there was the Social Credit leadership campaign, with Bill Vander Zalm, Brian Smith, Grace McCarthy and some others vying to replace the departing Bill Bennett. These were the days of Zalm-mania. Superficiality reigned at the Socred convention. Serious contenders like Brian Smith were swept aside because the media became fascinated with itself in its coverage of Vander Zalm. I tried to cut through the hype on my show. Don't get me wrong. Vander Zalm and I got on very well. He can be extremely charming. He's the only man I know who has sixty-four teeth on the top row, every one of them sparkling.

One of the most chilling and satisfying programs I did was on the Chernobyl nuclear disaster in the former Soviet Union. When the story came through on the wire, I got my producer to get on the phone and we spoke to a reporter at a newspaper in Helsinki, Finland. The reporter came right on air with his story, providing in-depth accounts of the incident before the major agencies could back up their news flashes.

During my third year at the station, Harvey Gold decided to take a different direction. They brought in Dave Abbott to work with me. Abbott was also a talk-show host and a very amiable fellow. He was to operate out in the community while I was in the station, and we would link up on the air. Abbott didn't chase fire trucks or ambulances, but if there was a big public event or a demonstration, he would be at the scene. Occasionally we would follow up these snippets by interviewing a key figure in the story, or Abbott would come into the station to provide greater depth. I was on from 9:00 A.M. till noon every day, and things can get boring if you don't watch out. Abbott was very pleasant to work with, but some of the directions he and Gold wanted to go in were not at all what I had in mind.

Our differences really became apparent when a story broke about a criminal case involving homosexual activities. According to unnamed sources in the story, Vancouver police were in possession of a book alleged to contain the names of prominent British Columbians. The book was supposedly written by a so-called madam who supplied young male prostitutes to clients with deep pockets. The book was also said to contain details about the sexual predilections of the clients. Police were not confirming the stories.

Abbott had been working on this story with a reporter from the Vancouver *Sun*, and they wanted to take it on the air. I hadn't seen any evidence to back up the story. It was all innuendo. So I refused to take part. I didn't want to subject myself or the station to libel or slander charges. And I told Gold I was not interested in programming that pandered to public voyeurism.

In January of 1987, CJOR and I reached an amiable parting. I was midway through my third one-year contract with the station. I had a long discussion with Harvey Gold and got a sense, although it was never stated, that station management wanted to hire someone else. Our ratings had not been bad, but it was obvious to me that Gold had lost confidence in my programming. They wanted the big bang and I hadn't delivered it. So I made it very easy for them. "Maybe we should just call it quits," I suggested. "Let's shake hands and I'll go on to other things." We shook hands all round. It had been a rewarding experience in a lot of ways, especially from a financial perspective. I walked away debt-free.

During my short time with the media I came to understand the kind of pressure working journalists must face. I was never subjected to such pressure; I was in a unique situation. But I now know how it must be for a minion dealing with an editor or a producer who decides, for whatever reason, to pursue a particular story. You simply cannot expect a journalist with a mortgage to pay and family to support to tell his or her boss to stuff it. It's a driven agenda, and to get along you have to go along.

During my time at CJOR I had an unusual encounter with Judy LaMarsh. Judy had been a Liberal MP during the Trudeau years, and we had met a few times while I was in provincial politics. It quickly became evident to me that she was a thoughtful, progressive Liberal in the same cast as Monique Bégin, who had been a cabinet minister under Trudeau during the 1970s. Judy talked openly about her time in politics and of her frustrations with Trudeau. She was also interested in the initiatives we'd taken with the Agricultural Land Reserve and ICBC.

In the fall of 1985, I had occasion to go to Toronto. LaMarsh had said if ever I was there to give her a call, so I did, and we arranged to meet for lunch. I don't recall the restaurant except that it was at the top of a series of escalators—a wide-open, trendy kind of place. We chatted awhile and she asked me to dance. I'm a terrible dancer. I have always been a shrinking violet on the dance floor. But Judy was earnest, so I got up and danced with her. She had lost a tremendous amount of weight and I complimented her on how she looked. Within a matter of moments, she began to cry very softly. "Dave," she said. "I have cancer and I'm dying."

I can't recall anything of consequence that we talked about after that. I do recall my overwhelming struggle to find an appropriate response. I was struck by how quickly she pulled herself together and smiled and went on chatting through lunch. Then she said good-bye and I hugged her and that was the end of it. I never saw her again.

Shirley and I had experienced our first personal tragedies during these years. My father died within a month of my going on the air. There are deaths that are described as blessings, and you could say that in my father's case. But it doesn't relieve the pain and angst of losing a parent. I recall one of the last times I saw my father, who was in the Louis Brier Home in Vancouver. It was during the 1983 election campaign, and Shirley and I, along with our eldest son, Dan, had left the campaign trail briefly to visit my dad. He had what I believe was Alzheimer's disease, and he had hardly spoken a word for six months. For some reason, to this day I do not know why, I leaned over to him and said, "Hey, Pop." The only answer you would get was, "Yeah." "Pop, it's Dave." "Yeah." "Pop, we've just come back from the Okanagan, Shirley, Dan and I, and we met a guy up there who bought a fish from you and he's really angry and he wants his money back."

I don't know why I said it. There was silence for a moment, then I heard this voice coming out of my father's body: "Dave, tell him to send the fish back."

Shirley's stepfather died while I was at CJOR as well, and that was also very painful. He was a wonderful, decent, honest man with a great sense of humour. Then my mother had a stroke. She was quite ill and we had to arrange for nursing home care, selling the house in Vancouver East. Ultimately, she followed my father into the Louis Brier Home. She died in 1989. Our only surviving parent is Hilda Hackman, who is still as alert as ever.

After I left CJOR, Shirley and I packed our things and returned to our home in Esquimalt. While we were pondering our next move, I got a call one day out of the blue from Tom Axworthy. It was April of 1987. After the Liberals were defeated in 1984, Tom had been appointed to the

Mackenzie King Chair of Canadian Studies at Harvard University. He asked if I would come to Harvard to address a seminar on Canada-U.S. relations.

I spoke at Harvard, talking about my experiences with the Jesuits and giving my views on U.S. and Canadian politics. Free trade talks were underway, and I predicted that Canada would suffer recession and soaring unemployment if the deal with the U.S. was ever signed. Afterwards, Tom asked me to stay an extra day to meet some people. He took me to the Institute of Politics at the John F. Kennedy School of Government and introduced me to acting director Terry Donovan, her staff and some students. Over lunch, Axworthy asked if I would like to teach at the Institute. "You've got to be kidding," I said. "I would love it."

Axworthy then told me about Harvard's Fellows program, which is designed for people who have been in public life. It is intended primarily for Americans, but Canadians with the right credentials are also considered. Fellows give a seminar one day a week on the subject of their choice, and spend the rest of their time in the four-month program conducting research on a topic of their choice. They have full use of the library and other facilities of the university, as do their spouses. "If you are interested," he said, "they might be interested in you." I replied, "Where do I sign?"

I was just bubbling on the way back on the plane. When I got home Shirley and I sat down, opened a bottle of wine and talked about this exciting new possibility. Soon after, I wrote a formal application as I was required to do. Then we waited, and we waited, and we waited. Finally, during the first week of August, Terry Donovan called to say that the six Fellows had been appointed and I was one of them. Well, you could have scraped me off the ceiling. Terry asked me to send a complete outline for the seminar right away. I decided to focus on socialized medicine.

Cambridge was a new world for Shirley and me. Suddenly we found ourselves on this incredible campus so rich in history and tradition, and with so many wonderful facilities. Shirley was interested in the Asiatic Studies department, where she audited courses on Chinese and Japanese literature and enjoyed studying calligraphy and Tai Chi. There were drama productions, music recitals and lectures. It was a cultural horn of plenty. I was provided with an office in the institute, where I decided to do some work on a guaranteed annual income. I set up my seminar on socialized medicine, in which I planned to give a political critique of how and why it had happened in Canada and why it wasn't likely to happen in the United States. Shirley and I both studied French, and I was awful.

Harvard Square, with its lively and animated mix of small shops, art galleries, restaurants, movie houses, delis and bookstores, was pretty close to what I would imagine Heaven would be. It was also a cross section of the United States' best and worst. The contrast was incredible. Unfettered capitalism had created the university and all the wealth it represented, as well as the beggars who existed in its shadow. There were sidewalk musicians, people reading poetry, people playing chess, young lovers, older people relaxing, people reading newspapers and engaged in intense conversations. It was a side of America that probably existed in town squares all over the United States a hundred years ago or in coffee houses and pubs in Britain, where conversation was still a part of life. Harvard Square was like a marketplace of ideas and human contact.

The director of the Institute of Politics was Dick Thornberg, who had been governor of Pennsylvania and later went on to become attorney general in the Bush administration. Among the other Fellows were Maxine Isaacs, who had been a press secretary for Walter Mondale when he ran on the Democratic ticket against Reagan, Jack Carlson and Thelma Duggin, both formerly with the Reagan administration, and Alan Karcher, a former Speaker of the House in New Jersey and the lawyer who argued for the defence in the Baby M case, in which a surrogate mother tried to obtain custody of her child.

The Fellows met as a group every Thursday, when we would have lunch with a guest speaker. One of the guests was John Kenneth Galbraith, who was a professor emeritus at Harvard. I invited Harry Fleischman to my seminar to speak on socialized medicine. Fleischman had been executive assistant to Norman Thomas, the socialist leader who was the American Tommy Douglas. Canadian journalist Marjorie Nichols gave a talk on Canadian media coverage of the socialized medicine debate, and Marc Eliesen spoke about socialized medicine from the administrative point of view.

My conclusion as to why Canada achieved socialized medicine and the Americans didn't is that we have such different political structures. Political parties are more accountable under our parliamentary system than are American parties. Individuals can go in any direction they choose in the U.S., and this is fertile ground for lobbyists. Franklin Delano Roosevelt tried to socialize medicine in 1933 under the original Social Security Act, but lobbying killed it. Lobbying is less powerful in Canada, but it is still a force to be reckoned with. Our health care system is under pressure today because the corporations want to peddle health care for profit just like they do in the U.S., and we Canadians have lost our collective memory about the struggle to achieve it.

The 1988 presidential election was only a year away when we were at Harvard, and the university sponsored a series of weekly panels for the Republican and Democratic hopefuls to strut their stuff. Shirley and I attended these forums, where we met Jesse Jackson, a brilliant speaker, and Pat Robertson, a very scary character with unblinking, deep blue eyes and a phony smile that evokes everything you've ever heard about the religious right. Michael Dukakis, who eventually won the Democratic nomination, was really on a high around that time. Among Dukakis's challengers was Paul Simon, who put me in mind of Lester Pearson whenever I saw his bow tie bobbing up and down.

Shortly after we arrived at Harvard, Harvey Oberfeld of BCTV came down to do a feature about me and the Fellows program. Afterwards, he asked me a number of questions about free trade. I didn't really believe the Mulroney administration would go through with the deal. I told Oberfeld that I was deeply opposed to it from both an economic and a social perspective. His reply was, "Well, they are going to do it." The next day I phoned Ed Broadbent, and he confirmed what Oberfeld had said.

A few weeks later I was scheduled to address a commencement class of graduating social workers at Carleton University, and while I was in Ottawa I arranged to meet Broadbent. He had asked me to run federally when I stepped down as provincial party leader, but I was not interested at the time. Now, because of my opposition to free trade, I was ready to step back into the breach. Shirley and I had discussed it, and I had her full support. I couldn't believe that any government would deliberately cause rising unemployment and deteriorating social conditions in Canada, and I wanted to do something about it. I told Broadbent that I had decided to reenter politics and run in the federal election expected the following year.

While I was in Ottawa I met John Thompson, who was a professor in the geography department at McGill University. Geographers seem to take everything and everybody under their umbrella, from engineers and economists to social workers and politicians, and Thompson asked if I would be interested in coming to McGill as a guest lecturer the following January. I immediately agreed to spend the spring semester there.

My seminar in Cambridge ended in December. I look back on our four months there as an intellectual and romantic honeymoon. Shirley and I returned home for Christmas, and then it was on to Montreal. We rented a furnished apartment on the eighteenth floor of a high-rise off Sherbrooke Street on the fringe of the Lincoln Village area. The Forum, home of the Montreal Canadiens, was a stone's throw away.

I gave a series of eleven lectures on public policy at McGill. I was defined as a visiting scholar, and my lectures concentrated on British Columbia. Most of my talks were open to anybody from the university. Between lectures I met with smaller groups of economics students, social work students and others.

It was while I was speaking to a second-year class in McGill's school of social work that I met Barbara Nichols, who was a professor in the department. I spoke about implementing social policy through political action, and Barbara and I had a nice chat afterwards. About a week later, Shirley and I ran into Barbara in the Atwater metro station, and Barbara said, "I think my daughter is going out with your son." This was news to Shirley and me. Barbara went on to tell us how her daughter, Mary, and Dan had met in a yoga class in Victoria and had been seeing quite a lot of each other. We were delighted. Dan and Mary married soon after and gave us two lovely grandchildren, Andrew and Hannah. Andrew was born on Remembrance Day in the midst of the 1988 election.

One of the more interesting people Shirley and I met at McGill was liberation theology professor Gregory Baum, who had left the Catholic Church some years earlier and married a former nun. We attended a conference on the English experience in Quebec since 1960, where Baum pointed out how little immigration there had been to Quebec compared with the rest of Canada, which has been changing almost constantly with the influx of new arrivals. Baum is a very witty speaker, clear and concise. He gave us valuable insights and our first real understanding of Quebec angst.

We also met a professor named Andrée Lévesque, a brilliant woman who had done a study of the CCF and its failure to win votes in Quebec. We had a number of discussions with her about the social, cultural and political history of the province. The NDP, like the CCF before it, still has much work to do to gain political ground in Quebec.

During this time I was asked to sit on a panel about social democracy in Canada sponsored by the students. There were three participants: myself, former federal Liberal cabinet minister Eric Kierans and Jacques Parizeau, who by then had succeeded René Lévesque and Pierre Marc Johnson as leader of the Parti Québécois. I was the only panelist who couldn't speak French, and I felt awkward about that. I do feel awkward that I don't know languages other than English. If I were to do it all over again, I would start studying Chinese, Japanese, French and everything else I could cram into my head, but that's a lament of the past.

Kierans, a brilliant man and a lovely human being, opened the proceedings by giving his presentation. I was next, followed by Parizeau. I had a student translator sitting behind me. The student would whisper in my ear what Parizeau was saying, except for the occasions when Parizeau would switch into his classical English. As I listened to Parizeau speak, I could not, for the life of me, figure out why he had been asked to address a panel on social democracy. I had met with René Lévesque in 1973, in an attempt to forge an alliance between the PQ and the NDP, and been very impressed with his genuine passion for social justice. Lévesque firmly believed that economic structures were meant to serve people rather than the other way around. But there was no such commitment forthcoming from Parizeau. He sounded like a stuffed shirt right out of the British Conservative Party. I jumped in the moment he made his pitch for Quebec nationalism. I recall my words exactly. I said, "Mr. Parizeau, if you have your way and achieve separation according to your agenda, it will only be a matter of time before you are totally absorbed, culturally and economically, into the United States. The last vestige of francophone culture after separation and absorption by the United States will be you, Mr. Parizeau, attempting to get the first franchise to sell Creole food in Montreal."

There were about 350 students in the room, and there was a real sucking of wind when I hit Parizeau with that. Parizeau said nothing. Perhaps he viewed it as an inappropriately political comment for an intellectual gathering. He was educated at the London School of Economics, and he prides himself on being an intellectual. There is an expectation in France that politicians will have an academic background, and this has carried over to some extent in Quebec. Réne Lévesque steered Quebec away from that mind set. He was a true populist and did not share the fascination for France so typical of some Quebec politicians. Parizeau represents a return to the traditional thinking.

Montreal was still more or less in the grip of winter when we left for home the third week in April. My year in academia had restored me for the struggles that lay ahead. I was deeply committed to joining the fight against free trade in the national arena.

Thirteen

Once More with Phoenix

During its first term in office, the Mulroney government announced a redistribution of seats in the House of Commons that carved the southern Vancouver Island riding of Cowichan-Malahat-The Islands into two new constituencies—Esquimalt-Juan de Fuca and Nanaimo-Cowichan. Jim Manly, the sitting NDP member of Cowichan-Malahat-The Islands, decided to retire, and that left the nomination in my home riding of Esquimalt-Juan de Fuca up for grabs. I informed the constituency that I would seek the nomination.

Esquimalt-Juan de Fuca includes the rapidly growing suburban municipalities of View Royal, Colwood, Langford and Sooke. Intermingled are the rural community of Metchosin to the west and similarly disposed areas such as Shawnigan Lake, Cobble Hill and Mill Bay along the northern tier. At the western end of the riding is Port Renfrew, a logging and fishing community. This part of Vancouver Island had long been an NDP stronghold, both provincially and federally, at the time I decided to run.

I was unchallenged for the nomination. The party executive decided to postpone the official announcement until after the election was called. It was agreed that Ed Broadbent would come out to give a kick-off speech for my campaign. Everyone was very upbeat about his impending visit. I had been received with warm enthusiasm in the riding, and I had the feeling I was being welcomed home.

I was anxious to get back into the fight and show people the folly of the free trade deal, which the United States had been promoting for decades and which had been rejected by a succession of Canadian governments, both Liberal and Conservative. Prime Ministers Diefenbaker, Trudeau and Clark had all defended Canada's interests. Then Brian Mulroney came along and capitulated. There was nothing in the deal that was "free" in the trading. It was structured by and for the corporate elite. Canada was to supply the resources, and ultimately Mexico was to supply the cheap labour to run the economic engine of corporate North America.

While I was at Harvard I had had a memorable conversation about the trade deal with Robert Reich, who was on the faculty at the John F. Kennedy School of Government's Institute of Politics at the time and is now secretary of labour in the Clinton administration. After hearing my litany of complaints about U.S. policy in general and the trade agreement in particular, he said, "What the hell are you worried about? Think about our problems. In the ten years it will take us to absorb your economy into our economy, we will take our eye off the ball in addressing our own economic problems here in the United States." What he told me, in effect, was this: "If you are foolish enough to hand over your country to us, we'll take it."

The election was called for November 21. There was an overflow crowd of more than five hundred people at my nomination meeting, held October 4 at the Esquimalt Recreation Centre. In addition to Broadbent, Jim Manly, Mike Harcourt and local MLA Moe Sihota were on hand. The atmosphere was white-hot. I introduced Broadbent, who got up and gave a very solid speech. It was well received and well presented. But it only briefly mentioned the Free Trade Agreement.

I was in a state of shock. In introducing Broadbent, I had set the stage for him by saying that this election was about Canada's loss of innocence. For the first time in history, I said, we had a government that was willing to cave in to the economic agenda of the United States. I outlined how Liberal dalliances with the Americans had turned Canada into a branch plant economy. In exchange for a constant supply of oil, gas, lumber and minerals at low prices, American corporations had reinvested in Canada to manufacture the same products they were selling in the United States. These were mere drippings off the table, but I predicted even the scraps would disappear under free trade. Until now, there had been the presumption that our branch plant economy would go on forever.

But Broadbent skirted the issue. Shirley and I returned home after the meeting and sat down at our kitchen table, puzzled about this. Then it dawned on me. Strategically, the only major support area in Canada for the trade deal was in Quebec. Much to their peril, the nationalists in Quebec have always entertained the notion that, should they separate, they would have a unique relationship with the United States. In my opinion, Broadbent had reached the conclusion that by muting the passion and logic of the NDP's opposition to free trade we could pick up votes in Quebec. I was still influenced by the old CCF-NDP school of politics that said damn the torpedoes, straight ahead is our issue and we don't care what the reaction is. Our campaign in B.C. continued to be totally driven by our opposition to free trade.

I was running against seven other candidates in Esquimalt-Juan de Fuca. I was clearly the front runner, and I knew it. I found I was much changed after my five-year absence from the hustings. My brief forays into the media and academia had been a wonderful, regenerative pause. I had, if not mellowed, at least matured in a way. I was far more measured in my responses to attack. The hair-trigger temper that had occasionally flared in debate was now muted. I no longer crunched an opponent unnecessarily and my combativeness was toned down. I enjoyed both the campaign and my opponents.

When the results were tallied on election night, I had won the seat with more than 50 per cent of the popular vote. And not only that: the NDP made its first-ever clean sweep of Vancouver Island, capturing all six seats. The other victors were Dave Stupich, former provincial NDP leader Bob Skelly, Bob's brother, Ray Skelly, John Brewin and Lynn Hunter.

When I walked into my first federal caucus meeting in January of 1989, I was struck by the number of people in the room. The party had risen to 41 seats in the House of Commons from 32, and this was the largest elected group of NDP members I had ever belonged to. Nineteen of us were from British Columbia, partly a reflection of the hostility in the province towards the Social Credit government of Bill Vander Zalm. But although the election had been a tremendous success in terms of our performance, it was a disappointment in the return of the Mulroney government. It was inevitable now that Canadians would be faced with the dreaded Free Trade Agreement, and the first rumblings were also being heard about NAFTA, the North American Free Trade Agreement that would include Mexico.

My first experiences in the House of Commons were rather amusing. I was immediately informed by some members of caucus that I was now at the "Big House," and what had gone on at the provincial level was of little or no consequence. This pompous attitude reminded me of a remark by Pierre Elliott Trudeau, who once told the House of Commons in frustration that "two hundred yards from here you are a bunch of nobodies." I think he was right, and his remark was equally applicable to all parties.

One of the things that most concerned me as a fledgling MP was the cautiousness within caucus. As I saw it, the NDP was the third largest party in the country; we had been strengthened in the recent election and the agenda was firmly before us in terms of the battles we should be waging. But I was concerned about a shifting agenda. I was ill at ease with a number of positions taken by caucus, one notable example being that on the OAS.

The Organization of American States was established in 1948 to promote social, economic and technical cooperation among the thirty-two member nations of North and South America and to act as a regional agency of the United Nations. It has a record of being wrong on every single issue in Central America. The CIA has had the tacit approval of the OAS since 1954, when they threw out Jacobo Arbenz, the democratically elected president of Guatemala. Other atrocities have been committed, in El Salvador, Nicaragua and Mexico, where 350 students were murdered in Mexico City during the 1968 Olympic Games. People talk about how horrible Tiananmen Square was and how we shouldn't trade with China. Well, what the hell are we doing trading with Mexico?

Canada had never been a member of the OAS. There had always been absolute opposition by the federal NDP caucus to the organization, and there had been nothing to warrant a change in our position. But when I was appointed to the House Committee on External Affairs and International Trade, I found a report unanimously urging Canada to join the OAS based on the argument that we would have some moderating influence on the United States. I got into a hell of a row with caucus over that. I then had a row with Broadbent. I lost on all counts; the caucus would not agree to reverse our position.

That was the first of a series of conflicts I had with my fellow MPs. These were bruising experiences, because I suddenly found myself isolated within my own party's caucus. There were a number of new members in the group, and many of them tended to view me as an irascible old troublemaker. But my friendship with Broadbent continued to be strong despite our differences of opinion.

My first session in Ottawa afforded the opportunity of renewing some old acquaintances. It was very good to meet John Turner again. It was a delight to have John Fraser sitting in the chair as Speaker of the House. He is a very capable, thoughtful person, and undoubtedly the best Speaker I have encountered during my time in politics. And I saw my old friend and political foe Senator Ray Perrault.

Shirley and I were indifferent to the social life in Ottawa. We had our own pursuits—the National Gallery, the Byward Market and the Rideau Canal were all pleasant winter diversions. I never went skating on the canal, though. I slipped on my ass in so many other ways I didn't want to do it physically.

The Mulroney government had announced their intention to bring in a Goods and Services Tax, and they were moving very quickly with the free trade legislation. The Liberals were divided on free trade. I sat on an all-party committee with Lloyd Axworthy, who was a very strong opponent of the trade deal, and Roy MacLaren, the current minister of international trade, who was a staunch supporter. I had the opportunity on that committee to watch what appeared to be MacLaren hosing Axworthy over the trade agreement.

It came during preparation of the final report of the committee. All the Tories on the committee, of course, were in favour. The Liberals, as the official Opposition, were allowed a minority report; it said, in essence, free trade if necessary but not necessarily free trade. With only two members on the committee, the NDP were not officially allowed a report, but I had prepared one anyway, kicking the hell out of the deal. My tactics were very blunt, possibly because of my boondock experience in British Columbia. As a result, when we met to discuss the minority report the Liberals were ready to deal.

Axworthy had been pushing for modifications to the Liberal position, and MacLaren suggested that my report could be included if it were shortened. Nope, I said. I wanted every single word printed. On the last day of accepting draft material, Axworthy was absent for some reason. MacLaren stopped me in the hallway and asked if I would be satisfied with a shorter NDP report if I made all the cuts. He said they would approve it, regardless of content, if all reports were finished that day. It seemed to me MacLaren wanted to finalize everything while Axworthy was away. But that had nothing to do with me, and since I would get what I wanted in writing, I agreed. That was the first time I had seen what looked to me like Liberals cutting their own members' throats. I figured the hard-core establishment of the Liberal Party wanted the free trade agreement.

John Turner had campaigned strongly against the deal, but he was by now an isolated, spent force in the party. He rarely came into the House, and he came to be viewed as treacherous by his own caucus. That is unfortunate. John Turner had done yeoman service for the Liberal Party and was treated very badly in the end.

In the spring of 1989, Ed Broadbent announced his intention to step down as party leader. He also let it be known he thought it was time the NDP had a woman as party leader. I think the idea of having a woman for leader as a concept is great. The idea of having a man for leader as a concept is also great. The question is, what do they stand for?

That question has always been paramount to any leadership fight I have experienced in the party. Gender had never been a factor, especially in British Columbia, where historically we have had women like Grace MacInnis, Dorothy Steeves, Eileen Dailly and Daisy Webster, to name but a few. These women were powerful individuals who had an identity of their own and were not there because of gender politics. They were human beings in their own right, fully equal to those of the other gender in the fight for social justice.

But all of a sudden we were confronted with a new dimension in politics. We had to have a woman, period. Anybody who suggested we slow down and take a look at a person's qualifications was immediately branded as sexist. I was very uncomfortable with that, but on the other hand I was not prepared to put my name forward as a leadership candidate. Furthermore, I had made a commitment to Shirley that I wasn't going to run. One of the first candidates to come forward was Audrey McLaughlin, a Yukon MP with only two years' experience in the Commons. Steven Langdon let his name stand around this time, as did Howard McCurdy, Ian Waddell and Simon de Jong. Later, Roger Lagassé, a B.C. French teacher, joined the race.

There were a number of people in caucus who approached me about running. I said no, but I, too, was getting worried about who was in the field. All were good people, but none, in my view, was sufficiently focussed on the issues. I started phoning around and I spoke to Roy Romanow, who was then Opposition leader in Saskatchewan. He was not interested.

Shirley and I then phoned Stephen Lewis and arranged to meet with him in Toronto. We spent four hours with Stephen. It was something of a reconciliation. David Lewis, Stephen's father, was a remarkable pioneer in our party, but he and I had had our differences, mainly on labour issues, since the sixties. We were also on opposite sides when an assault was made on the leadership of Tommy Douglas to get David Lewis elected as federal NDP leader. We put all this behind us that day, however, and Shirley and I urged Stephen strongly to run for the leadership. He had left his post as Canada's ambassador to the U.N. and was on the lecture circuit. But he didn't want to run, and we accepted that.

I continued to call around. Shirley could see that my commitment not to run was weakening. I contacted Jim Fulton of British Columbia and he, in turn, started bugging me to run. The declared candidates had started a road trip across the country. They had spoken in Saskatchewan. A group of Ontario labour leaders had attended that panel and come back publicly critical of the candidates, saying there was no depth. I heard there was a move to persuade Bob Rae to run for the leadership.

By now there was growing support for me in caucus. Several MPs came to my office and asked me to run. I said no. I said I appreciated their support, but I knew that when people give verbal support it is very unusual for them to actually deliver. I recalled a great story about Ted Kennedy when he was running for a position within the Democratic Party. He lost, although he had been promised significant support. Kennedy got up and said, "I want to thank the twenty-seven people who promised to vote for me, and the twelve who did."

MP John Rodriguez asked if I would consider running if he got other members to sign a paper pledging their support. At that point only a handful of MPs were supporting a particular candidate. I said, "You get me fifteen names and I'll look at it." I knew very well there wouldn't be fifteen MPs who supported me. Two days later, Rodriguez came back with sixteen signatures. Well, that just about knocked me over.

At the same time, I was getting pressure from party members right across the country. There was support from British Columbia, Alberta, Saskatchewan and isolated spots in Ontario and the Maritimes. There was none in Quebec, but no one else had any support from Quebec either. I knew that if I wasn't going to run, it was time I picked a candidate I could support and threw myself behind that person wholeheartedly. I couldn't sit on the fence forever.

One day I got a call from Bob Rae saying he was thinking of entering the race and asking me if I had made up my mind. I said I hadn't. Then I left my office and walked home. It was a bitterly cold fall day. There are really only two seasons in Ottawa, summer and winter. You have one week of spring and two weeks of fall. On the way home I decided to run. I stopped at a liquor store, bought a bottle of wine and went home to explain myself. I spoke to Rae later and told him of my change of plans.

Shirley took it in her stride. Her only response was to ask if I really wanted to do this. I said that not only did I want to do it, I had to do it. We discussed the party and the issues, and I remember thinking to myself how well I'd handled this, getting agreement from Shirley after all those promises not to run. I got up next morning, showered, shaved and put on my suit and tie. I said good-bye to Shirley, and just as I was going out the door I heard her reply: "Good-bye, asshole." I made my announcement with that endorsement ringing in my ears.

I kicked off my candidacy at a panel in Nova Scotia. I was yards and miles behind the pack. It was now September, and the convention was to be held on November 30. Fully one-third of the delegates had committed by then. Simon de Jong had support in Manitoba and Saskatchewan. Steven Langdon had support in Ontario. Howard McCurdy had support in little pockets of Ontario. Audrey McLaughlin had significant support across the country.

I had less than three months. I picked up every string I had in the party. We assembled a hodge-podge campaign committee. Diane Bradford headed up my campaign, and Dave Stupich was a prominent supporter, as were Bob and Ray Skelly and Jim Fulton. We worked as aggressively as we could in putting together a machine. I was the favourite target of the other candidates. McLaughlin said I hadn't paid my dues; I kind of wondered about that one. McCurdy said I was a regional candidate. He was from Ontario; I guess that's not a region of Canada. I was also criticized for not speaking French. But none of the other candidates could speak French either.

I discovered the base of my support was essentially British

Columbia and Western Canada. I had the backing of B.C. Federation of Labour President Ken Georgetti, one of the best and brightest executives the federation has had. John Fryer, another prominent labour leader, also lent his support, as well as Brooks Sundin and Cliff Evans of the United Food and Commercial Workers Union, John Shields of the BCGEU and Nick Warhaug of the Hotel Restaurant·Culinary Employees and Bartenders Union. There were many people at secondary levels of the trade union movement who were endorsing me, as well as several senior Ontario party activists. I got support very late in the game from Shirley Carr, head of the Canadian Labour Congress. I did not have the backing of Bob White of the Canadian Auto Workers, who later declared in favour of McLaughlin.

Many of my former provincial colleagues came forward: Alex Macdonald, Eileen Dailly, Bill King. But I was just too late in throwing my hat into the ring. The convention was held in Winnipeg, and I lost to Audrey McLaughlin on the fourth ballot by 244 votes.

I had been led to believe I would receive the support of Simon de Jong, who finished fourth after two ballots. De Jong had asked to be named as party whip in exchange for his backing, and I had agreed. He was wearing a CBC wireless microphone that transmitted our conversation. Our deal created quite a stir in the media and some sectors of the party, but that's politics. I was surprised and disappointed when de Jong threw his support behind McLaughlin, but that, too, is politics. After the convention, Simon's behaviour was brought up inside caucus. I remember standing up and saying forget it, the event is over as far as I'm concerned.

The pressure to vote for a woman was overwhelming. This was very intimidating for many of the delegates. I received a call the night before the vote from Stephen Lewis. He was extremely agitated. He did not feel McLaughlin had what it took to be leader, and he was upset with the other candidates. He told me he would come out next morning and support me. He never did.

I had the endorsation of the Vancouver *Sun*, but I don't think that was the fatal blow. The *Toronto Star* supported me after my convention speech. But what many people don't understand is that 70 per cent of the delegates are already wired when you go into a political convention. They are selected at local meetings, and I wasn't in the campaign early enough to have my organizational structure compete for them. By the time I jumped in, a significant percentage of the delegates were already committed, and they were not released until the second ballot. By that time the core support McLaughlin had worked so long and so hard for remained loyal. It was a hill I couldn't climb. It's remarkable I got as close as I did. I was not devastated at losing. By then my hide was pretty thick. I had lost for a very simple and basic reason: I didn't get enough votes.

The convention had a wonderful footnote. My thirteen-month-old grandson, Andrew, was there with his parents, Dan and Mary. When I walked into the convention, Andrew toddled over and I picked him up. As the reporters came over, Andrew squirmed away and started playing with a cameraman's gadget bag. The next day there was a picture of Andrew on the front page of the *Toronto Star*. He was chewing on one of my campaign posters, and he had a wistful look on his face. The caption read, "What happened, Papa?" That pretty well summed up the convention.

We had a series of banquets afterwards to raise money to pay off some of the debts arising out of my leadership campaign. John Fryer arranged one in Ottawa. John Turner was there, as well as Richard Hatfield, the Tory ex-premier of New Brunswick. Then Gordie Larkin of the B.C. section of the Canadian Labour Congress held a roast in Vancouver where seven hundred tickets were sold. NDP MP John Rodriguez was one of the speakers.

"Coming from Ontario," Rodriguez began, "I want to tell you a side of Dave Barrett that you in British Columbia don't know. Whenever we have a problem in caucus concerning agriculture, we go to Barrett. He knows all the answers, because he's a sexual intellectual. When we have problems with the economy we go to Barrett, because he's a sexual intellectual. When questions arise on foreign policy and we're in deep trouble, we go to Barrett for his expertise, and he gives it gladly because he's a sexual intellectual."

By now people were beginning to wonder what he was talking about, me included. Rodriguez concluded, "Finally I discovered why Dave Barrett knows so much. It's because he's a fucking know-it-all."

Back in Ottawa, tension arose in caucus almost immediately between myself and McLaughlin, and it lasted right through to 1993. I never said or did anything to undermine her leadership. After all, I had been a leader and there had been people who disagreed with me, but it was dealt with behind closed doors in caucus. I had expected that as leader, and I accorded that to McLaughlin. Eventually we got on quite well, but I continued to have fundamental differences with both her and the caucus on policy and strategy.

One policy disagreement came over an application through the province of Alberta for a major export of natural gas to the United States over an extended period of time. I was in favour of limiting not only the amount of the export but also the time frame. I also wanted a higher price. I was disappointed to discover that Ross Harvey, the NDP MP from Edmonton East, found this unacceptable. Alberta producers were in a slump, he said, and this was a welcome market boost. I raised the issue with McLaughlin but lost the argument. The Council of Canadians action group attacked us for backing this export giveaway.

My disagreement with McLaughlin over strategy concerned her staff and their dealings with caucus. She had two principal assistants—Michael Balagus and Les Campbell, both from Manitoba. At one point Balagus gave an interview to a Toronto newspaper criticizing some of the members in caucus. This was certainly brand-new to me. I had never even heard of staff giving interviews, much less bad-mouthing MPs. I raised this issue in caucus. There was discussion, and we were promised it wouldn't happen again. Well, it did happen again, a few months later.

The GST came down around that time. I argued vociferously that we should mount a strident campaign against it and called for a filibuster in committee. The House of Commons was too tightly controlled for a filibuster. After the advent of television, the House lost its spontaneity in the effort by politicians of all stripes to look good on camera. Question period offered some opportunity, but the most fertile battleground, as I saw it, was in the finance committee of the House of Commons.

Our members on the committee were John Rodriguez and Lorne Nystrom. You can exchange members by signing a simple form, and I arranged to replace Nystrom, who was uncomfortable with the filibuster idea. Rodriguez, who is just as puckish as I am, was in favour. McLaughlin was negative, and some caucus members produced buttons saying "Heckle with dignity," an oxymoron if there ever was one. W.A.C. Bennett had said to me many years before that politics is war, and he was right. Politics is war without loss of life. Parliament exists solely for the exercise of power. After a running battle for a couple of days, Rodriguez and I got the go-ahead.

The GST had been yawning its way through the House when we struck. There had been some public protests and the press had given pedestrian coverage, but until then there had been no major focus. There were fifteen members on the committee. The vast majority were Tories, and then there were a handful of Liberals and the two of us. Rodriguez and I had leaked that there was going to be a filibuster, and we arranged for someone to appear at the door with pillows and blankets at the start of committee. The cameras zeroed in on this, and away we went.

A filibuster is a very delicate thing to pull off. You have to be determined to sustain it. It takes a lot of energy. Rodriguez was a wonderful, spontaneous partner in this escapade. We played off each other with joy, zeal and pleasure. It was a throwback to my early days in the B.C. legislature. And we were causing exactly the kind of stir that filibusters should. The first day we went past the usual 5:00 P.M. adjournment until 9:00 P.M. The Tories took it in stride, but the Liberals were furious. It was then we discovered the Liberals really wanted the GST. Their agenda was to put up token resistance, register their vote against the GST, then get the hell out of there after it had been passed by the Tory majority.

The filibuster lasted nearly two weeks, and we had thrust the GST back to centre stage. We had also exposed the hypocrisy of the Liberals. These were exactly the kind of tactics I thought we should be using.

Our best fight as a caucus, in my view, was our opposition to the Mulroney government's support for the Gulf War. But we were frequently sucked in to the point of acquiescing to the government's agenda. The Charlottetown Accord was a prime example. It was basically Mulroney's response to the failure in 1990 of his brain child, the Meech Lake agreement. I argued strongly against our supporting the Charlottetown Accord, and to this day I regret that I stilled my opposition once the caucus reached its decision to support it.

The deal was a fraud, and we had been caught in a snare. It was a hodgepodge of ideas that pandered to separatist blackmail by giving Quebec a permanent guarantee of 25 per cent of Commons seats. It recognized the inherent right to aboriginal self-government, the only positive aspect from my perspective, but chickened out on settling land claims. It had more loose ends than a ragged quilt, and people were subjected to coercion by the likes of Mulroney and Constitutional Affairs Minister Joe Clark, who warned that Canada would fall apart if the deal was rejected. The media bought in, and Reform Party Leader

Preston Manning played on the whole scenario beautifully.

I went on the campaign trail in support of the accord with John Turner, and then Harvey Beech and I did a swing through northern British Columbia. I remember particularly a meeting in Houston. There must have been about eighty people there. They were mostly male. There were loggers, sawmill operators and some small businessmen. In the back of the room were the native men. There was a bloody-minded mood in the room, very much opposed to the Charlottetown Accord.

It wasn't until I stood up that I made up my mind what I was going to say. "This is a very funny country," I began. "There are a hell of a lot of people in Quebec who hate anybody who speaks English. And out here, there's a hell of a lot of people who hate anybody who speaks French. The common unifying factor in this country is hate."

There was dead silence. "Some of you remember as kids being called dago or wop or hunky. Others remember being called limeys. We have all shared in the common denominator of racial hatred in this country. Many of us recall as kids having to go to the grocery store with our mothers to read the English labels. Imagine the humiliation our mothers must have felt at having to rely on an eight- or nine-year-old child. Do you remember coming home really angry and hurt or maybe even crying that somebody had called you a name because of your ethnic background? Isn't it great that we share this? Well, this is an attempt to start healing."

The foot shuffling started with the loggers and miners in the front row. They had come to hunt bear, but the mood had passed. I meant everything I said, but in no way did I believe the Charlottetown Accord would help.

The Liberals went along holus-bolus, probably out of a cynical decision that it was a way to avoid being held up to any criticism in Quebec. But I felt as the third party the NDP should stand against it. The media was captured by the Mulroney plan. Every night the television channels pumped out the propaganda, saying the referendum was going to pass. Well, the people turned out to be smarter than the politicians they elected. They saw the Charlottetown Accord as the rushed, elitist, top-down deal that it was, a last-ditch attempt by Mulroney to save the Conservative party. I didn't say "I told you so" back in caucus, but I did say that we, the NDP, had pulled our umbilical cord right out from our grassroots.

One of the last acts by the Conservatives was NAFTA. I had occasion during the debates on the issue to get to know Brian Tobin, a Newfoundlander who is now the Liberal fisheries minister. We were on a committee together, and I was very impressed with his determined, tenacious approach. One day Trade Minister Michael Wilson had arranged for the bureaucrats to appear before the committee to answer questions. There were about forty-five of them in the room, and I asked Wilson why they were all there. The last thing an MP wants is to appear to be criticizing an expert civil servant, so I was cautious. I pointed out to Wilson that there were so many bureaucrats in the room they were falling all over each other. "Do you know how much money it costs to get all these people in here?" I asked. Then I suggested we save some money. "Is there anybody here who's against this deal?" Dead silence. "Well," I said to Wilson, "since they're all for it, let them get back to work and we can stick with just one spokesperson."

Wilson was fuming. At that point, Tobin leaned over and said, "I don't know exactly where you're going on this, but I think you are right, and I back you 100 per cent." On other days when I clashed with Wilson, Tobin would listen, make up his own mind and then enter the debate. Nobody in Canada should be surprised at the way Tobin handled himself in the turbot war with Spain. He's not afraid of taking heat when he thinks he's doing what's right.

The mood was very nasty as we went into the 1993 federal election campaign. Mulroney had stepped down, and British Columbian Kim Campbell was the new Conservative leader. Campbell had been a Socred minister in the Vander Zalm government before she was elected as a Vancouver MP in 1988. Mulroney had left in what has become the usual manner, with a flurry of junkets and patronage appointments. The Liberals spent their time during the campaign ducking the issues and attacking the Tories.

The NDP had started off way behind, and we stayed there. About the only bright spot in my campaign was an interesting clash I had with Paul Martin, now Liberal finance minister, while I was representing the NDP at one of CBC's weekly forums in Toronto. Martin was there for the Liberals, and Jean Charest appeared for the Conservatives. Preston Manning was there for Reform, and I was struck by the size of his entourage. I had never seen anything like it outside the United States. He was surrounded by security guards in black suits, and he came to the forum in a chartered bus. All this ostentatious spending from a party that said it was frugal. There were more hacks and flacks and handlers surrounding Manning than there were for Martin.

During the panel I had a sharp exchange with Charest, whom I like very much. That led into a volley with Martin. I turned to him and said, "Tell us how much your shipping firm has paid in corporate income tax in the last five years." Martin was furious.

When I got back to Victoria, Joyce Thomas, who was working on my campaign, said she had received a call from a guy with a heavy French accent from the Seafarers International Union in Montreal who wanted to know Monsieur Barrett's address. Three days later we got a campaign donation of $5,000 and a covering letter praising me for having the guts to take on Paul Martin.

I had a magnificent crew working for me under my very able campaign manager, David Howe (whose name, I predict, will be heard again in future). But the ugly mood that had manifested itself over the Charlottetown Accord was still alive, and I had a pretty rough ride. I took a lot of heat for supporting the Harcourt government on logging in Clayoquot Sound. The mixed-use approach angered both loggers and environmentalists. In the midst of that kind of controversy, you don't get any rational discussion.

On election night the NDP took a kicking, winning only 9 seats overall. In B.C., we dropped from 19 seats down to 2. Only Nelson Riis and Svend Robinson were reelected. We lost every one of the 6 NDP seats on Vancouver Island, 5 of them to the Reform Party. In my own riding, where I had garnered more than 50 per cent of the vote in 1988, I fell to below 30 per cent in 1993. Reformer Keith Martin led me by about 3,000 votes.

There was tremendous sadness on election night. Those who had worked on my campaign met at a local golf club, where I conceded defeat and congratulated the winner. I laid the political upheaval in Canada squarely at the feet of the Mulroney government, saying the former prime minister had virtually destroyed the Progressive Conservative party as we knew it. Regarding the Reform Party, I said that you cannot build a nation by cutting the ground out from under it. You cannot build a nation by assaulting the poor and the afflicted and those on the margins of society.

Voters turfed out the Conservatives in 1993 and went en masse to the Liberals, but has it made any difference? The capitulation of the Liberals to the U.S. agenda on NAFTA was positively shocking, particularly after Liberals Lloyd Axworthy and Herb Gray made such strong pitches to nationalist groups that they would demand a review and would not sign NAFTA without significant changes. Now the Liberals are tinkering with the hated GST in ways that threaten to make it worse. There is a saying that the great thing about being a Liberal is that you don't always have to be one. Only George Baker of Newfoundland and Warren Allmand from Montreal are speaking out from the Liberal benches, two lone voices in a government that is otherwise indistinguishable from its Conservative predecessor.

Fourteen

What's Left?

The 1993 election marked the end of an era and the passing of my age group in the NDP. Since then, I have not participated in either the national or the provincial party in any significant way. I made a conscious decision to pull back awhile and do some reflecting.

The NDP administration I headed from 1972 to 1975 in British Columbia has frequently been criticized for trying to do too much too quickly. I particularly was very much in a hurry, but I don't see that as a mistake; in my opinion it was historical imperative. Lurking in the back of my mind was always the nagging thought that sooner or later the forces that had governed this province until 1972 were going to coalesce to take our power away. It was a question of doing as much as we could while we had the power or waiting for another term in office. I came down on the side of forging ahead. And I think the proof is in the pudding. We passed 367 bills during our thirty-nine months in government, and most of that legislation has endured. But it took nineteen years for another NDP government to be elected, and that is regrettable.

On reflection, I think our administration should have worried problems through with the public a bit more. Any government that attempts to ram through a piece of legislation, even a good one, runs the risk of having the idea shot down because people feel left out of the process.

I regret that as leader I didn't use the talents of a significantly greater number of people in the legislature, both government and opposition. A nagging problem for any head of a parliamentary government is figuring out how to harness the talent, skill, desire and energy of government backbenchers. It is very difficult, and I wish I had found a way to bring in more people. If we had used committees more extensively, we could also have tapped into the considerable skills of opposition members like Liberal Leader Gordon Gibson, Scott Wallace of the Tories, ex-Socred Minister of Agriculture Francis Richter, Alex Fraser, a wonderful gentleman who became minister of highways after we were defeated, and Jim Chabot, who had been labour minister under W.A.C. Bennett.

Something else I regret is my own behaviour. I was sometimes very intemperate as premier. Youthful exuberance probably had a lot to do with that; I was pushing forty-two when we were elected government. I talked too much and was too accessible to the media. I was too available with an opinion on everything, and that was a mistake both strategically and tactically. As I look back, I think that by being such a wide-open, call-the-shots-as-I-see-them politician, I unwittingly created a climate of fear about myself and about the ambitions and intentions of our government.

Because of that, I was unable to leave a more balanced opposition in the House. The coalition of the right and the centre is one of the worst things that's happened in British Columbia. It would be much healthier if we had a three-way philosophical debate, but that was not our experience, and it is not the experience today. The so-called centre, the current Liberal Party, is trying to outdo the right-wing Reformers, and that is tragic. There is no rational debate on either the provincial or the national level, and I wish I had done more to bring about a mature, sensible dialogue in B.C. It may require a few generations for that to happen.

Our government certainly should have done more to explain how fragile are this province and its environment. Damage has been done to our fisheries and forests because of practices we assumed would do no harm. When the first criticism of existing practices came from the CCF and later the NDP, there was no environmental movement. Such people as John Squire, Rae Eddie, Tony Gargrave and Ran Harding stood up in the House and spoke about the interrelationship of everything on planet Earth. But the idea that the environment was fragile was alien to the conventional thinking at the time, and I wish we had done more to raise awareness.

The bold efforts of the current NDP administration in British Columbia in curtailing mining in the parks and trying to forge a sustainable future for our forest industry are commendable. The attempt to meet the requirement of the Bruntland Commission that 12 per cent of the land be set aside as park land is another step in the right direction. The Harcourt government has demonstrated that social democratic administrations can produce sustainable, sensitive employment and a vision for the future. Statistics show that British Columbia is now the largest single producer of jobs in Canada, and the province has the most robust economy of any provincial or state jurisdiction in North America. But the Harcourt administration, too, has been assaulted in the media. To its critics I say, "If you're not happy, just think of the alternatives." If you like the policies but not democratic socialism, like the Kamloops lawyer, just join the porridge party.

On the national scale, the North American Free Trade Agreement has changed the playing field for social activism dramatically. Political debates in this country up until 1988 took for granted that our economy could sustain the tremendous postwar advances we had made in socialized medicine, postsecondary education and housing. Not all of our social problems were solved by any means, but there was forward momentum from the Great Depression on. As long as our branch plant economy was protected, we were confident that we would see orderly economic growth in this country. This was especially true in British Columbia, with its rich and virtually untapped storehouse of timber and minerals.

The problem was that Canada had no control over its economy. We were at the mercy of Wall Street and the multinationals. As prime minister, Trudeau had tried to exercise some control through the Foreign Investment Review Agency, but the program was limited in scope and was scrapped by the Conservatives when they took power in 1984. Any pretext of holding U.S. subsidiaries accountable for their actions in the Canadian economy was abandoned when the Mulroney government was reelected in 1988 and signed the Free Trade Agreement. U.S. corporations were then free to close their branch plants at a whim and put the Canadian economy into a tailspin. The tragedy was compounded almost immediately by Canada's entry into NAFTA. That deal gave the U.S. corporate empire complete and unfettered access to Canadian resources and complete and unfettered access to cheap Mexican labour.

We lost 375,000 jobs and the Mexicans lost control of PEMEX, the state-owned oil company, which is in hock to its eyeballs. Now, instead of using profits to enrich the lives of Mexican citizens, PEMEX must repay its debt to the U.S.

There is now, in Canada, a massive assault on socialized medicine and other social services. Eighty-five per cent of Canadians support medicare, but they are perplexed. There is a persuasive advertising blitz attacking the cost of our health care system. Business and tax reform groups tell us to cut welfare, medicare and other social services without any reference to who pays for them. The recession of the early 1980s saw the return of food banks for the first time in nearly fifty years. I read somewhere that we now have more food banks in Canada than McDonald's restaurants. We are in a cesspool of chronic unemployment averaging around 10 to 15 per cent.

The Canadian government could have taken corrective action during the early eighties to tap into revenues generated by natural resources, like our government did with B.C. Petroleum. But the only response has been a stampede by politicians to reduce the deficit and the debt, without examining what caused them in the first place.

If corporations paid their fair share of taxes we wouldn't be in a deficit situation. Period. The time is long overdue for governments to end corporate welfare. We must stop the $2-billion handout to oil companies in Hibernia. We must end the massive tax loopholes that allow banks to escape paying a fair share of their profits back to the people of this country who made them rich. The same goes for the mining industry. There is more than $100 billion of deferred corporate income tax in Canada. If those companies were forced to pay just 10 per cent of what they owe, it would have a dramatic impact on the debt and the deficit. We don't have to raise the GST or the provincial sales tax, just collect the bloody taxes already owed to us.

The rich get richer, the poor get poorer and the middle class gets confused. Until 1988, every generation in Canada was able to say to its children, "Go to school, behave yourself, get an education, put your nose to the grindstone and you will be successful." Not any longer. We have more people with Masters degrees and Ph.D.s than the economy can absorb. We have a shrinking economy and an expanding pool of highly skilled people. On top of that, we've opened the door through NAFTA to even more skilled workers from our low-wage partner,

Mexico. We should be demanding that people rise up to our standards, not allowing ourselves to be dragged down to theirs. The Canadian debate about socialized medicine should focus on how Americans can be brought up to our level of care. Mexican wage earners, likewise, must rise to our union wage scales. But this debate has not taken place. Instead, our society and economy are being transformed to meet the new era of competitiveness.

The social malaise that exists in large urban areas in the U.S. is, in my opinion, directly related to the fact there is no basic security for every citizen in the form of medical and hospital insurance. I find it amazing that those on the right don't understand that if you want a stable society it has to be inclusive, not exclusive. The problem with the poor is that they simply don't have enough money. Social problems are based primarily on economics.

The Clinton administration in the U.S. tried recently to establish a universal health care program. After that effort collapsed, within six or seven months it came out that lobbyists had spent $79 million U.S. to quash Clinton's attempt. Of that $79 million, $54 million was identified as coming from the American Medical Association and the rest from insurance companies. In the U.S., corporations insist on their right to make a profit on everything, including human misery. They peddle health care the same way they do widgets. It's all done under the banner of free enterprise.

We are in grave danger of this happening in Canada. In the current fad of worrying over public indebtedness, I would challenge people to have a look at corporate indebtedness. Examine corporate debt-to-income ratio in light of long-term projections. These companies are feeding off the same economy, and they have incurred huge debt as an investment in future profits. Countries can operate the same way, with profits used to improve social conditions for their citizens. But the political will must be there, because the corporate elite doesn't want that. In their view, any profit has to be in the hands of the private sector.

Just look at how the corporations have manipulated the postal system. They get a special rate on advertising and we have to subsidize the distribution of their sales material. What bloody nonsense! The CPR is another example of how we have been screwed in this country. That corporation got huge land grants across Canada in exchange for providing high-quality passenger transportation in perpetuity. Then what did they do? They walked away from that obligation with their pockets bulging from the sale of those lands. Was there a logical, reasonable debate? No. It reminds me of what Alex Macdonald once said: "It's wonderful to know the law, but it's better to know the judge." Corporations have learned all too well that that adage can be applied to politicians too.

The economic dislocation created in Canada by free trade is adding fuel to the fire of the xenophobic forces in Quebec who are pushing for separation. The Bloc Québécois of Lucien Bouchard has bought into the entire right-wing agenda, including free trade, possibly because Bouchard realizes it serves his purpose of dragging Quebec out of Canada. The one binding thing we have in this country is our social policies. Take them away, and the balkanization threatened by Quebec is also fertile ground for Western separatists. We already share alienation from Ottawa. There already exists a Pacific Northwest Economic Region comprising British Columbia, Alberta and the U.S. states of Alaska, Washington, Oregon, Idaho and Montana. It's an economic union and trading bloc of 15 million people, ratified by the provincial and state legislatures. Who knows what future aspirations this group might have? What I do know is this: Separation by either Western Canada or Quebec will ultimately lead to Canada's absorption by the United States.

The media, as a full-fledged member of the corporate elite, is responsible for much of the confusion people feel about political issues today. Take a look at the sports pages. Every day you can see who has the best batting average in baseball or the most receptions in the CFL or who is the high scorer in the NHL. But have you ever seen a breakdown on the performance of politicians and how they voted? The introduction of legislation, the role of House debate and the consequences of the political process are great mysteries to 99 per cent of Canadians.

At one time a significant sector of the religious community provided leadership by questioning the economic system. Today, the only audible voices come from the religious right. Who's looking at the economy? Only those who have access to politicians and want to protect their positions and guard their control over resources. But who put the resources here on Earth? Was it the Seven Sisters, as Anthony Sampson so aptly called the oil companies in his book, or was it God? Whatever created Earth certainly didn't put the planet's riches into the hands of the corporate empire. As citizens, we have to accept that joint responsibility. We have frittered democracy away rather than demand that these resources be used to create a better life for all of us.

The only outrage in Canada and British Columbia today, which is fanned by the power brokers, is directed against what people see as big government and corrupt politicians. But that kind of short-sightedness only serves the status quo. Attacking government per se plays into the corporate agenda, maintaining power in the hands of those who have the most influence and are causing the problems we face. And it is not enough simply to attack elected politicians. It is very chic and popular to slam former Prime Minister Brian Mulroney. I certainly won't come running to his defence, but who elected him in the first place? The voters are ultimately responsible. People cannot walk away from their obligations in a democracy by attacking the politicians they voted for. Ninety-eight per cent of the people in Canada don't belong to a political party. Most do not attend information meetings or participate in public debates. They buy into the ads paid for by large corporations telling them how to vote. Then, when they get the predictable result, instead of looking in the mirror and blaming themselves they blame Mulroney. That's the easy way out, and people can't afford to take the easy way out if they are concerned about the futures of their children and grandchildren.

I think it is on the campuses and in the trade union movement that the pendulum will begin to swing away from the neoconservatives. Young, thoughtful economists and social activists are beginning to mount a political challenge to the current mood. I hope I live long enough to see the pendulum swing back and end the social and psychological devastation that has been imposed on our country. For now, there is a loss of hope and a sense of isolation. There is no clarion call to set about doing things properly and decently for people. That will return, and I hope it is soon.

Democratic socialists have an important role to play in this country, but we must set our own agenda in accordance with our historical and philosophical underpinnings, and forget about our image, superficial perceptions and poll results. In my opinion, part of the forthcoming struggle will be for a social charter with teeth inside NAFTA that will protect those segments of the population that have been savaged by the deal.

I'm currently wrapping up a proposal in conjunction with the University of Western Washington in Bellingham for bringing NAFTA together with NAFTU, the North American Federation of Trade Unions. The proposal calls for a tri-country structure to demand better working and social conditions for men and women inside the NAFTA bloc. I'm also teaching one day a week as an adjunct professor in the political science department at Simon Fraser University, focussing on the process of transforming an abstract idea into legislation. Political science is actually a misnomer. Politics isn't a science, it's an art. And it's all about power. I recall a remark by ex-Socred Attorney General Robert Bonner, who said politics is like sex: If it is done properly, it's very messy, but the results can be satisfying.

My career in politics has been both. I have enjoyed the access to power that only the British parliamentary system and a few other democratic structures can provide. But the political process is full of twists and turns, and it requires participation by informed citizens. Without that, we will end up marching to the beat of the corporate drum. Above all, beware of so-called non-partisan politicians. They are the most dangerous because they haven't committed themselves. And if you don't stand for something, you'll fall for anything. I am biased, and that is what drove me into politics. My bias was formed in the crucible of debate that began in the 1940s around social issues like national health care and improved education and housing. And my bias tells me the right-wing forces that permeate Parliament are going to have to be challenged. We won't win this struggle overnight, but let us begin.

Appendix

Elected Members of the Legislative Assembly of British Columbia, August 30, 1972

Electoral District	*Member*	*Occupation*	*Party*
Alberni	Robert Skelly	Farmer	New Democratic
Atlin	Frank Calder	Manager	New Democratic
Boundary-Similkameen	Frank Richter	Rancher	Social Credit
Burnaby-Edmonds	Gordon Dowding	Barrister	New Democratic
Burnaby North	Eileen Dailly	Housewife	New Democratic
Burnaby-Willingdon	James Lorimer	Lawyer	New Democratic
Cariboo	Alexander Fraser	Businessman	Social Credit
Chilliwack	Harvey Schroeder	Minister	Social Credit
Columbia River	James Chabot	Supervisor, CP Rail	Social Credit
Comox	Karen Sanford	Housewife	New Democratic
Coquitlam	David Barrett	Social Worker	New Democratic
Cowichan-Malahat	Robert Strachan	Carpenter	New Democratic
Delta	Carl Liden	Administrator	New Democratic
Dewdney	Peter Rolston	Minister	New Democratic
Esquimalt	James Gorst	Businessman	New Democratic
Fort George	Alf Nunweiler	Train Dispatcher	New Democratic
Kamloops	Gerry Anderson	Stationary Engineer	New Democratic
Kootenay	Leo Nimsick	MLA	New Democratic
Langley	Robert McClelland	Publisher	Social Credit
Mackenzie	Donald Lockstead	Plant Supervisor	New Democratic
Nanaimo	David Stupich	Chartered Accountant	New Democratic
Nelson-Creston	Lorne Nicolson	Teacher	New Democratic
New Westminster	Dennis Cocke	Pension Consultant	New Democratic

Electoral District	*Member*	*Occupation*	*Party*
North Okanagan	Patricia Jordan	Housewife	Social Credit
North Peace River	Dean Smith	Life Underwriter	Social Credit
North Vancouver-Capilano	David Brousson	Engineer Businessman	Liberal
North Vancouver-Seymour	Colin Gabelmann	Legislative Director	New Democratic
Oak Bay	G. Scott Wallace	Doctor	Prog. Conservative
Omineca	Douglas Kelly	Lodge Operator	New Democratic
Prince Rupert	Graham Lea	Broadcaster	New Democratic
Revelstoke-Slocan	William King	Locomotive Engineer	New Democratic
Richmond	Harold Steves	Teacher	New Democratic
Rossland-Trail	Christopher D'Arcy	Publisher	New Democratic
Saanich and the Islands	Hugh Curtis	Sales Manager	Prog. Conservative
Shuswap	Donald Lewis	Farmer	New Democratic
Skeena	Hartley Dent	Administrator	New Democratic
South Okanagan	William A. C. Bennett	Merchant	Social Credit
South Peace River	Donald Phillips	Auto Dealer	Social Credit
Surrey	Ernest Hall	Exec. Secretary	New Democratic
Vancouver-Burrard	Rosemary Brown	Counsellor	New Democratic
	Norman Levi	Social Worker	New Democratic
Vancouver Centre	Emery Barnes	Social Worker	New Democratic
	Gary Lauk	Lawyer	New Democratic
Vancouver East	Alexander Macdonald	Solicitor	New Democratic
	Robert Williams	Town Planner	New Democratic
Vancouver-Little Mountain	Roy Cummings	Merchant	New Democratic
	Phyllis Young	Researcher	New Democratic
Vancouver-Point Grey	Garde Gardom	Barrister and Solicitor	Liberal
	Patrick McGeer	Neurological Researcher	Liberal
Vancouver South	Jack Radford	C.L.C. Representative	New Democratic
	Daisy Webster	Housewife	New Democratic
Victoria	Newell Morrison	Businessman	Social Credit
	David Anderson	Public Servant	Liberal
West Vancouver-Howe Sound	Allan Williams	Lawyer	Liberal
Yale-Lillooet	William Hartley	Co-op Director	New Democratic

Acknowledgements

First of all, I want to thank the many pioneers and activists in the CCF and the NDP, whose hard work over the years has meant so much to this province and this country. I must single out Yvonne Cocke, who as NDP provincial secretary ran the brilliant 1979 campaign that took the party to its historic high of 46 per cent of the popular vote. Yvonne was ably assisted on that campaign by Soren Bech, Pat McLean, Kay Lackner, Arvena Tokarek, Pat Portsmith, Gilda Bryant, Brian McIvor and Bert Rougeau.

Deep appreciation is due to core staff who endured me as their boss in Victoria—Joyce Thomas, Jean Elphick, Joan McLaughlan, Dianne Davis, Jeannette Whelan, John Mika, Harvey Beech, John Wood and Arne VanCampen—and to the staff who so ably assisted me during my MP years: Joyce Thomas, Heather Manning, Jaz Manak, Debbie Parhar, Dale Vanelli, Denise Blackwell and Gay Christopherson. And a tip of the hat to Ken MacDonald, the Queen's Printer during our time in office, for his hours of overtime and his continued refusal to print three-dollar bills.

Invaluable assistance for this book was provided by B.C. Legislative library staff members Pamela St. Denis, Bill Williams, Jackie Johnson and Pat Somerton. Important legwork was done by independent researcher Holly Nathan. Joyce Thomas provided access to her appointment diaries, which span a twenty-seven-year period. Joyce, Arlene Yarnell and Deanna Chee performed the unenviable task of transcribing my rambling, sometimes incoherent monologues with diligence and perspicacity. A special word of thanks to Chris Main and George Henderson for their patience and skill in guiding a confirmed Luddite through the tangled web of high technology. Sincere thanks also to editor Barbara Pulling and publisher Scott McIntyre of Douglas & McIntyre. Thanks to Jim Munro, who provided the initial impetus for the book. And above all, thanks to literary obstetrician Bill Miller, who brought this book into being.

Index